POSITIVE PEDAGOGY ACROSS THE PRIMARY CURRICULUM

Sara Miller McCune founded SAGE Publishing in 1965 to support the dissemination of usable knowledge and educate a global community. SAGE publishes more than 1000 journals and over 800 new books each year, spanning a wide range of subject areas. Our growing selection of library products includes archives, data, case studies and video. SAGE remains majority owned by our founder and after her lifetime will become owned by a charitable trust that secures the company's continued independence.

Los Angeles | London | New Delhi | Singapore | Washington DC | Melbourne

POSITIVE PEDAGOGY
ACROSS THE
PRIMARY CURRICULUM

JONATHAN BARNES

Los Angeles | London | New Delhi
Singapore | Washington DC | Melbourne

Los Angeles | London | New Delhi
Singapore | Washington DC | Melbourne

SAGE Publications Ltd
1 Oliver's Yard
55 City Road
London EC1Y 1SP

SAGE Publications Inc.
2455 Teller Road
Thousand Oaks, California 91320

SAGE Publications India Pvt Ltd
Unit No 323-333, Third Floor, F-Block
International Trade Tower Nehru Place
New Delhi – 110 019

SAGE Publications Asia-Pacific Pte Ltd
3 Church Street
#10-04 Samsung Hub
Singapore 049483

Editor: James Clark
Editorial Assistant: Diana Alves
Production Editor: Gourav Kumar
Copyeditor: Clare Weaver
Proofreader: Derek Markham
Indexer: KnowledgeWorks Global Ltd
Marketing Manager: Lorna Patkai
Cover Design: Sheila Tong
Typeset by: KnowledgeWorks Global Ltd
Printed in the UK

© Jonathan Barnes 2023

Apart from any fair dealing for the purposes of research, private study, or criticism or review, as permitted under the Copyright, Designs and Patents Act, 1988, this publication may not be reproduced, stored or transmitted in any form, or by any means, without the prior permission in writing of the publisher, or in the case of reprographic reproduction, in accordance with the terms of licences issued by the Copyright Licensing Agency. Enquiries concerning reproduction outside those terms should be sent to the publisher.

Library of Congress Control Number: 2022947578

British Library Cataloguing in Publication data

A catalogue record for this book is available from the British Library

ISBN 978-1-5297-9502-8
ISBN 978-1-5297-9503-5 (pbk)

At SAGE we take sustainability seriously. Most of our products are printed in the UK using responsibly sourced papers and boards. When we print overseas we ensure sustainable papers are used as measured by the PREPS grading system. We undertake an annual audit to monitor our sustainability.

CONTENTS

About the author   vii
Preface   ix
Acknowledgements   xi

1   Positive values in a rapidly changing and diverse world   1

2   Positive pedagogy – taking control of the teaching and the learning environment through reclaiming teachers' values   21

3   Planning and building positive environments for learning   39

4   Connecting the Humanities – Geography, History, Religious Knowledge, Citizenship and Personal, Social, Health and Economic Education   57

5   Connecting the wordless disciplines – Art and Design, Drama, Music, Dance and PE   79

6   Science, Technology, English and Maths in cross-curricular contexts   105

7   Thinking carefully about the whole curriculum   125

8   Embodying positive pedagogy in a diverse UK   153

References   177

Index   193

ABOUT THE AUTHOR

Jonathan is a Visiting Senior Research Fellow at Canterbury Christ Church University and a National Teaching Fellow. He has taught and researched for the last 50 years throughout Asia and Africa and in primary, secondary schools and prisons in England. He was a primary head teacher between 1992 and 2000. Since then, he has combined work in primary initial teacher education with continuing research and teaching in the arts and humanities in primary and nursery education. His books and published research on Cross-Curricular Learning, teachers' values and diversity are widely used throughout teacher education. In 2017 with peace activist Alex Ntung Jonathan founded Education-4diversity, a charity dedicated to humanising, valuing and celebrating diversity through dialogue and education.

PREFACE

When I submitted plans for this book to five teacher education specialists, two of them used the term 'hostile' to describe the education policy environment into which it would enter. As I researched, observed for and finally wrote it, I more fully understand what they meant. During my enquiries in primary schools across England, before and through the Covid pandemic and in the recovery period after, very many teachers, assistants and heads expressed the view that primary education had narrowed to an intensive focus on often uncontextualised English, mathematics and subject-discipline facts. Although child well-being had nominally risen up the educational agenda, it was recognised that accessing help to address emotional and intellectual barriers to learning was increasingly difficult. At the same time it was commonly observed that teacher job satisfaction and indeed retention had declined. Teachers were feeling the strain of rising inequalities, reduced budgets, heightened accountability, standardisation and external judgements on the 'right' behaviour policies, knowledge and curriculum.

This book offers teachers, schools and children a positive route through such pressures. It stresses the fundamental need in any successful community to talk about, agree on and live a set of unifying and hopefully humanitarian values. It suggests that the 'values discussion' should be a frequent and essential part of school life and curriculum and that these values – varying for each school and community – should be the guide to action in both pedagogy and ethos. Fifty years in education has shown me that children of all ages are well-equipped and ready to think about and act upon agreed values. I will argue that applying humanitarian values knowledgeably and wisely to the big issues facing children's present and future, should be the overarching aim of each school curriculum. Children are ready to talk about how inclusive values can be applied to current concerns like warfare, conflict, climate change, racial injustice, social and economic inequality, migration or health. Teachers are equipped with the knowledge to help children deepen that interest and grow in wisdom.

Motivating, engaging and adding to the knowledge of all young people is central to the role of school. We know that those of primary school age thrive on practical and creative activity, meaningful experience, social interaction reflection and play, yet these modes of learning seem threatened in schools anxious about the next inspection and dwindling budgets. I hope that the case studies and philosophies in this book will demonstrate approaches to pedagogy and curriculum that establish lifelong values and significantly enhance knowledge at the same time as creating a positive, enriching experience for every child, teacher and assistant.

ACKNOWLEDGEMENTS

First and foremost, and in every way, I thank my wife Cherry Tewfik for her unending support, patience and simple love throughout the long and challenging process of writing this book. Her positive pedagogy has been its inspiration. In many ways Positive Pedagogy is the bringing together of a narrative she and I have shared throughout our lives as teachers and travellers over the last 50 years. Many of the ideas and illustrations come from her and her experience, all of the peace, space and positive spirit for the writing, rewriting and revising has been provided by her.

Our dear children Ben, Naomi, Esther and Jacob and grandchildren, Isaac, Tess, Theo, Charlie, Bella and Daisy have provided the constant and loving reminders of the real world and real lives within which education takes place. They have provided the illustrations, inspirations and impetus for this work.

I have been privileged to be closely involved in the wonderful work and children of dozens of primary schools and nurseries who have welcomed me to lead workshops, conduct lessons, research studies or observations or just as a friend. In the last five years and at a late stage of a life in education I have been hugely gratified to witness some of the best, most inclusive and creative work I have ever seen. Among the artists, arts practitioners, inspirational, highly positive teachers I have recently worked with, I must name with thanks: Adam Annand, Hope Azeda, Sam Bailey, Ben Barnes, Beatrice Bamurange, Margaretta Burrell, Angeline Conaghlan, Daniela Essart, Alex Evans, Mike Fairclough, Dan File, Gren Hancox, Matt and Esther Miles, Krishna Moorthi, Søren Nielsen, Stephen Scoffham, Glenn Sharp and Ibrahim Ssemambo.

Positive pedagogy places the child at the centre. The sparkling eyes of children as they have learned with these affirmative teachers and practitioners convince me that positive pedagogy is a possible, preferable and sustainable way of teaching. I know that for very many children, their relationships, confidence and futures were positively transformed by their time with those teachers. I thank Sage and Diana Alves for their support in bringing the knowledge and experience gained by my exciting lifetime in education to more of those engaged in education today.

1
POSITIVE VALUES IN A RAPIDLY CHANGING AND DIVERSE WORLD

Objectives

This chapter will introduce and discuss the primary curriculum themes and principles to be addressed throughout this book. The overarching themes are:

- The global context
- Our common humanity
- Our dependence on community
- The strengths of diversity
- Creativity as a meaning-maker

The underlying principles are that:

- Education policy and practice should be teacher-led
- Education practice should be founded upon research and evidence
- Schools and classrooms should be models of inclusion and positivity
- Diversity should be represented and championed across the curriculum
- Teachers should recognise and promote creativity in every child and at each stage of education

Introduction

This book outlines proposals for a primary curriculum relevant and right for today. An inclusive and positive curriculum entirely compliant with the current requirements of the devolved education authorities of the UK. A curriculum based upon values transferable to primary education everywhere and a belief that *every* child has creative potential that education should be centrally involved in releasing. The examples, discussions and proposals for the education of children post-2021 are constructed around themes arising from the experience of pandemic. These are:

- the reality of global interdependence
- the human desire to find meaning
- the universal importance of community
- the gift of diversity
- the benefits of personal and collective creativity

These themes will be linked to inclusive values recognisable across cultures (Brown, 1992; Pinker, 2002). The concept of inclusive values is taken to include: beauty, community, compassion, courage, equality, honesty, hope, rights, joy, love, non-violence, participation, respect for diversity, sustainability, trust and wisdom (Booth and Ainscow, 2020). Vignettes showing such values *in action;* their current relevance, effect on community and their relationship to collective and personal creativity, will lead teachers and students towards a principled curriculum whose ultimate destination is a sustainable future for the world and its people.

Changes to the content of curriculum alone are not enough. Current circumstances and the development of Artificail Intelligence require new thoughts about the intent of the curriculum, its implementation and impact (Ofsted, 2022). It could be argued that curriculum includes the whole culture of the school and that schools should consider the messages, attitudes and relationships within that culture very carefully. Currently, much potential is lost through the alienation or lack of engagement of rising percentages of children and young people (Gov.UK, 2019a). Even in primary schools hundreds of thousands each year are excluded, and absenteeism, or disaffection, affects millions more. Heightened attention to a core curriculum, raising measurable standards in English, maths and science, and increased rigour have benefitted some, but they have made school more alien to others. Across the country the 'long tail of underachievement' remains relatively unchanged in most areas by rigourous inspection, strategies, and the relentless raising of standards (Ofsted, 2013; Blatchford, 2020; Centre for Research in Underachievement, 2020). Large percentages of children – largely poor, with special needs and/or those from Black, Asian, Minority Ethnic groups and mixed heritage backgrounds – do not see their lives, experience and families acknowledged, let alone affirmed, in their schooling. Thus, this book challenges teachers, leaders of education and education administrators to consider establishing school cultures and climates that feel more secure, affirming and caring to all the children and young people that populate them. That challenge involves the idea of establishing what I have called positive pedagogy (Barnes, 2018).

This book's major focus on curriculum and pedagogy will be introduced by outlining some of the existential issues currently facing humanity.

The global context

Between 2020 and 2022 the world suffered a unique collision of crises. Lives and thoughts everywhere, were dominated by a series of global dramas: cost of living crises, pandemic, accelerating climate change, declining biodiversity, mass migrations, institutional racial injustice, culture wars, nationalism, unsustainable extraction, political extremism and heightened consciousness of ever-widening gaps between rich and poor. Our global interconnectedness was undeniably confirmed as Covid-19 with its many mutations, spread from nation to nation within days. The Russian invasion of Ukraine has had a similarly profound global impact on world economies, fuel security and grain supplies. Connections across the world were underlined by unrelenting news of racially motivated horrors like the public murder of George Floyd under the knee of a white policeman. Today, TV, social media and international conferences evidence the close relationship between threatened eco-systems and healthy human societies. Climate change is already generating multiple and wide-ranging environmental *and* human consequences that will increase through the century. The world, particularly between the tropics, is threatened with more frequent famines, droughts, floods and storms, but also unprecedented displacements, mass migration, mounting civil unrest and threatened or escalating warfare.

Governments and schools have been slow to respond to these long-predicted crises. Other priorities have prevented countries, systems and individuals from seriously tackling such global challenges until relatively recently. Indeed, it is possible to argue that it has taken the combined voices of a 19-year-old Swedish woman and a nonagenarian TV personality to push these issues towards the top of the international agenda. The united message now from the COP27, United Nations, business community, wildlife, environmental and aid agencies is that these huge and complex issues must be addressed urgently and education is central to the answer. A number of inter-related principles will link the case studies, research and theories that characterise this book.

Principle 1: Education policy should be characterised by sustained and teacher-led curricular, pedagogical and philosophical responses to the unique challenges of the 21st century

Values are central to the discussion. To address the multiple threats facing the globe it will be argued that inclusive values should be *actively* present in the curriculum and teaching of every subject, every lesson plan and each interaction. This book will show how these values are linked to major world issues and point to how a 3–14 curriculum might powerfully address them without the need to change or challenge more general national guidance. A theme that will recur throughout the book will be that these responses must be linked to the teacher's progressive understanding of our common humanity.

Common humanity

There is only one human race. Homo sapiens exterminated or hybridised other humanoid competitors tens of thousands of years ago. While every human has an almost identical genome, the cultures, languages and lifestyles we have developed are manifold. Success in diversity is a defining characteristic of our race. Within such diversity it may seem a miracle that there are commonalities; one is the continual human search for meaning (Frankl, 1992) but there are other human universals, many related to meaning-making (see Brown, 1992). Apparently, no human culture exists or has existed without language, music, stories, morals, emotion, spiritual understandings, allegiance to place.

There are other factors that conjoin us. Human emotions, for example, are often shown in very similar ways in the faces and bodies of people across cultures (see Ekman, 2004; Gladwell, 2006). Neuroscientists suggest a set of basic neural networks controlling and expressing fear, joy, sadness, anger that are recognisable across human and other animal cultures (Gu et al., 2019).

Emotion has been shown by neuroscientists (for example LeDoux, 2012), to be a driver of the human learning process. Damasio suggests that every object and each remembered action generates a unique 'emotional tag' through which we interpret and learn from the environments we inhabit (Damasio, 2003). Whether our environment is the grassy plains of Africa, the archipelagos of the Pacific, the jungles of the Amazon or the skyscrapers of New York, Dubai or Tokyo, our world is packed with emotional meaning. If the emotional relevance is strong, educational neuroscience suggests that learning becomes more profound, lasting and transferrable (Immordino-Yang, 2019). When emotions – positive or negative – occur in real-world contexts, psychologists assert that their 'mental representation' in memory serves as the basis of motivation, personality development and integration into daily life (Dweck, 2017a). If those emotions are positive – leading to what neuroscientists and educationalists would term variations of joy – then research shows connection-making, trust, growth, confidence and creativity are likely to ensue (Fredrickson, 2009).

Advances in other sciences suggest that the two linked hemispheres of the human brain result in a consciousness that seeks and combines a 'big picture' world of meaning and experience with a world of things and fine detail (McGilchrist, 2021). Such current and rigorously researched theories offer evidence on optimum conditions for thinking and learning and merit high-level attention among teachers and education decision-makers. Sadly, discussions on the application of educational neuroscience is under-represented in public policy, but so too are the views and experience of long-serving teachers. Teachers are of course in a unique position to know what engages and motivates diverse groups of children and what promotes learning.

Principle 2: Education practice should be founded upon evidence of the physical, mental and social commonalities that bind humanity and the human search for meaning

The importance of community

Pandemic quickly reminded us of the vital role of community. Suddenly, and with no planning, singing from apartment balconies, clapping on doorsteps, shopping trips for neighbours, distanced walking groups, Zoomed family quiz nights and phone call lists became common features of life. While people missed communal activities like choirs, football matches, shopping trips and festivals, inventive minds the world over, constructed online or socially distanced versions to keep community together. People quickly lamented what was missing and noted the high value of being physically and culturally together. Most communities also rediscovered how central schools were to the locality and particularly to the lives and healthy socialisation of children and young people.

Sociologists, psychologists and educational theorists have stressed the importance of social learning for centuries. More recently, neuroscientists (for example Goswami, 2015; Lieberman, 2015; Damasio, 2021) have highlighted the importance of their work in offering empirical foundations for long-held theories about the social and cultural nature of learning. Social cognitive or interpersonal neuroscience suggests, for example, that learning occurs particularly effectively through 'brain to brain coupling' (Pan et al., 2021), where two or more individuals temporarily link their brain activity to solve a problem or confront an issue. Such coupling occurs in other social species too and appears essential for survival and the creation of animal and human cultures. While lone, direct, 'Pavlovian' learning is part of every individual's experience, social learning via undirected observation, focused interactive activity and multimodal group interaction is much more common and usually more economical. For the majority social learning feels more pleasant too.

Humans are heavily dependent on social interaction. The development of language obviously made those interactions infinitely more efficient and bound communities more tightly. Vygotsky's observation of a 'Zone of Proximal Development' (1978) in which children were observed to learn linguistically and practically from and with more experienced others offered a 20th-century analysis of already well-known benefits of group interaction. But community is more significant to education than describing its collaborative aspects. Community often involves shared geography, larger numbers and a broader demography than a school. It involves usually shared values, cooperation, mutual experiences, distributed roles and, ideally, collective care and common goals. Community helps construct and sustain meaning for young and old.

As physical, social institutions schools become micro-communities whether they plan to or not. Communities are not always good, they can be inclusive or exclusive, positive or negative, secure or unsafe. Sadly, they can also be nondescript, poorly focused and directionless. In this book, it will be argued that the positive school should be a model of supportive, egalitarian, caring community, providing multiple daily examples of what good means. Within such a community, a classroom can become a model of a utopia that children can take into later life as an exemplification of how to live together in sustainable, trusting, joyful, respectful and kind ways (Barnes, 2020).

Principle 3: Teachers should strive to make their schools and classrooms models of inclusion and positivity
The gift of diversity

Diversity is a welcome fact of human life. Diversities of race, culture and creed are often obvious, but equally important are the less obvious diversities highlighted towards the end of this book. Each individual human is wonderfully different from the next. Even identical twins, clones of each other, usually brought up in the same physical and emotional environment, develop different selves because they each occupy what Pinker called a 'unique environment' of thoughts, sights and happenings that only happen to them (Pinker, 2002). *Within* each of us there is diversity too – depending on our mood different things engage us. Differing settings and emotions will evoke contrasting responses to the same issue; particular people or situations may trigger unpredictable reactions and consistency is a problem for many. Established teachers expect such diversity, even in the most mono-cultural of communities.

The diversity within us is not usually acknowledged in the curriculum. Neither are our more visible diversities adequately represented. Despite frequent reminders about curriculum 'whitewashing', Black, Asian, Mixed Race, disabled or unusual youngsters only occasionally find themselves present in story books or history topics. Recently, and partly as a result of movements like Black Lives Matter, youngsters from diverse backgrounds have begun to see themselves more widely represented in advertising, TV, or as characters in schoolbooks. Without doubt, such attempts to offer a fairer picture of the UK's super-diversity are common in some urban schools, but dead, white and male heroes are still heavily over-represented in music, history, literature, drama, science and art. The best of diversity-conscious schools have corridor and classroom images representative of a range of cultures and all kinds of family arrangement in the UK. Their classroom resources include story books that star diverse characters and they use multicultural examples and illustrations across every curriculum area. In inner city schools it is common to find positive interactions in the languages of local community members, visits, visitors and class discussions that acknowledge a cross-section of local cultures and culturally sensitive tests and assignments. However, in significant numbers of schools such reflections of British society only appear in 'Black History Month'.

The huge educational and social value of diversity will be illustrated and discussed throughout this book. Just as the world's eco-diversity demonstrates the beauty and wonder of nature, human diversity richly exhibits the multiple ways humans can be both individual and part of communities. We know that biodiversity would flourish perfectly well without humans, but humans cannot survive without halting and reversing the current loss of species, habitats and ecosystems. The 8.7 million species of plants and animals surviving in the natural world not only provide endless fascination and awe, but provoke new thoughts, connections and solutions. Safeguarding present biodiversity preserves and re-establishes balance and raises the potential of the environments we coexist within. Careful husbandry of the land and its ecosystems delivers life-affirming contexts for community, life-preserving oxygen, nutrients, food-rich rivers and seas, shade, medicines and foods for all. Ultimately, protecting the remaining species of the world enhances the chances of peace and plenty for all.

Preserving human diversity is equally important in sustaining our species. Sustaining the differences between and within us offers benefits parallel to the benefits of environmental conservation. Just as life burgeons in rewilded landscapes or restored forests, when human diversity is seen as a gift not a threat, our lives are enriched with better ways of being human.

Principle 4: Diversity should be represented throughout the year in every subject across the curriculum and in the pedagogies and people that implement it

The value of creativity

Psychologist Mihaly Csikszentmihalyi summarised a lifetime's work on creativity and happiness in the words, 'Creativity is a central source of meaning' (Csikszentmihalyi, 1997). While definitions of creativity differ, there is ubiquity in the look of satisfaction on the faces of people everywhere as they consider something they have made. Witness the pride of the parent of a new-born child, a goal scorer, a problem solver, or a successful do-it-yourself-er anywhere and it is difficult to disagree that using one's own resources to make something new is both satisfying and very often meaningful.

Creativity can however be an exclusive concept as in Feldman's definition:

> the purposeful transformation of a body of knowledge, where that transformation is so significant that the body of knowledge is irrevocably changed from the way it was before.... (Feldman, 1994, p. 86)

Gruber (1981), Simonton (1984), Gardner (1993) and Csikszentmihalyi (1990), early researchers and theorists on creativity, have broadly supported this statement, but of course Feldman's kind of creativity excludes almost all of us. More inclusive, everyday definitions of creativity are probably more helpful in an education setting. In the groundbreaking *All Our Futures* report of the National Advisory Committee on Creative and Cultural Education (NACCCE), Robinson defined creativity as:

> imaginative activity, fashioned so as to produce outcomes which are original and of value. (NACCCE, 1999, p. 29)

This definition opens creativity to all: the youngster who has just built their first sandcastle, or settled an argument between friends, the child whose story had an unexpected ending, or who made a novel connection between a picture and some music, or found an unusual way of getting the right answer in a maths test. When a young person is told that something they have done is original (even to them or their group), appreciated (even by one other person) and used their imagination – the body language of pride often follows. A teacher or other adult is often the person that recognises and highlights such humanising acts.

Seventy years before Robinson, Vygotsky concluded that repetitive, imitative, combining and imaginative kinds of creativity were 'fully manifest in early childhood'. His transcribed lecture of 1930 details children's small innovations in a wide range of curriculum subjects in Russian primary schools. For Vygotsky:

> Any human act that gives rise to something new is referred to as a creative act, regardless of whether what is created is a physical object or some mental or emotional construct that lives within the person who created it and is known only to him. (2004, p. 7)

This open definition resulted not just from Vygotsky's observations that creativity brings *the creator great happiness,* but from his belief that developing creative imagination in children was essential for 'the entire future of humanity' (2004, p. 87).

The Covid pandemic forcefully reminded us of the importance of creativity to human survival. The scientists, planners, designers, inventors, technicians and health practitioners that created and continue to create safe responses to a novel and fast mutating disease, demonstrate the huge value of creative solutions. Throughout 2020 and 2021, key workers in the utilities, waste disposal, retail and hospitality, charities, volunteers, the self-employed and of course those involved in education rapidly imagined new ways of working, serving, communicating and earning. We discovered that waste disposal operatives are as vital as teachers and nurses and that creativity is as much a part of family life as of the arts and culture. We now know how dull life can be without collective experiences in concerts, galleries, theatre, sports venues, markets and street arts. We understand precisely just how interdependent we are and how often interdependence promotes creativity.

Principle 5: Every teacher should recognise and promote creative acts, products and connections in all subjects, in every child and at each stage of education

The current context in UK primary education

Human commonalities underpin our stories, ceremonies, values, religions and ordinary daily lives. These shared qualities might be expected to result in very similar approaches to the education of children in our primary schools – but they have not.

Progressive versus traditional

In the West for at least 300 years tensions have existed between education binaries such as: 'progressive' and 'traditional'; knowledge versus experience; subjects versus themes; conformist or flexible; practical or intellectual; tacit or explicit approaches. More inclusive and considered analysis leads to more of a balance between these extremes. My writing and research on the curriculum have at times been taken to imply that cross-curricular and creative approaches are all that is needed to make primary education effective, relevant and engaging. This is not the case. While I maintain that cross-curricular and creative approaches more easily sustain motivation and learning, I also know that developing a bank of discrete knowledge and skills within each subject discipline is crucial. Both my books on the primary curriculum culminate in what I call *double focus cross-curricular learning* where newly acquired subject knowledge is rapidly applied in real-world and cross-curricular contexts. I agree with Tim Oates that, 'knowledge is an essential component of performance' (Oates, 2015, p. 68), but 50 years in classrooms have shown me that the knowledge needed for excellent and fulfilling performance is both specific and very varied. My interest in disciplined knowledge and skills does not mean unquestioning support of a privileged subculture's definition of what knowledge is defined as core.

Core knowledge

The concept of 'core knowledge' is of course contested. There are probably as many definitions of what knowledge should be core as there are thinkers about knowledge. Not very long ago, for example, Sir Chris Woodhead then Chief Inspector of Schools, suggested that knowing that Edward VIII was the most recent monarch to abdicate (Woodhead, *Sunday Times*, 3 April 2005) constituted what he called 'worthwhile knowledge'. Only seven years earlier, Roy Strong the then Director of the Victoria and Albert Museum stated:

> It is more important for a young person to be made to wonder at the architecture of something like the Palace of Versailles or glimpse what underlies ... a single scene in a Mozart opera than to paint another bad picture or bang a drum in the false interests of self-expression. (SCAA, 1997)

What is judged 'core knowledge' is likely to relate closely to the information most valued by those currently holding authority in a society. Knowledge of details of British Royal history or European palaces might be important to some, but may have an excluding effect on others. In a highly diverse Britain where 14% are Black, Asian or from a Minority Ethnic group (BAME), 23% live in poverty and increasing numbers of children are excluded (RSA, 2020), disaffected or suffering from mental ill-health (UK Parliament, 2021), definitions of core knowledge will vary from family to family, community to community. It is difficult to imagine that the record 66,463 primary school children on fixed term exclusions in 2019 (Parsons, 2018) will have been persuaded to change their ways by being given more core knowledge. Indeed, Bourdieu's concept of 'cultural capital', the knowledge one needs to ensure easy passage up the social and economic ladder within a culture, can only effectively apply where power is held by a relatively homogenous elite. Decision-makers with existing educational, economic and social advantages are likely to respond positively to a curriculum based on 'traditional' approaches to education because they have already profited from them. Those disadvantaged by exclusion, poverty, special educational needs (SEN), those 'in care', or from BAME, Mixed Race, Roma or traveller communities may be less likely to be captivated by a culture that takes little account of people like them. If political ambitions like 'levelling up' and supporting the most disadvantaged are to be realised, the process should start in education. Teachers should be centrally involved in serious debate on what needs to be known and understood to make a more equitable society. This book is offered as a contribution to that debate; the positive pedagogue will take the debate further.

New expectations from government and inspectorate

Despite the complications of pandemic, government proceeded with some major changes in education, some responding to more market-led, competitive education philosophies imported from the USA. The *Core Content Framework* (CCF) (DfE, 2019a) sets out a new baseline expectation for all teacher education and adding to existing Teachers' Standards. The CCF sets out the areas that must be developed and supported in all teacher education whether in university or work-based settings. The Early Career Teacher Framework (DfE, 2019b) adds funding and detail to what novice teachers in the first two years of teaching should expect from their schools and authorities in the primary education context. Both frameworks stress: pedagogy, assessment, behaviour management, curriculum and professional behaviours. They highlight maintaining positive relations, creating effective learning environments, challenging all pupils, activity, modelling, the essential skills, knowledge and principles of each separate subject, formative assessment, meeting the needs of individual pupils including all vulnerable groups and reflective practice. However, this encouraging guidance was seen by many as being rather undermined by Ofsted's Chief Inspector's view that halving the number of schools previously judged 'outstanding' would be a more realistic appraisal of the quality of education nationally. It is equally undermined by the absence of balancing words like creativity, compassion, community and care. In addition, newly appointed Social Mobility Tsar Katharine Birbalsingh whose view that the, '… idea that the state should look after your child's schooling is ridiculous', surprised many (Mirror, 2021).

The *Initial Teacher Training (ITT) Market Review* of 2021 (Gov. UK, 2021a, 2021b) stresses evidence-based training and established 'teaching school hubs' to participate in delivering ITT and provide a mentor network. The stress on certain words gives a flavour of current expectations: the word 'quality' is used 161 times, 'requirement', 'rigorous', 'accreditation', 'assessment' 'highly targeted' are also popular. Creativity is not mentioned and only passing reference is made to flexibility or choice. In contrast, in 2021

Ofsted published the latest in its subject reviews, this time on music. It dwells on the technical, constructive and expressive aspects of music and music making and expects teachers to help children at all levels to 'explore their own creative potential' – again, the emphasis is on quality products and experience but refreshingly the words 'creativity' and 'diversity' are mentioned frequently, imagination and meaningfulness hailed and the need for balance between freedom and constraint highlighted.

In its Annual Review for 2021 Ofsted commented on what it called a 'wholly different year'. Schools were at first not guided on distance learning by the Department of Education and what Ofsted called *hokey-cokey education* of open and closed classes and schools followed throughout the year. Missing weeks, teachers, friends and activities throughout the year meant that almost all children's education was 'hampered' and those with SEN often had no support. The need for 'catch up' or a 'recovery' is clear, but even more concerning is Ofsted's observation that many children had 'disappeared from teachers' line of sight'. Indeed, both the Children's Society and Ofsted warned of tens of thousands of children that have 'fallen off the radar' and may have slipped into gangs, criminal activity and exploitation during the pandemic.

The Ofsted press release of 7 December 2021 stressed:

> it's important the focus is not solely on bridging gaps in academic learning. Schools must offer children a rounded experience, including a rich curriculum, sport and physical activity, and extra-curricular opportunities that broaden their horizons. (Ofsted, 2021c)

Disaffection

Unhappiness amongst children currently in UK schools is a serious and growing issue. Since 1945, the World Health Organisation (WHO) has published four annual. International comparisons on children's health behaviour (WHO, 2020). The latest report shows that before the pandemic British, particularly English, 11-year-olds reported poor levels of life-satisfaction, English children at 11 years are near the bottom of 45 countries (Scottish and Welsh children are halfway down the league). English children also express low levels of liking school and high levels of pressure from school. In the WHO report, English children also claimed low and declining levels of parental, teacher and peer support compared with other European countries. There are numerous interpretations of such self-reported feelings, but if large minorities of a child population *feel* unenamoured with school at 11, the effect on classroom behaviour, engagement and progress is likely to be negative. Suggested explanations for these concerning figures include a perceived narrowing of curriculum away from subjects that engage by practical activity and perceived relevance (Barnes and Scoffham, 2017), an increasing focus on assessment and the pressure of school league tables. Others highlight unsupportive inspection regimes (Cohen, 2019), poor funding, poor teacher retention and generally poor morale in schools (Ofsted, 2021d).

Disaffection shows itself in many ways at school. Children may be difficult to motivate, uninvolved, badly behaved, absent for minor illnesses or for no good reason. They may develop speech, language and communication or other 'special' needs. We know too that cases of anxiety, depression and eating disorders have grown significantly during the lockdowns and the suspension of normal school activities during the Covid-19 pandemic (Nuffield, 2022b). Rising numbers of children find themselves in care (County Councils Network, 2021), more are suspended from school (Parsons, 2018) and child poverty continues to increase (End Child Poverty, 2022). Taken alongside the WHO figures a picture emerges of a specifically British educational crisis to add to the global ones outlined earlier – the loss of enthusiasm for education among significant percentages of children. Weakened interest in education is of course likely to result in diminished potential perhaps to a third of children (Blatchford, 2020).

Addressing children's disengagement requires careful thinking about both the official and the 'hidden' curriculum. A curriculum is not just the subjects taught, but the ways they are taught, the illustrations chosen, the physical conditions of learning and the attitudes demonstrated as well as the facts. The curriculum does not have to be the same in each school. Schools are microcosms of the community in which they are placed and the positive curriculum should reflect the many differences between communities, as Sherrington observed:

> We don't need all young people to read the same books or study the same periods in history; in fact, across the nation, we are probably better off with a diverse curriculum so that collectively we have a broader range of expertise; our collective cultural capital is greater. (Sherrington, 2015)

Schools might begin addressing disaffection by seeing children's own locality as their most treasured and accessible curriculum resource and an extension to their classroom for every teacher.

Education funding

Many schools and teachers report the impact of shortfalls in education funding (e.g. Guardian October 2021a; Institute for Fiscal Studies, 2021; NASUWT, 2021). Education as a whole now receives 8% less funding than in 2010 and 1% less of national income. The pandemic has undoubtedly cost every nation and system dearly – in the UK this amounted to 370 billion pounds – more than £5,000 for every man woman and child. One of the consequences of this astronomical bill, added to pre-pandemic, 'austerity' cuts, is that a wide range of public services have seen reduced income or smaller rises than expected.

Less money in the system has resulted in shrinking children's services. Children in most need have suffered most. For example, from the early 2000s families in the greatest difficulty could expect coordinated support from a 'Team Around the Child' (TAC). This group was formed in each school, to provide a plan for the protection of individual children at risk. However, TACs are currently seriously overstretched and under-resourced (see Action for Children report 2020). In addition to parents and foster carers, the professionals in a TAC might include: midwife, health visitor, school nurse, nursery teacher, school teacher, SEN coordinator, speech therapist, CAMHS (child and adolescent mental health service) representative, Teacher Assistant, and any other support worker. The waiting list for a CAMHS appointment is commonly over two years, by which time a child's mental health is likely to have deteriorated. Issues of underfunding affect parents, children, foster parents (see *Observer* 5 December 2021), and all professionals involved in a TAC. Discussions over low morale, cuts to funding, less-than-inflation pay rises and shrinking resources are familiar across education.

While a positive approach to curriculum and pedagogy will not affect education funding, I contend that it can and does benefit recruitment, retention and staff well-being – and thus children's security and engagement in education.

The need for positivity

Children are not immune to news of a troubled world. When consulted most are aware of wars, refugees, climate change and extinctions via social media, overheard conversations, playground conversation and popular press (Hicks, 2018). In addition, feelings of high stress amongst teachers inevitably pass on to the children in their classes. There is little doubt that the times of lightness, freedom, discovery and joy that should define childhood are in shorter supply because of the combination of crises outlined above. A relaxed and happy childhood is even less available to those facing multiple physical, economic and social disadvantages. A positive pedagogy approach offers hope for these often 'unseen children', and that hope can arise from inexpensive, relatively minor but heartfelt, changes to the climate and culture of schools.

All children benefit from a positive environment. We know from experience and scientific research that an atmosphere of security, care and love impacts positively on the minds of all of us. From the classically most able to those with profound and complex barriers to learning and participation, affirmative conditions promote broader, deeper, more creative thinking (Fredrickson, 2010). Teachers also know from experience that, 'learning is a consequence of thinking' (Perkins, 1992) and by inference the deeper the thought, the wider, more transferable and lasting the learning is likely to be. Under the headings: *values, humanising the curriculum, celebrating diversity, connecting, experiencing the world around us*, we offer a five-point plan to guide novice primary teachers towards the state of positive pedagogy. This will begin by helping you think about changes to the present school lives of children that will quickly generate a positive culture that involves and inspires all.

Values

If values lead and sustain the good in us then the values discussion must be a frequent part of the life of the positive school. A value can be defined as:

> a deeply held belief that acts as a fundamental guide and prompt to action. They spur us forward, give us a sense of direction and define a destination. (Booth and Ainscow, 2020)

Many teachers begin their careers with enthusiasm and idealism; I believe it is vital to maintain that idealism. Aligning your daily working life in school with the personal values that led you to choose teaching is sustaining (Barnes, 2012). In interviews for Initial Teacher Education (ITE) successful early career primary school teachers frequently speak of a love of learning, a joy in communicating with children and a wish to be part of an affirmative educational experience for all children. Most teachers want to use education to make the world a better place and inclusive values lead us there. Talking about our personal values helps turn them into action and schools making frequent use of 'values discussions' are more likely to live the values they claim.

The link between values and *action* is central on an institutional as well as personal level. If the school's values are to give coherence to curriculum and pedagogy then they must be visible in every aspect of school life at any time. Take just one of the inclusive values listed earlier – compassion. If we claim compassion is a key value of the school then that irreducible concept should be the judge of everything we do. Did we show compassion in the way we dealt with the 'difficult' parent? How do we show compassion in our choices of resources, lesson illustrations, displays and themes? Could we show more compassion in the way we line up after playtime? Is compassion a defining and recognisable feature of the activities and relationships in our school culture, policies? Is compassion growing daily in our practice? Similar interrogation is valid for any other school values.

Using the values discussion to set up a values-creating school:

1. Each staff member (including TAs, secretary, caretaker and other support staff) independently names the four or five personal values that drive and direct their decisions.
2. Groups of staff share their most prized values and seek agreement on areas of overlap.
3. Whole staff meets to pool the most well-supported values and agree on 4 or 5 that are shared by all. These become the school values and are publicised to all stakeholders.
4. Staff meet each week to address one of the chosen values. They work independently and then in teams to *visualise in an idealisation of the school or classroom involving how that value is lived out*. Staff spend time on the fine detail and make the visualisation present tense: What is the weather like on this ideal day? What are the dominant smells? What do the classrooms look like (colour, arrangement, access, decoration, etc.)? Feel like? Are adaptations needed to the building/furniture/equipment? What do faces of children and staff look like? What do casual interactions in the corridor, staffroom or playground

sound like? Imagine a typical interaction between children in the classroom when the teacher is not there. How is that value applied to teaching, curriculum, resources, the building, the playground, relationships with community, parents, governors, children and between children?

Humanising the curriculum

The differences between us are to be expected and honoured, but what we share is greater than what divides us. The aspects of humanity we share are relevant across the curriculum. Geography, for instance, concerns the inter-relationship between people and places. History considers the past of different groups of people and changes in their lives over time. Science is used to make sense of the physical and natural realities around us. Physical education helps us maintain and develop physical strength, balance and coordination, but also shows that we can express ideas through our bodies and find joy in movement in games. Each subject and area of the school curriculum relates to human needs and interests. How do we emphasise the common aspects of humanity through our work in each subject?

First, we humanise any subject by involving our powerful and uniquely complex emotional system. We should continually aim at emotional engagement throughout our teaching. When we are emotionally engaged commitment is more intense, physical and sustained and deep, transferable learning is more likely. So, how do we generate emotional engagement? I suggest trying out the following approaches that can be introduced into the teaching of any subject:

1. Find the relevance to the child – where does the aspect to be learned intersect with the child's life?
2. Use objects – introduce a subject by putting something relevant in children's hands. 'No objects that surround us are without their emotional tag' (Damasio, 2003, p. 55).
3. Use touch, smell, taste, sound and detailed examination through visual observation.
4. Enhance visual examination by drawing in science, geography, history, English, foreign languages, RE and design technology as well as art.
5. Consider wordless ways to deepen understanding – music, art, movement, dance, mime, games, physical exploration, even non-literal poetry, can effectively capture mathematical, scientific and social truths. Aspects of the humanities can be powerfully expressed and understood through the arts.
6. Use stories across the curriculum – including personal family stories, improvised tales, narratives acted out by class members and visitors, the stories of others. Stories frequently involve human commonalities: values, emotions, needs, meaning-making, community, diversity and creativity – familiar themes across cultures.

Celebrating diversity

Take a walk around the school to identify and record settings, displays, relationships, signs and symbols that celebrate diversity. Seek examples of cultural, racial, religious diversity but also diverse skills, interests, personalities, friendships and families. Ask groups of children to do the same. Ask some of the following diversity questions taken from *The Index for Inclusion* (Booth and Ainscow, 2020).

1. Do all curriculum development activities address the participation of students differing in background, experience, attainment or impairment?
2. Do all curriculum development activities address the reduction of barriers to learning and participation?
3. Do staff development activities support staff in working effectively together in classrooms?
4. Is partnership teaching, followed by shared review, used to support teachers to respond to student diversity?
5. Do staff observe each other's lessons in order to reflect on the perspectives of students?
6. Do staff receive training in devising and managing collaborative learning activities?
7. Are there shared opportunities for teachers and classroom assistants to develop more effective collaboration?
8. Are there opportunities for staff and students to learn about peer tutoring?
9. Do teaching and support staff learn about using technology to support learning (such as cameras, television, video, overhead projector, tape-recorders, computers/internet)?
10. Do staff explore ways of reducing disaffection by increasing the engagement of students in curricula?
11. Is disability equality education provided for all staff?
12. Do all staff learn how to counter bullying, including racism, sexism and homophobia?
13. Do staff and governors take responsibility for assessing their own learning needs?

Connecting

'Only connect…live in fragments no longer,' said novelist E.M. Forster and there is truth in this bold condensation of philosophy. In many ways everything can and should connect. The theory of 'six degrees of separation' is also often confirmed, especially as one gets older. With imagination we might connect the oak tree in the school grounds with aspects of any curriculum subject, but we don't all have the same creative imagination. Sharing teachers' subject expertise across a primary school is essential. The mathematics specialist, for example, will more easily connect a skill in their subject with a poetic idea, artwork or a musical composition and the musician might see the maths in music more quickly than the historian. The language, skills and attitudes of any curriculum subject may be applied to any of the physical, mental and spiritual realities around us (see Gardner, 2000a).

Some connections are weak or insubstantial, however. Connections between curriculum subjects must be carefully planned and workable. In previous work (Barnes, 2015 and 2018) I have stressed that planning, delivering and assessing cross-curricular learning is best done by applying the knowledge, language and skills of just two subjects – with the addition of English if reading, writing or speaking is used at all. So, for what I have called *The Connecting Curriculum*, consider the following ideas to guide your decisions on connections:

1. Connect subject learning to a powerful personal experience (usually) at the beginning of a cross-curricular unit of work – perhaps a video, visit, visitor, event, object, presentation or out-of-class activity that you have made relevant and exciting for children. The energy and interest generated by engagement in this experience will motivate and sustain interest through the unit of work that will follow.
2. Plan and teach the specific skills and knowledge that will be used to make sense of the cross-curricular experience you have planned.
3. Ensure children know which two subjects will be connected to the experience.
4. Have discrete learning objectives *that extend* the knowledge and skills in the two subjects you want children to use in their responses to the experience.
5. Make connections authentic – replicating connections evident in the real world or deliberately challenging current practice by connecting unusual subjects – 'how can I represent this tree using the skills and knowledge of dance and geography?'
6. Consolidate new subject learning by applying it in new situations – this will help you accurately assess the degree to which the learning has been internalised.
7. Connect each curriculum subject to at least one other in a cross-curricular project within a school year.

Experiencing the world around the child

The word experience has been used many times in this introduction. Experience is necessary to make real connections and human life is a string of personal experiences out of which we try to build meaning – our values are born from experiences that have a particularly powerful meaning to us.

Experiences with an educational purpose normally require careful planning. Sometimes, however, unplanned experiences shared with age-mates can provide motivation and interest to engender many questions and the desire for deeper understanding. Sadly, current global and national issues have curtailed many planned and unplanned educational experiences. Between 2020 and 2022 many schools plays, musicals, concerts, sports days and processions were cancelled due to Covid restrictions and fears. School trips and adventure holidays were cancelled and collaborations with other schools limited. In addition, tightening inspection rules and statements regarding expectations and accountability may have had the effect of making schools more risk-averse – avoiding experimentation, the unknown, untried or open-ended. The positive teacher will strive to maintain a series of powerful experiences to capture attention, motivate and sustain learning – and be the aspect of education remembered tens of years later.

Consider the following simple and easily arranged experiences to provoke involvement in further learning:

1. Make a visit to meet representatives of a local temple, Gurdwara, church, or mosque. Making drawings of small details and collecting stories from people who use these places (RE and English).
2. Use a wild walk to gather colours, shapes, textures or sounds and to use and make maps and make classifications (science and geography).
3. Plan a school-based exercise where groups construct maps of grounds that include some of the invisible boundaries known by children and not adults (PSHE and geography).
4. Collect a group of unusual objects borrowed from the local museum for children to investigate, draw and question. Later they design and curate a display of their loaned collection and introduce them to children in other classes (history and art and design).
5. Mount a research exercise to find appropriate food for a Roman/medieval/Victorian party. Find a recipe, make it and plan to eat it in an appropriate setting (technology and history).
6. Establish an internet link up with a school in Africa where children ask each other questions and perform prepared musical items for each other (music and geography).
7. Make an exhibition of paintings capturing the fine detail of science investigations accompanied by performances of musical compositions based upon microscope observations (science, music and art).
8. Visit a complex building like a factory, shopping arcade, palace, large religious centre, or grand house to identify, photograph and collect as many geometric shapes and patterns as possible. Use the shapes to design wallpaper or fabrics (maths and design and technology).
9. Select the biggest tree in the playground on a sunny day. Measure its girth, its shadow, the diameter of its shadow, the size and shape of its leaves. Estimate its height, count, classify and record the numbers of life forms it supports. Collect the pollution deposited on leaves using a tissue, compare the temperature beneath it with the temperature in the open sun. Express these findings in graphs and diagrams (maths and science).
10. Watch the wind move through long grass or grain crops, observe the patterns and movements it makes. Make a list of words that describe the scene and take a series of photos to be used as part of a story written back in class. Experiment on site with dance movements in response to what is observed (PE and English).

Summary

This chapter has introduced the idea of positive, inclusive values and put these values alongside some of the things we have learned through the Covid pandemic of 2020 and 2021. Refreshed understandings of the important and universal aspects of human life have guided fresh thinking about education in the UK. Ideas about core knowledge and catch-up have dominated the thinking of education policy makers, but the negative mental health effects of the pandemic, disaffection, underachievement and reduced funding in primary schools have preoccupied many involved in schools on a day-by-day basis. The case has been made for a rethink of education that starts with using teachers' expertise on the diverse needs of children. It was suggested that a positive approach to education would place community, global issues and human commonalities centrally in curriculum and that reassessment should include significantly more attention to inclusion, diversity, positivity and creativity. The chapter closes with some practical suggestions to support novice teachers in becoming positive pedagogues.

2

POSITIVE PEDAGOGY – TAKING CONTROL OF THE TEACHING AND THE LEARNING ENVIRONMENT THROUGH RECLAIMING TEACHERS' VALUES

Objectives

This chapter will lead you to think carefully about:

- The relationship between your personal values and your work as a teacher
- The kind of teacher you want to be
- The environments you will create as a leader of learning

It will outline the case for establishing a climate of positivity in your classroom and discuss how affirmative approaches to curriculum experience can be applied in every lesson and learning environment. Combining aspects of the history of education, recent research in education, educational neuroscience and psychology with real-world case studies, the chapter will discuss how inclusive values in schools can release potential through generating an atmosphere of security, possibility, achievement and hope that enables the long-term learning of key concepts and skills.

Talking about your values

We all live by values whether or not we are aware of it. We saw in Chapter 1 that a value is a fundamental belief that serves as a prompt to action in the real world of our daily lives. If you deeply believe, for example, that all animals have the right to life and freedom, that belief may prompt you to become vegetarian or vegan. Your belief will also inform your choices of clothes, partners, holiday destinations, the books you read and friends you make. If you believe that pleasure is your main aim in life, that value will influence every small and big decision. A value indicates the general direction in which our decisions will lead us. Those who believe, for example, that compassion is an essential element of the moral life are likely to be heading in a different destination to those for whom accruing power or wealth is an ultimate goal.

We rarely think about our values. Perhaps during an interview you considered what motivated you towards teaching, but since then you may have had few opportunities to think about values. Most successful applicants to ITE courses express quite clear reasons for their career choice and these often concern fundamental beliefs in concepts such as equality, fairness, access, participation, community, hope. Perhaps you chose teaching

---

Exercise 1: Take some time to think about your values now.

- Draw around your outstretched hand and after reflection write a word or idea in each digit that captures a fundamental belief that you think directs many of your actions in everyday life.

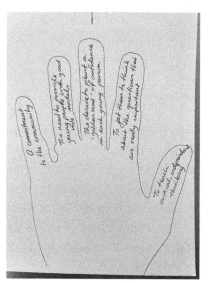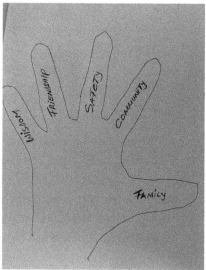

Figure 2.1 These values hands were made by Japanese and Congolese teachers (Photo: Barnes)

- When you have filled the fingers of your hand with four or five values that are important to you (see Figure 2.1), share them with a colleague or friend who has done the same thing. Discuss any similarities and differences. Try to arrive at one or two that you can both agree on, perhaps you will have to re-express the chosen value/s during this conversation.

for other reasons, but comparing your motivations with those who follow other career paths will reveal interesting differences in values. You have probably already met people who say that education in the 'real world' does not fit the idealistic hopes of teachers, but my research suggests it is worth holding to those ideals. When long-serving teachers were asked, 'What sustains a fulfilling life in education?' (Barnes, 2012) it was found that those whose personal values continued to match the values lived and honoured in their school institutions, were most likely to stay, develop and be happy in their job.

Current pressures on schools may at times overpower your treasured values. Assessment, accountability, standards raising, behaviour policies, inspections, compliance and performance targets on top of covering for staff absence and pupil illness can easily drive our guiding values far from our minds. Key questions are: How can trainee and early career teachers sustain what might be called 'humanitarian' values in an environment that may at times, seem hostile to empathy, kindness or fairness? How do we retain, build upon and broaden the values that brought us to teaching in the first place?

Teachers' values overlap all over the world. Between 2005 and 2012, I asked about the values that sustained teachers in 40 English primary schools. Later I asked the same question of teachers in five non-western countries throughout 2017 and 2018 (Barnes, 2019). The answers came clearly. A majority of teachers believed in the importance of kindness, happiness, community, love, equality and humility. Around half my sample shared beliefs in service, patience, trust, tenacity, faith, democracy and peace (see Figure 2.2).

Figure 2.2 Values wordle

Regardless of culture, the established and well-respected teachers interviewed suggested that fulfilment in their job involved an awareness that their personal values were upheld and lived throughout their school. They recognised that heartfelt values thrived within supportive friendships and affirmative relationships. Their prized values were best expressed in school settings where they could develop their artistic, social, intellectual, academic or practical creativities. You will find a range of examples of such personal values in action and the conditions that nurtured them in the following chapters.

Thinking about values in general

Curriculum advice and practical examples in this book are based on positive values. This term needs briefly explaining. Positive values are beliefs and actions that across many cultures are seen as virtuous, constructive, morally good. From the earliest recorded times particular virtues have been singled out as desirable for a healthy community by wise sages, philosophers and religious leaders. Greek and Roman philosophers and later interpreters like Thomas Aquinas elevated what became known as *the cardinal virtues*: prudence/wisdom, temperance/self-control, courage and justice. These virtues became guides to moral behaviour in public life throughout medieval Europe. St Paul identified a set of more intimate values, what he called the 'fruits of the spirit': love, joy, peace, patience, kindness, goodness, faithfulness, gentleness, and self-control (Galatians, 5.22–3). In Asia, Buddhist and Confucian ideas offered similar, action-based guidance adding notions of propriety, fidelity, benevolence, calmness, righteousness. The *Ubuntu* philosophy of central and south Africa emphasises human inter-relatedness and the fundamentals of survival, solidarity, compassion, respect and dignity. The central beliefs that have survived as 'virtues' across time and culture all identify courage, self-control or temperance, compassion or kindness, respect, wisdom, justice and freedom.

Influential educationalists recognised such virtues as of primary importance. Rousseau (1712–1778), for example, wrote of the natural goodness of humanity, and innate qualities of wisdom, benevolence, justice and freedom. Pestalozzi (1746–1827) also believed in the basic goodness of children and centring their education on free choices in affirmative settings, self-reliance and community. Later, Froebel (1782–1852) highlighted values related to human unity and connectedness, while Steiner (1861–1925) focused on inclusivity, gratitude and respect for diversity. Maria Montessori (1870–1952) majored on respect for young people and establishing a caring environment that nurtured independence and curiosity. More recently, education writers and researchers have emphasised time-honoured values like Wisdom (Craft, et al., 2007; Sternberg and Gluck, 2019), Love or Care (Noddings, 2005), Goodness (Gardner, Csikszentmihalyi and Damon, 2002; Gardner and Goleman, 2012), Hope (Halpin, 2003; Kidd, 2020), Joy (Iunez and Goulah, 2021) and Inclusion (Booth and Ainscow, 2020). Among the more heartening public responses to the Covid pandemic many have noted a resurgence of awareness of such 'virtuous values', those values that exemplify moral goodness across many cultures.

Values are not necessarily virtuous. We probably all have values we are not proud of. Deeply held beliefs in personal wealth, discrimination, selfishness, unfairness and hate are evident daily on social media platforms. Such values intentionally exclude others from states of well-being. Many of the values that dominate our economies and societies are far from those of ancient philosophers, sages and saints. Indeed, exclusive values like hierarchy, competition, surveillance, authority, monoculture, power, exploitation, consumption, selection and compliance could be argued to be represented throughout history and particularly widespread in periods of colonial and economic expansion across the world. Many have noted that similar exclusionary forces have dominated UK and particularly English education policy since the 1980s (see for example, Booth, 2018). Only lately have companies, governments and international organisations recognised the importance of inclusivity and allyship – principles that many teachers have sought to establish for decades. The application of inclusive values such as sustainability, respect for diversity, compassion, non-violence and equality could hardly be more relevant for today's world. Ethical Environmental, Social and Governance (ESG) policies currently high on business agendas across the globe, represent attempts to reset the values balance in favour of more virtuous principles (see Table 2.1).

Exercise 2: Offer your first thoughts on how business ESG policies on environmental and social matters might apply in primary school environments, curriculum and policy.

Table 2.1 Linking values and education with major global issues

Environmental concerns	Values to be applied	Write your thoughts on how these issues might be addressed in curriculum, environment and policy in the primary school?
Climate change	Sustainability, courage	
Carbon emissions	Wisdom, beauty, honesty	
Water shortage & pollution	Participation, rights, hope	
Air pollution		
Deforestation		
Social concerns		Write your thoughts on how these issues might be addressed in curriculum, environment and policy in the primary school?
Lack of inclusion	Love, joy, hope, equality	
Discrimination	Participation, compassion	
Unconscious bias,	Trust, community	
Endangered mental and physical health		
Impoverished communities	Respect for diversity	

Teachers' values matter. The opportunity of regular values discussions during training and in school life as outlined in Chapter 1, would help focus and refocus on the principles that teachers think matter in education. Frequent values conversations will make key shared values explicit and raise the expectations and standards of all. Sadly, these discussions rarely happen. When honestly debated and clearly expressed, our collective expectations of education would shape, sustain and direct a virtuous school life and remind us of the ultimate destinations we aspire to for the children in our care.

Valuing diversity

The rich cultural mix in modern Western societies has proved a vital asset. Though this idea is challenged in Chapter 8, the United Kingdom has been described as a super-diverse society (Vertovec, 2007) because of the high numbers and broad range of cultures and races for whom it is home. Currently 14% of the UK population are of Black, Asian or other minority ethnic (BAME) heritage. In London and the big conurbations of the UK, those percentages are higher – about 40% of London's population is BAME (Diversity in the UK). Increasing numbers of children belong to families with a mixed heritage and population experts estimate that by 2050 over 30% of the UK will see themselves as having a Black, Asian, minority ethnic or mixed background (Rees et al., 2016). Though Black, Asian and other minority ethnic individuals have lived, worked and occasionally ruled in Britain for thousands of years, the vast majority of families from BAME backgrounds trace their family origins to Commonwealth countries, reflecting Britain's long history as a colonial power. The education systems, exams and curricula of ex-colonies continued to deliver an Anglo-centric curriculum and for many years after their independence, English was spoken in their parliaments, courts and universities and often by well-off and well-educated elites. For the first few decades after independence, British versions of democracy, justice, education and social organisation were seen as the 'gold standard' by many. The British Nationality Act of 1948 gave citizens of the colonies British citizenship and many new British citizens were encouraged to fill vacancies in the newly created National Health Service (NHS), the transport system and industry. Through the 1950s and 1960s, these campaigns attracted 500,000 UK citizens (BBC, 2021) from the Caribbean and beyond. At the same time, the UK also became an attractive destination for further education, career development and secure employment. Some continue to benefit from the legacy of this period.

Ethnic diversity is part of the UK's past, present and future. The content of school curricula and the resources, illustrations, examples, environments and personnel of school life ought to represent that diversity, but they often do not. The curricula of the devolved nations of the UK contrast strongly with each other, but it should be uncontroversial to suggest that every subject is taught in a way in which children from all backgrounds, abilities and diversities can feel represented and 'at home'. The case studies illustrating the positive, inclusive and connecting themes of this book aim to reflect the rich diversity of our population.

There are other types of diversity too. Children differ in intellect, interest, interactions, and general character. They have divergent ways of seeing and interpreting the world, very often coloured by their experience, but probably genetic too. As Desmond Tutu remarked, 'We inhabit a universe that is characterised by diversity' – embracing that diversity reminds us of our need for each other (Tutu and Allan, 2011).

These diversities and those within us, can and should be accommodated in our teaching if something close to the potential of each child is to be released (see Table 2.2). This approach would be positive for each child, but on a community level diversity is probably our most valuable human asset because our differences so often spark creative advances.

Exercise 3: Reflect on some ways you are different from most other people.

Table 2.2 How am I different from others?

	In what ways am I **different** from other people around me?
Character	
Skills	
Background	
Physical appearance	
Experience	
Family	
Likes and dislikes	

Investigating the power of positivity

The positive psychology movement is a relatively young branch of the science. Founded around 2000 by eminent American psychologists like Seligman, Csikszentmihalyi and Sternberg, it sought to establish ways of using psychology to help study and increase psychological well-ness rather than its usual focus on mental illness. Well before 2000 psychologists such as Isen (1987) and Csikszentmihalyi (1990) showed how a range of positive states like interest and involvement enhanced and extended cognitive focus and function. At the same time, other psychologists (e.g. Ekman, 1989) and neuroscientists (e.g. Damasio, 1995) renewed interest in Darwin's (1872) work on the role of emotions in human and animal behaviour. Research in the early 2000s identified the neurological and visceral basis of what were understood to be fundamental human emotions – sadness, anger, fear, and joy. Though learning takes place in each emotional context, in conditions broadly categorised as 'joy' it was observed that brain and body appeared to be in the '… optimal physiological coordination and smooth running of the operations of life' (Damasio, 2003, p. 137). States of joy appeared to generate significantly increased activity in the prefrontal cortices and there were 'marked deactivations' (p. 101) in the same brain areas during conditions of sadness and fear. Extended conditions of fear and sadness were seen to impact negatively upon relationships, self-image, ideation and the immune system (Segerstrom and Miller, 2004). Such observations are highly significant for teachers because of their dependence on students' attitudes towards learning. Since the prefrontal cortex is responsible for essential aspects of thinking and learning such as planning, reasoning, problem solving, comprehension, judgement, creativity and perseverance (see also, Le Doux, 2002; Damasio, 2010, 2013; Immordino-Yang, 2015; Immordino-Yang, 2019; Goswami, 2019), developing environments in which positive emotions dominate and stress is diminished would seem to be essential for optimal learning conditions.

Learning involves changes in mind and body generated by new knowledge, skills and/or attitudes through experience. There is strong evidence that in positive emotional states like joy, gratitude, serenity, interest, hope, pride, amusement, inspiration, awe and love, we learn better. Simply put, when we are happy, body and mind function better (Fredrickson, 2013). Part of functioning better, is that learning is deeper, more easily transferable, more connections are made intellectually, socially and intra-personally, we take more notice of our environment, we have more and better ideas, more sustained concentration, heightened confidence and creativity. Research (Fredrickson et al., 2003) also shows that in positive states we can more easily 'call up' past positive experiences from memory adding to resilience and validating and prolonging present positive states. Each type of positive emotion whether mild or extreme generates comparable effects on the brain, flooding it with neurotransmitters like dopamine and serotonin that trigger feelings of satisfaction and well-being.

So, positive affect can have a powerful influence on learning. In her pioneering work on the 'Broaden and Build Theory', Barbara Fredrickson has shown that positive emotions from mild interest through to elation, activate this wide range of affirmative physical and mental responses. In various conditions of positivity she argues that we tend to broaden our range of possible behavioural responses (for example: trial and error, experimentation, collaboration, (safe) risk-taking or speculation). In positive states our attention, even our peripheral vision, becomes broader, we notice more detail and build more accurate maps of a location. Thinking becomes more flexible, integrative and open to the unusual. When we feel positive we make friends more easily and broaden our range of trusted people and we remember more accurately. Fredrickson's research confirms that positive emotions have the effect of making it easier to retrieve positive memories and build on existing physical, social, intellectual and psychological resources like optimism, confidence and resilience. We have more hope for the future (see also Seligman, 2004; Kidd, 2020).

Cultivating a positive atmosphere has probably been an aim of successful teachers through the ages. Positive psychologists have built on this truism and sought to discover the sources of positivity and hope in individuals, Currently, there is broad agreement that the such conditions often involve:

- spiritual or religious belief
- the presence of models of positive thinking and positive responses
- communities where sharing is normal
- plentiful opportunities to observe others doing good
- a focus on gratitude
- encouragement to pursue realistic goals
- practices that encourage relaxation and reflection
- frequent occasions to engage in favourite activities
- a habit of calling up the *best times* from memory. (Fredrickson et al., 2003)

Positivity-inducing conditions like these offer an interesting focus for both curriculum and pedagogy and indeed for a society in recovery from crisis.

Even when short periods of positivity are artificially induced by a happy video or the promise of a small reward, indicators show clear improvements in the connection-making and memory described (Fredrickson, 2013; Nunez and Goulah, 2021). If such effects indeed result from affirmative emotional states why would teachers *not* want to assess the impact of positive approaches to teaching, curriculum, school environments and relationships in school?

Clearly, negativity is also important; some balancing thoughts are necessary. Negative emotions have been crucial for human survival. Sadness, fear, anger, disgust and contempt each have significant, sometimes lifesaving, functions. Learning happens through these emotions too. Without occasions of negative emotion, we would not be safe or healthy, experience would be one-dimensional and we would be ill-equipped to deal with adversity or disappointment. Negative emotions have driven some of the major developments in creativity and invention. Indeed, some of the greatest works of art, technology and culture have arisen from disappointment, grief, horror and even hate. Thankfully, as we have found during the global pandemic, threats often spawn new solutions, innovations, and fresh responses. Sometimes teachers may deliberately construct a negative response – for example confusion, cognitive conflict – in order to provoke a (positive) creative outcome. Occasional positive developments from negative beginnings do not, however, contradict the generative properties of positivity. Teachers know from daily experience that frequent or continuous negative life events have a crushing, demotivating and damaging effect on children. Most are familiar with the way that even mild occasions of personal stress inhibit our normal thought processes. Perhaps, for example, you remember a time in your own education when a teacher's impatience with your inability to 'solve a simple problem' led to a temporary shutdown of sensible thought! We are probably all aware that in 'fight or flight' mode, physical or emotional self-defence is the dominant motive.

Security generates very different responses. Think of those calm, peaceful, relaxed moments perhaps just before you fall asleep, when for many people new thoughts and solutions unexpectedly present themselves. Remember times in your childhood when time stood still as you were happily immersed in accomplishing something you loved doing for its own sake. Hopefully, you still experience times of deep and willing involvement in an activity where the processes of life, ideas and answers seem to flow naturally and you feel you are in the right place. Csikszentmihalyi (1990) indeed called this highly positive feeling the state of 'flow' – a state recognisable to children and adults equally. In flow, at any age we enter into an autotelic activity and use existing skills and knowledge to face a challenge that is perhaps 10 or 15% greater than we have previously faced. During periods of flow, difficult things feel possible, time seems altered, we feel 'at one' with the activity, we know what we will do if things go wrong, the normal worries and preoccupations of life take a back seat, we feel less self-conscious and more confident. The evidence is that we look back on such periods as times when we were happy. Csikszentmihalyi postulated that in flow both children and adults were able to think more deeply, broadly, collaboratively and that creative thought was more likely. He also observed that the body responded positively to flow in improved biological systems and lowered blood pressure. Table 2.3 will help you examine this theory from a personal perspective.

Exercise 4: Think of an activity which you enjoy. Describe your feelings when you are fully involved in that activity.

Table 2.3 Flow and me

What activity have you chosen?
While you are involved in this activity……..
How would you rate your skills (appropriate to the activity) on a scale of 1–10?
Do you set yourself some kind of challenge? If so what?
For what reason are you involved?
What does time feel like?
Describe your state of confidence
Say something about what you do when something goes wrong
Where does feedback come from?
On a scale of 1–10 where would you place your self-consciousness?
What about your day-to-day worries?
Do your answers to the personal questions above suggest anything about how you might go about teaching children?

If being involved in a flow activity is good for body and mind how might this knowledge affect teaching, the learning environment, the examples we choose, resources we use, stories we tell, relationships we make and encourage? A teacher's thinking and decisions on such aspects of learning come together in the word 'pedagogy'.

Why pedagogy?

The word pedagogy is not common in the English educational vocabulary. In the second half of the 19th century the word 'pedagogue' was more often used to describe dull, fusty, pedantic, rigid approaches to teaching. Pedagogy as a concept has, however, survived more positively in most other European languages and beyond, to mean everything involved in the processes, resourcing, environments and reception of teaching. University departments and first and higher degrees in the science of pedagogy are common throughout the world.

A school claiming positive approaches might expect teachers to be role models of good moral, social, physical, intellectual, spiritual and emotional behaviour. We would hope such teachers would create environments that offer children a working example of an inclusive and virtuous society. In the terms of this book, positive educational approaches require more than teaching methods and behaviour adjusted towards the affirmative, but also imply detailed attention to the multiple environments that affect children's physical, emotional and intellectual development. 'Positive pedagogy' therefore involves teaching in a way that recognises and aims to generate the potential of every student, through affirmation and affirmative modelling of moral behaviour. It includes an assumption of teacher agency in creating and continually developing the moral, social, physical, academic, spiritual and emotional environments in which the best can be experienced by all. The idea of positive approaches to pedagogy has a long history.

By the end of the 19th century, the word pedagogy was used to express powerful claims about the aims of education. Dewey in *My Pedagogic Creed*, for example, suggested education should be '…a process of living and not a preparation for future living' (1897, p. 22). For him, teachers had the responsibility of shaping and utilising the positive, active learning experiences he outlined. Luminaries in the 20th century such as Freire (1970) and Giroux sharpened the concept of pedagogy by linking it to criticality. 'Critical pedagogy' summarised their proposals that teaching should be a revolutionary activity that would bring social justice to society. Within a critical pedagogy, teachers were seen as 'transformative intellectuals who develop counterhegemonic pedagogies that empower students' (Giroux, 1988, p. xxxiii). Their transformative role was intended to replace:

> ...schools as extensions of the workplace or [...] front-line institutions in the battle of international markets and foreign competition,

with

> schools as democratic public spheres [...] constructed around forms of critical inquiry that dignify meaningful dialogue and human agency. (Giroux, 1988, p. xxxii)

Less radical but equally political definitions of what positive pedagogy could look like were expressed by Japanese educationalist, Makiguchi (1871–1944). He argued that the purpose of education, and therefore pedagogues, was the happiness of the child. Happiness was to be felt in the present moment, not in terms of hedonistic pleasure but in a growing consciousness of each child's personal flourishing and their contribution to the flourishing of their community. Like Dewey and his contemporary Gandhi, Makiguchi suggested that instead of preparing children for involvement in economic, nationalistic or military competition, schools should aim at what he called 'humanitarian competition' by creating value and contributing to human happiness and working towards the alleviation of human suffering. In Makiguchi's value-creating (*soka*) schools in Japan and elsewhere teachers aspire to become and help children become:

> ...truly desirable people of ability [...] creative people who untiringly pursue lofty ideals, who have rich individuality and who can make free and effective use of their knowledge and skills. (Ikeda, 2020)

For both Makiguchi and Gandhi the values of peace and non-violence were fundamental to education as was the development of positive character. The teaching of 'human values' that Gandhi listed in his pedagogical principles in 1937 placed belief in compassion, kindness, fair mindedness, truth and the dignity of labour as central to what he called Basic Education. Indeed, his statement of 15 years earlier commented that, 'Literary training by itself adds not an inch to one's moral height and [...] character-building is independent of literary training' (Young India, 1-6-21, p. 172).

Teachers cannot guarantee that education is a positive experience for every child. Many would wish for a far more nuanced and balanced approach, understanding that failures, difficulties and disappointments are an essential part of the learning process within a wider climate of positivity. This book suggests positive pedagogy as an educational philosophy that seeks excellence and challenge through the use of affirmative choices, methods and intentions in teaching. It recognises the multiple cultural and social environments in which children learn and that stimulating the innumerable diversity of human minds requires social, emotional, moral, physical, intellectual and spiritual environments in which the *chances* of positive outcomes are significantly greater than the chances of negative ones. Teachers can and should use and create this wide variety of settings. What then might the co-construction of these liberating environments look like in ordinary schools or classrooms? Consider the following brief case studies from around the world:

Some international case study statements on liberating educational environments

Positive approaches to teaching

1. When teachers change their attitudes, they are able to connect with the students because the teacher focuses on what the student needs. … Treasuring the differences between each person. If there is someone that is very rational, they might get it faster. If the student is more artistic, then there are other ways to teach the student and the teacher has to adjust. The teacher has to reinvent another way to teach depending on the student. You can't force a student to learn something.

Brazilian teacher Olivia (Mokuria and Wandix-White, 2020)

2. It really depends on the child you have in front of you. Meeting their needs and every child has different needs… My philosophy is that all of them can learn. All of them can succeed. And there's no child who's not being able to be the best they can be. Every child is an incredible treasure in a way and I honour them. I guess my job is to identify what skills they have and then build on them… The goal should be that they lead a happy successful life and it's not about having good grades and doing things in a certain way, looking at each child and looking at how I can help develop them into their best.

Teacher Corina working in a private elementary school in California. (Takazawa, 2016, p. 89)

Building a positive moral environment

A Year 3/4 class in a seaside town in Sussex illustrates the impact of confronting big news issues in humane and sympathetic ways.

A small rubber boat of migrants from Syria, Afghanistan and Iran landed on the beach near a school on the south coast of England. The dinghy's asylum-seeking occupants were intercepted by police and border authorities and taken to an emergency reception centre. The children in school knew all about this event from the media and local chatter. School was able to help the children make sense of this event.

Working with a geographer and an artist, a Year 4 class decided they wanted to make a humanitarian response. The class looked at maps of the migrants' journeys, learned about reasons for leaving their country and modes of transport, the visiting artist was introduced. The artist had devised a practical and personal way to help children understand the human issues behind the people in boats, within the overarching theme of her work – 'Can we make the world a better place through small creative acts?' (O'Donoghue website).

Children were shown how to make a basic, paper origami boat. On one side of their completed boats they were asked to write a word for a relationship between two people: friend, sister, aunt, uncle, mother, father, etc. On the other side each child wrote a personal message about asylum seekers for others to read (see Figure 2.3 and Figure 2.4). All were assured that their statements would be seen by grown-ups in the town. The origami boats were then neatly glued and arranged onto huge rolls of transparent fabric for display in the town library and other public buildings.
www.education4diversity.co.uk

(Continued)

Figure 2.3 Some origami boats with their messages

Figure 2.4 Children tallied the values expressed in the messages written on the sides of the paper boats

Positive relationships between adults and children

We set up a system called Hard Talk where student representatives reported issues highlighted by their age mates (4–12-year-olds) at the beginning of each term to a school staff and governors meeting. In the first Hard Talk session children complained that they had had too many replacement teachers and that when novice teachers were brought in they were often sacked when discipline went wrong. The students argued this was wasteful and that each new teacher should be given extra training within school by mentors on inclusive methods of classroom control and making lessons relevant to the students. School staff and governors accepted this advice and changed their systems.

Year 5 teacher, Rwanda

Positive physical surroundings and resources

In Eastbourne, Sussex, up to 1/3 of lessons take place on the marshland just a few hundred metres from our Junior school. Here, children learn about animal husbandry among a small herd of water buffalo. They look after the grass snakes, black bees, frogs, newts and butterflies that share the natural habitat of the marsh and learn *in situ* and through practical experience, about the life of their Bronze age forebears. Children compose music about the marsh, build shelters, paint or draw, make bronze, light fires, measure, record, describe, construct and enjoy physical challenges, shoot clay pigeons and explore every detail of the marsh. The effect of this huge outdoor classroom is that every child in the school has ample opportunity to shine either as a way-finder, an observer, writer, analyst, maker, carer, builder, artist, scientist, musician or athlete.

Head teacher Eastbourne, England

Positive intellectual atmosphere

A holiday club for 'gifted and talented' pupils run by a university gathered a disparate group of 10–13-year-olds for a course on creativity. They drew, potted, painted, acted, wrote Haikus and composed. One day they were invited to attend the dress rehearsal of an opera by Handel – though the organisers were reluctant to take up the offer (few of the children knew what opera was, none had ever seen one) they agreed to give it a try. The director of the opera came to speak to them, 'Handel was not just a brilliant composer he was a wise human being and made this opera Theodora to show what happened when a minority is victimised by a powerful majority – so I have decided to place this eighteenth-century opera as if it was taking place in the first Iraq War 2003'. The children were captivated as scenes of suicide vests, explosions, state executions and terrorism were juxtaposed with classic opera. Their experience led to an animated debate on diversity in the UK and a subsequent series of powerful magazine articles on discrimination and unconscious bias. (Hancox and Barnes, 2003)

Positive emotional climate

During the lockdowns in 2020 and 2021 nine schools combined to hire an artist in residence to help students find ways of wordlessly expressing their feelings about isolation. In the project 'Our Shared Isolation' students were asked to produce self-portraits surrounded by the symbols of things and ideas that helped them through the lockdowns. From home they watched introductory videos from an educational psychologist on emotional health, and from artist Esther Miles on symbols and portraits and received support in painting and drawing techniques. The students largely worked alone to produce a series of highly original imaginative images for a post lockdown exhibition (see Figure 2.5 and Figure 2.6). Many remarked that this project powerfully provided the security and confidence to express aspects of their mental state too difficult to put into words. (East Kent Schools Together, 2022)

(Continued)

Figures 2.5 and 2.6 Self-portraits in lockdown (East Kent Schools Together)

Positive spiritual environment	In our Gandhian home and school for destitute children in south India, our 5–14-year-old students start each day in the multi-faith meditation room with prayer. Muslim, Hindu and Christian children gather together, cross-legged and surrounded by religious images of their faiths. Today, children offered extemporary prayers in the manner of their faith for the health of the rabbit that has just given birth, they gave thanks for the local cotton factory owner who provided this week's food and to the cotton mill workers who had donated money for school uniforms. I don't know who belonged to which faith, I don't ask. We just sit at the back of the room – one of us Christian one Hindu, silent, cross-legged, eyes closed, just part of the proceedings.
	Krishna, Tamil Nadu, India

Summary

This chapter introduced the central theme of inclusive values, the all-important foundation of ideas throughout this book. It asked you to think about the values that led you towards teaching and those of other teachers before you. It encouraged you to talk about values and share them in order to concretise them and encourage you to live them out in corridor, class and school. Evidence was presented that the core values held by respected teachers in diverse times and cultures overlapped regardless of culture. When personal values corresponded with the lived institutional values of the school, teachers felt sustained and fulfilled in their work.

The importance of respecting diversity was highlighted. Arguments for a powerful relationship between diversity, positivity and pedagogy were presented. Embracing and celebrating diversity was advocated as the most appropriate educational response to a clearly interdependent world. Affirmative personal and social attitudes to diversity were shown to lead to significantly broadened possibilities for creative thinking and deep learning. Recent evidence on the role of positive emotions in improving relationships, thinking, connectivity and good intellectual, mental and physical health was cited and linked to teaching approaches that go beyond instruction to include the teachers' role in creating and using a widened range of settings for learning. The chapter ends by offering the concept of Positive Pedagogy as a way of expressing styles of teaching that seek to create conditions where positive emotion can thrive and the learning potential of each individual is maximised.

3
PLANNING AND BUILDING POSITIVE ENVIRONMENTS FOR LEARNING

Objectives

In this chapter you will consider positive physical, social and mental environments for learning. Building on evidence on the social and emotional conditions required for inclusive, transferable, long lasting, useful learning, outlined in Chapter 2, you will be guided towards approaches to planning for high-quality teaching and optimising the learning impact of positive physical and emotional environments by:

- Considering a wider range of flexible and stimulating spaces for learning knowledge and skills within and beyond the classroom
- Developing an understanding that hearts, minds and bodies can also be seen as learning environments
- Teaching from personal strengths and enthusiasms and sharing them across the school
- Increasing time spent in generating and applying learning in 'real world' contexts beyond the classroom and immediate locality
- More frequently employing the diverse, multiple, social, sensory and intra-personal strengths of all members of the school community
- Becoming more conscious of cultural, emotional, intellectual, moral, spiritual and physical frameworks for learning by undertaking small-scale research projects of your own

Introduction

Computers may have led us to think too much in terms of binaries. In line with the global and humanitarian themes and principles outlined in Chapter 1 you will assess the benefits and limitations of 'traditional' classroom learning alongside those of more progressive styles. You will read of various approaches to planning and teaching and consider where a fusion of styles may be possible, perhaps preferable. The chapter will provide examples of how to plan teaching approaches and environments to maximise the conditions for learning. It will suggest that these styles and settings can involve community, diversity and creativity and how such contexts enrich learning. Invitations to do your own classroom-based research are intended to help you discover that inclusion, humanity and sustainability can be learned and lived in settings that are both rigorous *and* fun, challenging *and* emotionally involving, knowledge-rich *and* creative. The chapter will help broaden your thinking and action regarding effective learning environments and help you set up learning settings that are right for you, your community and the children in your class.

The traditional versus progressive debate

The word 'traditional' often means, 'how it was before'. With regard to education, seeking the traditional might involve mentally returning to a fictional 'golden time' (often in the 19th century) when things are thought to have been better, more ordered, predictable, deferential, hierarchical and mono-cultural. When asked to give detail, the champions of traditional methods in school may mention desks all facing the front, teacher as authority, instruction rather than discussion, rote learning, strict and adhered-to behaviour practices and facts, facts, facts. We know from Dickens' *Hard Times* (1854), and other 19th-century sources that the esteemed traditional methods were frequently unkind, demeaning, restrictive and narrowly focused. They were also effective, especially from 1870 onwards, in building a society of largely literate, numerate, obedient people equipped to advance British industrialisation, military power, colonial administration and wealth. Traditional procedures also successfully maintained, even bolstered, pre-industrial, social class, wealth, race, gender and ability hierarchies. Similar education approaches were copied throughout the then British Empire and are still recommended by some politicians and education leaders 150 years later. As education secretary and long-time supporter of traditional methods, Michael Gove said in 2010:

> I'm an unashamed traditionalist when it comes to the curriculum. Most parents would rather their children had a traditional education, with children sitting in rows, learning the kings and queens of England, the great works of literature, proper mental arithmetic, algebra by the age of eleven, modern foreign languages. That's the best training of the mind and that's how children will be able to compete. (Gove, 2010)

The supporters of such models today value the certainties of former era (Birbalsingh, 2020). They use words like 'proper' and references to 'most parents' or concepts like 'the best that has been written and said' (DfE, 2013a, p. 6), but education traditionalists often fail to define how they arrive at what is 'best' or 'proper'. The schools embracing such methods pride themselves on their high standards, clear boundaries, punctuality, 'tough love', consistent behaviour expectations, uniform, silent corridors, absence of mobile phones and prioritising concepts of what they feel constitutes a 'cultural contribution'. Opposing arguments based on years of education research and teachers' genuine experience in the classroom over many years, are sometimes dismissed as 'Marxist', politically motivated, representing 'the enemies of promise' (Gove, 2013). Politicians and commentators who set themselves up as arbiters of what is best for children or the feelings of 'most parents' often have little experience (outside their own education) of classrooms or of working with a wide cross-section of families on a daily basis. Teachers alone amongst the professions have continual, intense and daily contact with a regular but highly disparate group of parents, carers and children throughout a year. This accumulating experience quickly creates in most teachers a deep knowledge and understanding of a wide variety of conditions, needs and opinions across the UK's superdiverse society.

Mass education was key to social and economic change in the 19th century. While some Victorian approaches are clearly effective today in developing order, uniformity, cultural capital, discipline and compliance – the question remains whether these are the skills most required for the 21st century. As discussed in Chapter 1, the world faces a unique set of existential crises many of them resulting from the political, environmental, social and economic excesses of the 19th century. In an age of instant, unregulated communication, artificial intelligence, political instability, cultural diversity and severely weakened trust in the traditional institutions of authority, the UK and other post-industrial economies promote increased consumption while simultaneously struggling to undo the environmental and social damage caused by the very industrialisation from which they benefitted. Schools may be the only institutions capable of generating the broad-spectrum of knowledge, creativity and positive attitudes that will produce sustainable, ethical and widely supported solutions to the world's multiple crises. Education can only play such a role if the opposing sides of the debate work together under a genuine consensus and as it will be argued, a truly inclusive value-set.

Educational fusion

It would be foolish to dismiss everything about traditional methods. Successful adherents rightly point to the way that their schools provide the security of structure, self-discipline and high expectations absent in some children's lives (for example, Hirsch, 1988; Birbalsingh, 2020). At times many of us learn effectively through rote and repetition. The separate subject disciplines are time-honoured ways of understanding our world and their specific language, concepts, skills and knowledge must be learned and understood if they are to be applied and used to solve the small and big problems we face

(Gardner, 2009). Context and direct relevance are not always essential and the possession of an Anglo/Eurocentric 'cultural capital' continues to buy positions in some professions, especially those commonly accused of perpetuating race and gender inequalities (Kings College London, 2021; UK Parliament, 2021; Roach, 2022). It would be wrong to suggest that the relatively progressive approaches introduced in Chapter 2 were the answer to every child's education needs. Liberal methods of education, including cross-curricular learning, are effective for many, but not all and not all the time. 'One size fits all' and binary attitudes to education practice inevitably result in exclusion and limit potential. If our ultimate education aim is the happiness of every child or making the world of their future a fair and sustainable place, the experience of teachers suggests such destinations will not be reached through single routes. Nuanced, numerous and sometimes bespoke approaches to teaching and learning are probably more appropriate than inflexible ones.

There is little doubt that we need to pay closer attention to the ways children respond to teaching and experience. In this book, you are encouraged to do that by seeing yourself not just as a teacher but as a teacher-researcher (Chartered College of Teachers, 2021). Throughout the chapter, small-scale research questions will help you evaluate the approaches most likely to generate a positive climate for learning for you as well as those you teach.

Building positive environments in schools

We learn more expansively and creatively in secure, affirming environments. Sadly, schools do not provide such positive feelings to all. Primary school inspections, for example, suggest that around 12% were 'inadequate' or 'requiring improvement' in 2020 (Gov. UK, 2020). Figures from other surveys claim that one in eight British 5–16-year-olds feel generally unhappy with school life (Children's Society, 2021). One in five young people may have self-harmed and 16% suffer from a recognised mental health disorder (Gov. UK, 2022b) and though often caused by issues beyond school, often show themselves powerfully in school. During the Covid pandemic for a variety of reasons school was unattractive enough to mean that 250,000 children or more were missing from school rolls. This is only partly explained by a roughly 60% rise in registration for home schooling (Gov.UK, 2022b). A recent four-yearly study (WHO, 2020) presented evidence that up to 15% of British 11-year-olds had recently been bullied twice or more times in school, a significant rise on 2014 figures. Schools cannot be affirmative places when bullying, pressure, self-harm and general unhappiness affect a substantial minority in every class. These adverse features of schooling for some in the UK are measurably on the increase (Brooks et al., 2020; WHO, 2020). Though each issue is likely to result from complex family, social and economic causes, comparisons with figures from the devolved education authorities of Scotland, Northern Ireland and Wales, suggest that curriculum, pedagogy and public policy are key additional factors in the particularly worrying child well-being figures for England.

Figures like those in the previous paragraph are depressing, but teachers and school leaders are in a strong position positively to transform the experience of many more children and young people. This book is partly a plea for teachers to be given more space to effect these transformations. How then, can we construct a school environment that is favourably perceived by higher percentages of students? Education needs radical change, led by those in its front line – teachers, head teachers, teacher assistants, support staff and teacher educators. These practitioners are experienced in the day-to-day lives of children and their families; their philosophy generally arises from experience. Teachers quickly become daily collectors of evidence, potential researchers, best placed to know what changes will positively impact upon children. Children and young people also have clear views and respond constructively and often imaginatively to being part of the dialogue. The evidence-based proposals for change below, sit easily within current curriculum expectations and inspection frameworks, but require significant shifts in attitude and philosophy about what education is for. Education change inevitably provokes hostile responses from the champions of 'traditional' or 'training manual' methods, but informed, inclusive, humble, professional discussion must happen if the moral and economic failings of our system are to be addressed. Even subtle modifications may feel demanding, but the suggestions below are intended to provoke teacher discussion and reflection on how to address the exclusion, unhappiness, inequality and resultant, long tail of underachievement in UK schools. Classrooms should be settings where positive experiences are more likely than negative ones and moments of joy, engagement, curiosity, interest, humour and serenity are common for every child (and teacher) each day. The changes proposed require sensitive, incremental changes of practice in:

- Leadership
- Curriculum
- The physical, social and intellectual environment of the classroom
- Pedagogy

Changing the approach to leadership

It is evident from inspections, reports and research that 'good' leadership transforms a school culture (Bennett, 2017). A consistent, always visible manager that models, promotes and provides clear values and expectations, gives stakeholders the feeling that they matter and are supported, probably marks out good leadership in most institutions, but schools have a wider social and moral purpose, being charged with enriching individual minds for the present and enhancing communities for the future. Some important issues for primary school leadership, are, however, missing from Bennett's useful list of qualities (2017, p. 7). A good primary leader will be an enthusiastic expert in several curriculum subjects. They will clearly demonstrate that children do not just 'matter' but that they are committed to their well-being. The effective school leader will not just 'support' and 'engage' staff but be an inspiration and exemplar. They will have a clear idea of the aims of their curriculum and of individual pedagogical strengths throughout their school. Enabling school cultures need leaders who are sympathetic communicators to parents and carers from a wide variety of backgrounds. The language they use is of fundamental importance and meaningful words like security, belonging, kindness, care, enthusiasm, inspiration, sympathy, character strengths and love should characterise their interactions.

The well-being of both child and adult stakeholders is central to the positive school. Within the teacher-led principles of positivity, diversity, inclusion and creativity underpinning this book, an effective primary school leader might embody some of the humanising practices listed in Table 3.1. Grade them in importance to you and add your own suggestions.

Teachers and support staff lead too. Ideally, they build environments of well-being in the spaces they control and adopt similar principles. However, positive learning settings are only sustainable when the leadership constantly upholds the inclusive values upon which they are built. Significant research questions arise from analysis of your developing self as a leader in the classroom – you might start by rating yourself against the starred attributes in Table 3.1 above and monitor any changes over the period of your school experience.

Table 3.1 Evaluate the following school leader characteristics

Some possible characteristics of school leader	Assessment of importance of this characteristic on a 1 – 10 scale
*likes children and communicates with them as individuals	
*is slow to make judgements about children and young people	
likes their staff and communicates well and often with them as individuals	
is present, visible and approachable in all areas of the school	
*is optimistic	
congratulates staff and students on small but explicitly identified achievements	
*is honest	
has a metaphorical and actual open door policy	
refers to agreed school values in small and big statements or decisions	
*actively demonstrates agreed school values in their interactions and choices	
*is an expert on pedagogy	
*is an expert on one or two specific curriculum areas	
*has clear and consistent expectations of positive behaviour towards others	

Curriculum changes

Each country of the United Kingdom has its own national curriculum. Each curriculum reflects national priorities – a political construct. Thankfully, all leave space for local interpretation. It is in these spaces that a transformative and positive curriculum can be planned and shared. School by school decisions are required on the intent, implementation and intended impact of curriculum (Ofsted, 2019). Curriculum change will vary according to the priorities of the leader and learning community, but will ideally address the global, national and personal issues that apply to all. One such issue is creativity.

Creativity is a central source of meaning in our lives (Csikszentmihalyi, 1997) – it drives developments and problem solving across the globe and yet still in many schools it remains sidelined as an aim. Ken Robinson spent his life arguing for the importance of promoting creativity in education reminding us that creativity is not something only to seek in the arts:

> Creativity is possible in all areas of human life, in science, the arts, mathematics, technology, cuisine, teaching, policy, business, you name it. (Robinson and Aronica, 2015, p. 119)

The development of creative responses should be part of curriculum intentions for all subjects and infirm assessments in every school. The diversity of communities and individuals means that there will be multifarious additional aims and objectives but in effective schools, these decisions must be understood, agreed and owned by every teacher – a principle succinctly expressed in 2010:

> In relation to anything he/she does, a teacher should be able to give a coherent justification citing: 1. evidence, 2. pedagogical principle, 3. educational aim, rather than the unsafe and undemocratic defence of compliance… (Alexander, 2010, p. 308)

In Table 3.2 are some suggested aims, means and intended effects of a primary curriculum. You can think of your own suggestions in the intent, implementation and impact columns.

Every school will need to prioritise. The character of the school and its role in the community will be defined by these priorities. Teacher commitment and enthusiasm is essential in promoting the aims, methods and hoped-for impact of these choices (Keller et al., 2016). Teacher, parent, carer and child involvement is essential for the success of these choices.

Decisions about ways of accessing the curriculum are equally important. Learning happens in a wide range of different ways and if the curriculum is presented through a narrowed and specific set of 'learning styles' or traditional approaches it is inevitable that some children will fail to encounter the approach that catches their interest. This is particularly true regarding the presence or absence of opportunities to play – in its early and later years the human species among many others learns powerfully through play (Froebel, 1887; Project Zero, 2018). Often evident in play, teachers should always watch

Table 3.2 Thinking about the intent, implementation and impact of your curriculum

	Curriculum aspect	
Curriculum intent	*Curriculum implementation*	*Curriculum impact*
Focused on developing:	Through:	Becoming:
• Environmental consciousness • Understanding of social justice • Cultural knowledge • Broad and balanced knowledge in every discipline • Happiness/positivity in each child • Personal, moral values • Creative thinking and collaboration • Community awareness/responsibility • Global citizenship • Unique personal strengths in each child • A range of practical, transferable, analytical skills	• Separate subject disciplines • Direct instruction • Experiential/practical learning • Cultural visits • Games and play • Thematic, cross-curricular approaches • A range of different teaching approaches • Locality and local community-based • Forest school and other outdoor activities • Social learning – group and paired work • Problem-based learning • 'Traditional' approaches • Attention to global issues	• Responsible, collaborative, citizens • Effective communicators • Global citizens • Resilient people • Fulfilled people • Sustainability champions • Flexible, creative individuals • Knowledgeable people • Critical thinkers • Happy, confident, contributing community members • Reflective, spiritual, moral people • Aware of and able to use personal strengths

for the 'Eye Sparkle Quality' (ESQ) in children's expression, or other non-verbal signs that an individual has been captured by something heard, seen or done. A mini-research question might be: 'What are children doing when I see the ESQ?'

Planning for positive physical, social and intellectual classroom environments

In schools most learning happens in the classroom. Classrooms, however, often do not represent the world of children's lives outside school. This is not necessarily a bad thing. There are convincing arguments that schools should offer a standard, moral, unified experience to all. This shared space can provide a living example of a perfect society (Barnes, 2020): inclusive, enabling, fair, growth-focused and life-affirming.

Physical features of the classroom

We saw in Chapter 2 that personal emotional and existential relevance are key routes towards lasting learning. It therefore makes sense to suggest that contexts familiar in the everyday lives of children offer good starting points for learning. A revealing, mini-research question related to a positive classroom might be:

'In what physical ways does this classroom include recognisable, visible and positive references to the everyday lives of the children?'

The physical environment affects our mood and attitudes. We know from everyday life that beautiful environments often positively affect us. Beauty in a classroom can act similarly. Teachers have little influence on the dimensions and plan of their classroom, but its attractiveness includes its furniture and arrangement, decoration, display, views from its windows and overall appearance. These aspects involve teachers, students and others thinking about the sensory pleasures offered by decisions on aspects of beauty such as balance, order, freshness, cleanliness, variety, security, colour, texture, form and shape. There is also potential for finding beauty in the moral character of learning settings.

Values-conscious classrooms

Affirmative settings should generate feelings of security and optimism. Situations where negativity dominates are more likely to engender sadness and anxiety, emotions that evolved in response to threat and necessarily limit risk-taking, alliance-formation and trust. Even subtle negatives such as shyness, embarrassment, lack of confidence, confusion, distraction or boredom, tend to activate mechanisms that privilege mental/physical survival over activities that broaden and build thinking (see Fredrickson, 2010). Positivity on the other hand generates a 'can-do' or growth mindset – one that counters helplessness and fosters possibility, extension, invention, innovation and creativity.

A positive environment is arguably dominated by inclusive values – values that provide a sense of involvement and welcome. The choice of inclusive values shown in Booth's (2018) framework (illustrated in Chapter 7) can form a powerful starting point for discussion.

Daily experiences of hope, respect, gratitude and trust are satisfying to all, but perhaps especially today's children. In a values-conscious environment teachers will encourage children to live out inclusivity in the classroom and in so doing, provide antidotes to anxieties they may experience socially or virtually (Scioli and Billier, 2009). You may wish to add your own inclusive values to those suggested above.

Values will also take us into controversial areas. Sustainability is an inclusive value and yet as the Royal Society of Arts reminds us, 'Classes remain silent when it comes to the values and knowledge we will need to move into a post-carbon circular economy and society' (RSA, 2014, p. 40). Children of primary school age show their understanding of the importance of sustainability in the hundreds of Forest school activities throughout the country, but also in their interest in the global movements for change. Well over a million schoolchildren across the world joined the 'Fridays for the Future' climate action campaign in 2019. Since these campaigns, UNESCO and charities like Save the

Children have added greater pressure on education authorities to include serious modules on environmental sustainability, climate change and the loss of biodiversity into all curricula from nursery through to university education (see Kwauk, 2020). Whole school activism (cypnow, 2021) has become more common as teachers with their classes have discussed the link between values and action.

Those seeking to create a classroom characterised by positive values might observe and ask: 'To what extent, and where, have I witnessed [one or more inclusive value] in action?'

Emotionally positive classrooms

Emotional relevance may be more felt than seen. It is often entirely invisible, expressed in mood, atmosphere or other non-verbal signals like the ESQ. Highly influential psychologists have researched and written on the importance of emotions to education. Dewey suggested emotions are fully engaged during experiential learning; Jung argued that independence and intuition engendered commitment to it (1971); Piaget (1954) argued for discovery; Feuerstein (1999, 2003) collaboration; Bruner (1996) storying; Gardner (2000b) multiple ways of knowing; Sternberg (1997) creative ways of understanding; Bandura (2003) self-confidence; Craft (2005) possibility thinking, positive mind sets; and Dweck the creation of positive, '...mental representations of experiences that serve as the basis of motivation, personality, development and help integrate disparate views' (Dweck, 2017b, p. 689).

A similar range of emotionally salient foci have been confirmed more recently by educational neuroscience (Immordino-Yang and Gottlieg, 2020) that stresses the impact of personalisation. Each approach to classroom and curriculum planning will invigorate some children, but not others – no single focus will reach all and experienced teachers know this.

It is possible, however, to maximise the chances of emotional engagement for all. Plan your classroom or outside area so there are places where positive emotions like peace, calm, curiosity and joy are likely to be encountered. Plan sessions and spaces that will provoke moments of discovery, joy, engagement, movement, experimentation, inquisitiveness, interest, humour and serenity each day. At times, arrange furniture and groupings for quiet collaboration or storytelling and stimulating areas for playful discovery and experimentation (see Table 3.3 for some examples). Teacher-researchers might usefully test the effectiveness of their decisions in small-scale research by asking questions like:

> 'In what ways does the atmosphere here encourage personal security? How does the ethos here promote safe levels of mental and physical risk-taking? What examples of self-awareness, social awareness, confidence, collaboration or participation can I see?'

Table 3.3 An emotionally positive classroom

Emotion	What spaces or arrangements might help emotional engagement?
Reflection, serenity, peace, calm, self-awareness, empathy	Reading corner, carpeted area, library, quiet area of playground, 'friendship seats' in the playground, mindfulness/yoga/reflection session, emotion words, quiet listening area with earphones, mirrored area for learning about the facial and postural elements of emotion, circle time, 'hot seating', worry boxes
Excitement, discovery, playfulness	Musical sound play area, sand or water play, construction toys and equipment, games, PE, adventure playground, forest school, 'way-finding' sessions, dressing-up box, themed role-play area, distorting mirrors
Curiosity, interest, fascination	Nature table, wild area, forest school, beach school, class museum, weekly class walks, light boxes for display, mystery objects, 'feely boxes' themed displays, school garden
Collaboration, sharing, cooperation, friendliness, community, responsibility	Small group arrangement of tables, collaborative 'work stations', thinking partners, buddy system, temporary mime, role-play or acting area, art and craft area, agreed 'Class rules' display. Circle of seats in hall, playground or cleared classroom for collaborative drumming or music making, climate change or eco-diversity activism centres, school council

Socially positive classrooms

Humans are social creatures. For the vast majority, learning is socially mediated (Goswami, 2015). We learn through the proximity and contributions of others. In family and friendship groups we support each other using our individual, specific strengths. Vygotsky (1978) captured the mutual nature of human learning in his time-honoured concept, 'the zone of proximal development', the learning that occurs in the company and influence of more knowledgeable others. Feuerstein (1970, 1999) extended this idea by showing how intelligence could be positively modified through the involvement of others in deliberately structured, mapped or 'bridged' learning experiences where personalised and novel links are made between existing experience and new knowledge. The facility to invent unique and emotionally relevant 'hooks' to connect the learner's life with what needs to be learned, has become a hallmark of effective teaching.

Establishing satisfying links with others is also essential to emotional health. Our need for social interaction is biologically programmed from before birth and synchronicity with parent or carer operating on both behavioural and cognitive levels (Bowlby, 1988; Benson, 2020) continuing for the rest of life. Friendships and good relationships provide a fundamental element of what we call well-being (see Ryff, 1989). So, classrooms should be places where these positive relationships thrive and foster the secure conditions needed for creativity, link-making and learning on all levels. Children and adults develop through affirmative interactions modelled around them and your role of teachers in a positive classroom is to make it a space of social intelligence, an exemplar of a good society – a place of transformation as well as transmission.

The best classrooms are the starting point of multiple learning journeys. Such journeys will guide young people towards achievement within the curriculum but also developing their own character strengths, their interests, passions, personal happiness and their role as good citizens. These socially positive surroundings are enhanced by opportunities to share positivity in:

- daily 'gratitude books'
- role play
- daily positive diaries
- once a week 'Special Person' time (where through a year the attributes of each child in turn are named by their classmates and recorded on a certificate to take home)
- cross-curricular exploration of key inclusive values
- 'golden time' when children and young people can follow and share their own interests
- frequent opportunities to take breaks to refocus and relax (Immordino-Yang et al., 2021)
- thinking partners
- moral, spiritual and religious education themes
- 'circle time' discussions on issues raised by individuals
- a 'sustainability' or 'community' focus across the curriculum.

A positive classroom is flexible in layout and character. Some shared activities need grouped tables for collaboration, or open space for performances of understanding. Thinking work is often done in pairs (Clarke and Muncaster, 2018). Other collaborations happen after solitary reflection, study or whole class instruction. The arrangement of furniture will change accordingly and ease of movement will influence furniture choices. When children return from a lunch break to find their room transformed into a theatre auditorium, café, conference chamber or round table meeting, the impact can be electric. Conversely, rigid furniture arrangements, fixed groups and predictable groupings can inhibit the growth of new friendships and creative collaborations. Ideally, groups should change often to represent the multiple diversities in every gathering of children and provide opportunities for new connections. To research the socially positive character of a classroom we might ask:

- How are friendships, relaxed relationships and flexible groupings encouraged in class?
- What is the evidence of support for personal, social and mental development in this classroom?
- What themes dominate the gratitude books?

Intellectually positive classrooms

Children should feel they are flourishing. A palpable sense of mental development, with challenges slightly beyond current ability and rewards for all kinds of achievement will produce a positive intellectual environment. An intellectually positive environment does

Table 3.4 Some thought-provoking words and phrases

Thought-provoking words	Thought-provoking phrases
Find	Talk about…
Bring	I wonder if…
Plan	I wonder what…
Show	I wonder how…
Say	I wonder when…
Tell	I wonder where…
Collect	What if…
Draw	Share with…
List	Can you show me…
Describe	Make a shape like…
Compare	Make me a picture of…
Classify	Why do you think…
Contrast	I don't understand…
Examine	I wish I knew…
Analyse	I don't know…

not avoid difficulty, disappointment or failure. Jung argued that energy, 'can proceed only from the tension of opposites' (1953, p. 29). Csikszentmihalyi (2002) showed that those in conditions of flow often see failure as productive as does Dweck (2017b) in her work on positive attitudes toward setbacks. If learning results from thinking then challenges enrich it.

Physical and invisible environments created by the teacher can provoke deep, lasting, transferable and distributed thinking or stifle it. An intellectually positive classroom will generate positive dispositions toward all kinds of experience (Ritchhart and Perkins, 2008) and you can support the development of these dispositions through your choice of words. Thought-provoking words and phrases such as those in Table 3.4 (above) can be surprisingly generative.

Table 3.5 Possible teacher responses to challenge

Challenge to teaching	Possible positive teacher response
A child says they are bored with the task you have asked them to do…	• Raise the level of challenge you give them • Teach them a new skill to address the task in a different way • Tell them the task is an essential foundation for the next much more challenging assignment • Show them how the task relates to their everyday life
A child refuses to enter into a practical or physical activity you are expecting of them…	• Repeat the instruction avoiding eye contact • Praise another (and perhaps unexpected) child who is already fulfilling the task

(Continued)

Table 3.5 Possible teacher responses to challenge *(Continued)*

Challenge to teaching	Possible positive teacher response
	• Ignore the child for a short time and allow them to see your positive responses to other children who are engaged in the refused activity • Offer to do the activity with the child • Give the child the choice of doing the activity now or later during lunch or break time
A child keeps saying they do not understand a mathematical problem you have given them...	• Show them practically how to address the problem • Place them with others to complete a comparable problem and return with the others to the original problem after scaffolded success • After direct demonstration of how to address the problem give several similar ones to work on (perhaps with others) as a special task that you will celebrate with the rest of the class later
A child continually turns round to talk to others...	• Have frequent changes of group • Reiterate and reward by praise, the class rule of following instructions first time • Give attention when the child is not talking to others • Provide an achievable target of a specific amount of time to refrain from talking
A child never seems to bring in homework or responses from home...	• Have spare sets of letters/homework exercises always ready to reissue • Make a class grid of positive work attributes (including remembering responses from home) with space for individuals to write their name when they have achieved the target • Have visual/symbolic reminders on the desk • Consult parent/carers about the importance of bringing responses, homework back to class

If you were seeking to identify an intellectually inclusive classroom you might ask:

'What examples are there that show this is a place where children feel their strengths are recognised, valued, used and challenged in ways that promote thought and growth beyond expectations?'

Pedagogy and positivity

Pedagogy goes beyond teaching to include the methods, attitudes, activities and environments used by teachers. Teacher-created learning environments were discussed above, but the practical approaches, rules and attitudes they might use form the substance of the following section.

Praxis and pedagogy

Effective teachers need to be flexible. Rigid methods of delivery and expectation exclude and alienate. Back in the last century, eminent psychologist Robert Sternberg (1997a, 1997b) suggested that intelligence could be framed in creative, analytical and practical ways. Sternberg also showed that teachers not only taught creatively, analytically or practically, but their preferred approach bestowed considerable advantages on children that tended toward the same style. So, 'analytical' children taught by an analytical teacher performed well. The same children did less well with teachers that used creative or practical styles of delivery. Although classifying teachers and children into the categories of Sternberg's 'Triarchic Theory' of intelligence greatly oversimplifies the complexities of teaching and learning, the suggestion that a child will learn better from a teacher who teaches in ways they will understand, is uncontroversial. Around the same time, when Gardner identified his eight ways of showing intelligence, it would not be surprising to suggest that teachers with, for example, a strong musical or spatial or bodily kinaesthetic intelligence (Gardner, 2000b) inspired children with similar strengths.

Knowing that there may be three, four or eight or more ways of showing intelligence is important for teachers. The danger of such theories is that they too easily become ways of categorising and limiting children. Being labelled 'Naturalist' or 'Inter-personally smart' suggested fixed units of aptitude that were the very opposite of Gardner's intentions to broaden adults' understandings of intelligence. Both Triarchic and Multiple Intelligence theories have been dismissed by some in recent years because of such misuse by teachers, but Gardner and Sternberg's intention to steer teachers away from 19th-century beliefs in an immutable intelligence have mostly succeeded. We now know that intelligence is teachable, learnable, more broadly defined and subject to change. Stressing its cultural, subcultural and practical nature, Gardner's definition still holds true, intelligence is:

> the biopsychological potential to process information that can be activated in a cultural setting to solve problems or create products that are of value in a culture. (Gardner, 2000b, p. 28)

What then would practical intelligence look like in a teacher? Sternberg might say it is the teacher who uses largely tangible, physical processes to learn or teach a task or solve a problem. An analytical teacher would carefully plan, monitor and evaluate their tasks using a range of metacognitive strategies and a creative teacher might prefer the use of imagination, knowledge and experience in less orthodox ways. Viewed through the eyes of multiple intelligences, each teacher is likely to display a different profile of malleable personal strengths and weaknesses across Gardner's eight or nine proposed ways of showing intelligence (his ninth, the spiritual/existential intelligence did not pass all the qualifying tests). Consider Figure 3.1 below and think about the profile of your strengths and areas for further development. Comparing your bar graph with a colleague offers a powerfully personal route towards discussions on styles of teaching.

Each individual will teach in a different way. Each adapts their teaching as a result of experience and feedback from self, colleagues, children, remembered theories and memories of their own education. These adjustments happen continually through a career and contribute to the sense that teaching is an art; a dance or act of theatre that responds creatively to the challenges of the moment. Some of these challenges are troubling, but keeping the humanity of students in mind and holding to the values that brought them

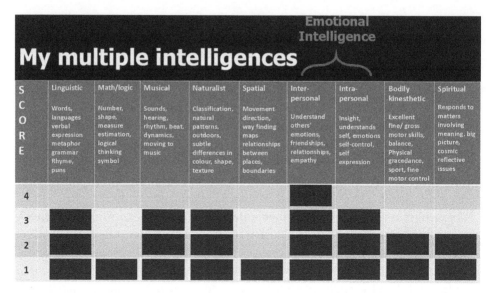

Figure 3.1 Thinking about your own profile of intelligences. Where are your strengths?

into teaching, sustains many teachers through times of doubt. The ability to hold to fundamental personal values needs institutional and collegiate support, however, and teachers tend to stay and flourish in schools that cherish the values that they hold dear (Barnes, 2012).

What about behaviour?

Teachers of course worry about behaviour. It has been a major focus of debate for centuries and currently 'discussions' on social media often centre on the use of exclusion, isolation booths, silent corridors, parental involvement or lack of control. These unregulated debates regularly provoke pages of vitriol on progressive and traditional sides of the argument. The poor behaviour of some pupils is a significant challenge for schools (Bennett, 2017). It has been linked with poor teacher retention and recruitment for decades (NUT, 2001). There is a public perception, shared by some teachers and educationalists, that the last 20 years has seen an 'erosion of teacher authority' and a 'perception that children's behaviour is out of control' (Policy Exchange, 2018, pp. 9 and 11), but many longer serving teachers will know that these things have always been an issue. An accurate picture of behaviour and relationships in school is complex and requires deeper analysis through observation, refection and research.

Perceptions of challenging behaviour rest on views of the role of education itself. Education may be seen as, 'the passing on of an intellectual birth right', the 'transmission of knowledge from teacher to pupil' and the place where 'children submit to the authority of subject experts' (Policy Exchange, 2018, p. 9), or a preparation for the 'opportunities, responsibilities and experiences' of adult life (DfE, 2014). It may equally be believed to be a diversity-conscious, child-centred project to include, bring out and enhance the best in every child and community (Ainscow and Booth, 2020). Could education involve all of these aims? Could it be about more than the contested definitions above? Such questions are fundamental in the philosophy of education, but are often missing from school-based and other types of initial teacher education (ITE).

Many maintain that good, non-disruptive, respectful, inclusive behaviour arises from deep involvement in activity. When a child is fully engaged, relationships, thinking, imagination, focus and ideation tend to become more positive for them and those around them (see for example Laevers, 2004). Flow theory (see Chapter 2) suggests that when occupied in attention-capturing activities our physical, social, intellectual and emotional selves take on more efficient and affable characteristics. The impact of deep engagement is highly evident, for example, when young people are giving very close attention to aspects of the natural world through drawing or examination through microscopes or magnifiers. The precise circumstances of any engagement is important – the state of flow arises in morally bad or questionable contexts too, but participation in morally *positive* activities or processes that capture a child's physical and mental attention will generally result in improvements in behaviour. It is the experience of many teachers, for example, that youngsters behave better on school trips, fieldwork and other activities outside the classroom. Reflecting on the evidence for this observation or the details of specific conditions for good behaviour can form the basis of a helpful mini-research study.

Sadly, it is impossible to involve all children in flow activities all the time and at the same time. Behaviour policies are necessary, but when well-planned and consistent, become simply part of, rather than the focus of, community life in the school. Effective policies are values-conscious. They emphasise the consequences of bad behaviour but also provide clarity, and promote confrontation-avoidance and fairness.

Consider some examples of common teaching challenges in Table 3.5, and evaluate the proposed, often inter-changeable, positive responses. Sometimes the quiet and sympathetic response might be to share a brief story about your own memories of fear, embarrassment, failure when a child, but there is often little time for such interactions. Generally, teachers must react quickly and in the spirit of this book, calmly, fairly and consistently to mild disruptions. More serious disruptions will require strict reference to school behaviour policies and head teachers are responsible for their consistency and effectiveness. Using Table 3.5 discuss other possible responses and their probable effect, thinking about likely public and private reactions in a child and also the maintenance of school-wide standards. Should we always adopt a positive, formative and calm approach? When might negatives be appropriate and how can they be framed to avoid confrontation or escalation?

The Table 3.5 responses to these everyday challenges give just a flavour of the attitudes that might characterise a positive pedagogy. The personal demands arising from maintaining such attitudes are high. Consistency is an ongoing battle and positive practitioners often fail, but the pointers in the summary below arise from research and experience and may restore our trust in the well-established path towards a positive pedagogy.

Summary

In this chapter you considered how to make the visible and invisible learning environments you create for children more positive. Throughout you were asked to consolidate your learning by asking and applying simple research questions. After discussing the false binaries of progressive versus traditional approaches you were asked to reflect on the possibilities of fusion of the best of both. Whatever the style, the major global issues of the 21st century alongside poverty, the underachievement, educational inequalities and the unhappiness of a significant minority of children in the UK, demand fundamental change in education. Specific changes in leadership and teaching style, organisation and attitudes towards the meaning and purpose of education have been suggested. In outlining the character of a positive learning environment the chapter stressed the importance of linking teaching to the real world experience of the child (Dewey, 1938) but also of disciplined knowledge. Creative – original, imaginative and valued – ways of presenting and using information and skills were recommended alongside approaches designed to generate long-term memories that embody important life principles. Inclusivity and sensory involvement were argued to be central to classroom conditions of positivity. You were reminded that frequent short breaks in activities allow refocus and relaxation. You were encouraged to seek out diverse ways of representing knowledge and aim at generating conditions of flow for a variety of children every day. Plentiful opportunities for social collaboration, fun and play-like conditions were highlighted along with the vital role of your own passion for learning and communicating shown often and in many different ways. Your own resilience and children's engagement was argued to be primarily sustained through such enthusiasm.

'Behaviour improves markedly when children are fully involved in activities and experiences.'

4
CONNECTING THE HUMANITIES – GEOGRAPHY, HISTORY, RELIGIOUS KNOWLEDGE, CITIZENSHIP AND PERSONAL, SOCIAL, HEALTH AND ECONOMIC EDUCATION

Objectives

In this chapter we will consider:

- What 'humanising' education could mean
- The concepts, skills and attitudes the humanities bring to education
- Some ways in which disciplines and themes that form the humanities can be positively linked
- Case studies that demonstrate how humanities subject can be combined to address some of the big issues facing the world today

Introduction

This chapter will ask you to consider the humanising qualities of the humanities. It will focus upon how geography, history, religious knowledge, citizenship and the groups of themes known as personal, social, health and economic education (PSHE) and social, moral, spiritual and cultural education (SMSC) offer answers and approaches to the question: 'What is distinctive about humans and human societies?' It will define the humanities further and outline the vocabulary, skills, and attitudes of each of the disciplines associated with human impact on the world. The chapter will show how each discipline throws a different, but essential, light upon human existence in and human stewardship of the world and its people.

The chapter will then offer case study examples of disciplinary and integrated learning in the humanities at all stages of primary education. These authentic examples will show how newly learned disciplinary knowledge can quickly be applied and combined in inter-disciplinary, multi-disciplinary and thematic contexts. A form of assessment through performance will be outlined.

The humanities: disciplines founded upon people and multiple routes towards understanding our world

The humanities today are subjects primarily concerned with the lives of humans. In the classical world of the Greeks and Romans, the humanities (*studia humanitatis*) brought together a list of skills taught almost exclusively to the male children of the rich and powerful. The humanities defined the knowledge expected in the cultivated leader: drama, history, logic, music, philosophy, rhetoric and sometimes astronomy. By the Renaissance the humanities, still only available to the wealthy, involved the study of grammar, poetry and other literature, rhetoric, Greek and Roman history as well moral philosophy. By the 18th century 'Enlightenment', humanities in Western countries had contracted to Greek and Latin literature and language. The concept of humanities widened in the Victorian era to involve study of human experience, values, systems and beliefs, distinguishing them from the physical and social sciences that measured and explained the world's empirical or material characteristics. The humanities at that time included arts, languages, literatures as well as history, philosophy and religion, and their attempts to make moral, spiritual and intellectual sense of the world. Learning in and through these subjects was expected to help humans better understand each other.

Today, in primary education in the UK, the humanities are taken to involve the national curriculum subjects of history, geography, religious education and citizenship. Each discipline has its heroes and gatekeepers. Each its own epistemology that generates a distinctive language, skill set, core knowledge and attitudes. Children in the primary years need frequent reminders on the key concepts and foci of the separate disciplines. Each brings a different way of making sense of the human world:

- Geography considers the impact humans have made on places in the physical world and the impact those places have had on humans.

- History concerns what humans have done in the past, how human life has changed over time and how the past affects humans today.
- Religious education (RE) teaches about the spiritual and religious world humans have created to make sense of existence and traces the sources of moral and cultural features of human life.
- Citizenship concerns itself with the ways in which humans order, sustain and peacefully and cooperatively develop their lives in various kinds of community.

The cross-curricular themes of personal, social, health and economic (PSHE) education and spiritual, moral, social and cultural (SMSC) education also come under the purview of humanities. These are not curriculum subjects or disciplines, but affect our perception and interaction with all subjects, so that we may look at geography or history from spiritual, moral, cultural or social perspectives and RE or relationships education from personal, social, health or economic standpoints. Some major aspects of the distinctive concepts, language, skills and attitudes of each humanities subject are outlined below.

Geography

Key concepts

Geography (Gov.UK, 2013b) is fundamentally about *place* and *interactions* between *humans* and *places*. Places can be as small as a table or the corner of a garden, a room, a house, a street and as big as farms, forests, shopping streets and malls, car parks and protected landscapes, sacred spaces, damaged environments, open spaces, forbidden locations, routes, rivers, lakes, seas, coasts, counties, countries, continents and oceans. Each kind of place has unique and shared associations for people and affects them in different ways. Places have a past and a future and connections with other places; therefore, human geography involves concepts of the international, internationalism and global interdependence (Bonnett, 2008).

Other concepts central to geography include the map, fieldwork, plans and diagrams. Such visual simplifications of place record natural features, or human-constructed patterns, real and imagined boundaries, human links, occupations, preferences and disputes linked to places. The weather, its patterns and processes and impact on humans is also part of geography. The geography of places often involves the landscape alone and physical geography studies the processes of land formation, geology, seas and oceans, often called geomorphology. Physical and human geography overlap when landscapes are affected by humans; the stewardship, protection and restoration of landscapes and built environments are additional key concepts. In the light of growing consciousness of the negative human impact on the world, the sustainability of natural and human places has become an increasingly important focus of geography over the last 20 years.

Key vocabulary

The language of geography arises from its key concepts. Geographical words colour the ways we perceive the world around us and children only begin to see the detailed and varied aspects of that world when they have words for them. There are words for different kinds of map, geographical diagram and digital image. A specialised language describes the detail of the natural landscape and the processes that affect it. Names for aspects of the settlements we live in are continually being added and help us understand the influences, patterns and changes of human habitation. When considering physical and economic links between humans and their communities we use words for different transport types and routes but also the language of speed, distance, direction, cost and environmental impact. Since geography also concerns thinking about the future, Hicks (2002, 2018) reminds teachers that the possible, probable and preferred future of places is a central theme of geography. Table 4.1 is a sample of the vocabulary that captures some of the unique contributions of geography to understanding our world. Predictably the words *change, global, international* and *sustainability* occur in more than one section.

Table 4.1 A sample of vocabulary for geography at Key Stages 1 and 2

Maps	Diagrams	Landscapes & landscape processes	Settlements	Links between places	Water
Journey stick	Picture	Mountain	Town	Left	River
Key	Graph	Hill	Centre	Right	Lake
Atlas	Label	Valley	Village	In front	Pond
Globe	Cross-section	Plain	Street	Behind	Ocean
Symbol	Graphic table	Plateau	Avenue	Under	Sea
Sketch-map	Layered	Slope	Lane	Through	Watermill
Plan	Flow chart	Desert	City	Beside	Drainage
Direction	Processes	Island	Marketplace	Journey	Well
North	Comparison	Cliff	Industrial	Road	Dam
East	Chart	Beach	Estate	Motorway	Water-table
South	Profile	Bay	Factory	Railway	Hydro
West	Elevation	Field	Office	Track	Wave
Height	Plan	Woodland	Conurbation	Footpath	Meander
Depth	Shape	National park	Nucleated	Ferry	Floodplain
Shape		Track	Linear	Route	Stream
Weather		Road	Scattered	Airport	Estuary
Contour		Motorway	Planned	Harbour	Flood
Topographic		Canal	Terrace	Port	Erosion
Political		Mine	Detached	Trade	Deposition
Physical		Slagheap	Urban	Change	Harbour
Economic		Vegetation	Rural	National	Basin
Route		Countryside	Left	Global	Sustainability
Land use		Land-use	Right	International	Change
Geology		Volcano	Change	Interdependence	Conservation
Cartogram		Earthquake	Conservation	Interaction	Evaporation
Compass		Erosion	Local	Collaboration	Conservation
Scale		Weathering			
Grid		Change			
Continent					
Equator					
Tropic					
Pole					

(Continued)

Table 4.1 A sample of vocabulary for geography at Key Stages 1 and 2 *(Continued)*

Change	The future	Climate	Systems	Boundaries	Photographs Geographical information Systems (GIS) Video
Different	Probable	Wind	Electricity	Fence	Aerial
Before	likely	Rain	Pylon	Hedge	Compare
After	Possible	Fog	Power station	Edge	Contrast
Used to be	Preferable	Cloud	Gas	Limit	Pattern
Environment	Climate	Hurricane	Internet	Border	Isolate
Improvement	change	Mist	Water-supply	Zone	Identify
Deforestation	Carbon	Snow	Windfarm	Area	Interpret
Pollution	footprint	Ice	Mine	Locality	Sketch
Conservation	Sustainability	Hail	Minerals	Limit	Plan
Preservation	International	Season	Eco	Continent	Caption
Damage	Cooperation	Weather	Pipeline	(The	Similarity
Sustainability	Global	Change	Energy	continents)	Difference
Globalisation			Water cycle	Country	Detail
International			Biome	County	Space
			Sustainability	Region	Digital
			international	Biome	Global
				International	

Key skills

Map making, map reading, way-finding and the use of imaginary maps are geographical skills. They are often used in association with the skill of fieldwork. Learning to use symbol, scale, grids and directions focuses these skills back to the real world of children's lives. Similarly, diagrams that visually represent data or processes connected with place, or offer simplifications of landscape features, support young people in understanding, generalising, and classifying the physical world around them. During fieldwork collecting, photographing, videoing, sketching, tallying, observing, imagining and measuring provoke and deepen thought and generate feelings of agency. Practical and intellectual involvement in places in these ways can often result in a new sense of belonging.

Dominant attitudes

Since it majors on interactions between humans and place, positive attitudes towards people and places should be explored and taught in geography. The attitudes most dominant in the best of geography teaching involve emphasis on international and community cooperation, examples of environmental and community sustainability, and the appreciation and conservation of biodiversity. In the face of current global social and environmental threats, geography can guide young people towards hope for a better future through highlighting the positives of human impact and a gratitude for the beauties of diverse landscapes, peoples, lifestyles and affirmative human interactions. The championing of positive attitudes to people and places everywhere are appropriate for primary geography, but there are strong arguments that youngsters should take an active interest in the damage humans have done to places. Awareness of examples of polluted water supplies, seas, degraded landscapes or declining biodiversity and how people have addressed them will enhance a sense of control and perhaps direct children towards personal action. Such issues are not currently included in the English national curriculum; indeed, addressing 'issues' was excluded from the statutory guidance at Key Stage 1 and 2 though allowed as part of fieldwork. Government defence of their omission of climate change and from the geography primary curriculum was expressed in the following words:

> ...schools are encouraged to link action to reduce emissions with the school curriculum, with the guidance stating that 'linking what is taught in the classroom to carbon reduction activity underway in the wider school environment can build momentum for change through pupil leadership and involvement'. (Gov.UK, 2013c)

Sustainability, climate change and human responsibility for the loss of eco-diversity, however, *do* form major focuses within the geography aspects of the curricula for Wales, (Education Wales, 2022), Scotland (Education Scotland, 2022a), and part of the 'Change Over Time,' focus in the Northern Ireland Curriculum. (Northern Ireland, Curriculum, 2019).

History

Key concepts

The key concept in history is time, specifically human time. The chronology of events, developments, stories, processes, interactions, inventions, peoples, cultures, human-made arts and artefacts through time, form the substance of what historians study. Despite its connotations of fiction, the word 'story' within the word history is no coincidence. The Greek and Latin *historia* and the French *histoire* all convey the idea of a narrative, a supposedly true chronical of real events. So, the second key concept is that of narrative, a story generally told in chronological order. Weighing up the truth of such stories is the work of historians, who use evidence, interpretation, a range of primary and secondary source material to consider the accuracy of different perspectives, arguments and accounts of what happened in the past. History also centrally considers change, continuity and trends in human affairs. It looks for causes, consequences and the longer-term significance of particular events. The judicial handling of different kinds of evidence helps develop critical thinking, and greater awareness and appreciation of the diversity of other points of view. Historical evidence, narrative and questioning hopefully help us learn from human attempts to solve problems or respond to the unexpected. History should also help individuals and societies build a sense of identity and relationship to the past. The widest possible representation of diversity in our history teaching is crucial to building a cohesive society.

Key vocabulary

Words that arise from chronology are: time, order, narrative, sequence, beginning, middle and end. The term narrative itself suggests a vocabulary related to storytelling, but the narratives of historic events require a wider vocabulary covering the organisations, structures, systems, traditions, cultures, groupings, issues, priorities, artefacts, settings, timescales, characters and challenges involved in a range of national and international events. Finally, history's dependence upon evidence, analysis, enquiry and questioning requires the language of investigation and judgement. A sample of important history vocabulary for primary school students is suggested in Table 4.2.

Table 4.2 Some suggested vocabulary for history at Key Stages 1 and 2

Time & periods	Chronology & narrative	Change & continuity	Evidence & judgements	Interpretation & arguments	Sources & questions
Old	Story	When I was…	Find	Made up	Map
Ancient	Before	Remember	Sort	Story	Book
Long ago	Since	Same	Guess	Myth	Letter
Century	When	Different	Judge	Folk law	Journal
Millennia	Past	Similar	Weigh up	Composed	Diary
Before	Present	Repeat	Evaluate	Improvised	Film
Common Era (BCE)	Now	Again	Describe	Bias	Picture
Common Era (BE)	Then	Still	Suggest	Ally	Portrait
Decade	After	Consequence	Compare	Enemy	Illustration
Generation	Old(er)	Trend	Contrast	Disagree	Verbal
Prehistoric	Last	Fashion	Cause	Agree	Oral history
Stone/Bronze/Iron Age	Once	Tradition(al)	Influence	Support	Written newspaper
Medieval	At first	Familiar	Link	Argue	Why
Modern	Later	Replace	Assess	Dismiss	What
Middle Ages	Then	Continue	Value	Truth\Lie	How
Period	After	Lost	Better	Guess	When
Level	In the end	Disappeared	Accurate	Debate	Where
Dynasty	At the same time as	Progress	Prove	Adjudicate	Which
Classical	When	Decline	Sum up	Oppose	Archaeology(ist)
Contemporary	While	Loss	Discriminate	Account	Photograph
Roman	During	Journeys	Decide		Artefact
Saxon	In	Explorers	Judge		Building
Viking	Time-line		Contrast		Landscape
Egyptian	Memory		Examine		Architecture
Greek			Investigate		Quiz
South American/ Mayan			Archaeology		Buildings
Indian			Connection		
Chinese			Places		
Victorian					

(Continued)

Table 4.2 Some suggested vocabulary for history at Key Stages 1 and 2 *(Continued)*

Perspectives & accounts	Contrasts & diversity	Trends & fashions	Systems, individuals & organisations	Events: significance & consequences	Artefacts & inventions
Good	Different	Modern	Empire	War	Pottery
Bad	Contrasting	Old fashioned	Emperor	Peace	Iron
Helpful unkind	Alternative	Odd	Inventor	Restoration	Bronze
Violent	Instead	Unusual	Leader	Poverty	Agriculture
Difficult	Other	Common	Originator	Wealth	Container
Dangerous	Surpris(ing)	Popular	Artist	Plague	Wheel
Powerful	Original	Vogue	General	Disease	Painting
Influential	Unusual	Clothes	Ally	Rebellion	Code
Conservative	Creative	Freedom	Country	Battle	Gunpowder
Radical	Appropriate	Equality	Parliament	Fire	Bow
Accurate		Justice	Democracy	Battle	Arrow
Detailed		Emancipation	Communism	Victory	Spear
Genuine		Education	Autocracy	Defeat	Fire
Collaborative		Tradition	Dictator(ship)	Loss	Industry
Characters			Revolution	Discovery	Factory
Relationships			Subjects	Invention	Mechanisation
			Peasants	Medicine	Machine
			Aristocracy	Science	Engine
			Worker	Arts	Vehicle
			Middle Class	Culture	Gun
			King/Queen	Music	Canon
			Emperor	Space	Crossbow
			Monarch	Exploration	Bomb
				Raiders	Ship
				Settlers	Vessel

Key skills

The key history concept of chronology requires the accurate sequencing of events. Young historians will learn how to place the elements of a historical happening into timelines or how to bring elements together in themes, contexts and periods. Both novice and experienced historians use analysis: sorting, questioning, evaluation, investigation and comparison, to weigh up the evidence from different sources including buildings and real artefacts. They become increasingly expert at identifying, collecting and handling a range of spoken, written, illustrative and artefactual sources. Sometimes, especially where evidence is sparse or incomplete, the narrative aspects of history require the less analytical skills of generalisation, hypothesis or intelligent guesswork. Historians should also know how to present their investigations so that others gain from their labours. Transferable skills in narrative, report or summary-writing are useful but not essential, for history can be communicated powerfully in labelled exhibitions, displays, posters, annotated collections, visual presentations, mime, role play, drama and the spoken word.

Dominant attitudes

The English National Curriculum in History highlights historical knowledge and understanding of Britain's past and that of the wider world. Attitudes of curiosity, critical questioning and making informed judgements towards that knowledge are key. The study of history is argued to help young people gain a better understanding of diversity, change and complexity of people's lives in the past as a route towards developing their own identity and responses to life's present-day challenges. The Scottish Curriculum for Excellence places history within its interdisciplinary Social Studies curriculum (Gov.Scotland, 2019) focusing attention on '…other people and their values, in different times, places and circumstances', but also on a more general, 'history, heritage and culture of Scotland', and an appreciation of 'local and national heritage within the world.' For the Early Years in Wales, history skills are incorporated in the cross-curricular theme, 'Knowledge and Understanding of the World' (see Figure 4.1), and skills of enquiry and curiosity should be developed to help children become, 'aware of human achievements and the "big ideas" that have shaped the world' (Wales Education, 2022a, p. 32). At Key Stage 2, the Welsh Curriculum expects children to have 'experiences' in school, '… that make history enjoyable, interesting and significant' (Wales Education, 2022b, p. 10) and alongside standard history skills like enquiry, using multiple sources, and understanding chronology, youngsters are encouraged to 'organise and communicate their skills, knowledge and understanding in an increasing variety of ways' (Wales Education, p. 10). In the Northern Irish Curriculum (2007), the theme 'The World Around Us' incorporates history, and its *Cultural Understanding* objectives seek to develop an, 'awareness and respect for the different lifestyles of others, similarities and differences in families and people in the wider community'. The Northern Irish Curriculum emphasises healing attitudes potentially developed by history teaching: understanding the '…cultural traditions and histories of others', 'people who have helped us in the past' (2007, p. 87), change over time and 'stopping unwanted changes' in addition to proposing historical examples that show how '…we can influence change' (pp. 89–90).

Figure 4.1   Drawing for science in an historic location (Photo: Barnes)

Religious Education

Key concepts

Religious education (RE) exists in British schools to give young people opportunities to learn about the different religions, beliefs, values and traditions of the world. In a superdiverse country like the UK it is considered essential for community cohesion that we understand and respect the similarities and differences in people. This understanding can come from familiarity with a diverse range of religious objects, stories and practices. Respect is a key concept and especially important when discussing the religious views of others. Since much of religion involves the unseen and immaterial, symbols are key to expressing the inexpressible and used in probably all religions.

Children and young people should have the chance to explore their own beliefs and ask questions about life, death, meaning and faith in RE sessions. They are likely to be asked within lessons to reflect on issues related to good and bad, values, truth, ethics and moral behaviour. Additionally youngsters will be expected to interpret, evaluate and communicate views on awe, faith, belief and unbelief. The concept of a spiritual view of the world and existence, whether religious or within an appreciation of realities bigger than ourselves, is an important focus in all locally formulated RE guidance. Increasingly in our secular society children will also consider the position of the absence of belief, how that affects the spiritual response and what it may mean to our actions and principles in daily life.

Key vocabulary

The key religious word 'spirit' comes from the Latin *spiritus* – breath, so that 'spiritual' literally means to see the breath, or life in things. To 'inspire' is therefore to breathe life into. Terms that express wonder and other felt but not seen aspects of life, are central to thinking about faith and religion (Keltner, 2023). While many will feel they know the major religions of the world, fewer know that shamanism and ancestor worship remain very widely used religious practices. RE often turns to the vocabulary of things unseen, not fully understood, but deeply felt and real to many (consider the use of words in Table 4.3).

Globally, life's key moments are marked with ceremony, celebration and special gatherings. These may be religious or secular occasions but in every society they are important ways of establishing meaning, focusing on the life and specialness of individuals. Everyday terms are often used to express religious experience, but each culture and religion has specific words, music, settings and activities linked with such celebrations. The language of faith itself is equally specific to the religions, but common words like symbol, belief, prayer, soul have meaning across most religions. Religions frequently identify or build special or sacred places with meaningful objects and fitments for worship, prayer, preaching and meeting – these have a rich and evocative vocabulary of their own. The metaphor of a journey gives rise to a language of faith full of images and stories common across religions.

Table 4.3 Some suggested vocabulary for Religious Education at Key Stages 1 and 2

Spirit	Religions	The unseen	Celebrations	Faith	Story
Holy	Ancestor-	God(s)	Sad	Symbol	Symbol
Life	Worship	Awe	Happy	God	Tale
Soul	Baha'i	Wonder	Birth	Belief	Lesson
Ghost	Buddhism	Honour	Initiation	Acceptance	Metaphor
Spiritual	Christianity	Holy	Transition	Prayer	Simile
Divine	Confucianism	Magical	Marriage	Sacrifice	Parable
Heavenly	Hinduism	Sacred	Death	Heaven	Moral
Celestial	Islam	Worship	Gift	Paradise	Traditional
Inspire	Jainism	Venerated	Anniversary	Saint	Culture
Unworldly	Judaism	Sublime	Holy day	Holy	Epic
Reflective	Shamanism	Ecstasy	Memory	Miracle	Ramayana
Special	Sikhism	Miraculous	Memorial	Parable	Folktale
Godly	Taoism	Invisible	Symbol	Blessed	Lessons
Religious	Traditional	Supernatural	Light	Scripture	
Mindful	Zoroastrianism	Immaterial	Darkness	Offering	
Meditative		Silence	Sadness	Creed	
Thoughtful		Reflection	Dance	Rite	
Significance		Meaning		Conviction	
		Unexplained			
		Profound			

Symbol	Ceremony	Journey	Values	Buildings	People
Cross	Birth	Walk	Good	Mosque	Priest
Trinity	Initiation	Enter	Bad	Synagogue	Rabbi
Crescent	Transition	Join	Wrong	Church	Imam
Ohm	Marriage	Footsteps	Right	Temple	Vicar
Star	Death	Path	Kindness	Pagoda	Monk
Lotus	Worship	Destination	Compassion	Pavilion	Nun
Parasol	Feast	Pilgrimage	Faith	Cave	Hermit
Conch	Table	Crossing	Courage	Shelter	Saint
Wheel	Procession	River	Honesty	Sukkah	Prophet
Prayer flag	Bow	Shelter	Love	Chapel	Patriarch
Banner	Prostrate	Stranger	Temperance	Hospice	Goddess
Knot	Offerings	Guest	Humility	Tomb	Hero
Star	Memorial	Welcome,	Charity	Gurdwara	Heroine
Hand	Sacrifice	Companion	Generosity	Chantry	Example
Menorah	Prayer	Flood	Justice	Cathedral	Mystic
Torah	Reverence	Climb	Pacifism	Hall	Shaman
Kippah	Dance	Mountain	Peace	Mihrab	Medium
Sword	Song	Lake	Forgiveness	Minaret	Elder
Comb	Hymn	Chariot	Sorrow	Wudu	Healer
Bracelet		Boat	Selflessness	(washing area)	Sage
Prayer mat			Individuality	Ka'bah	Follower
Stool					
Candle					
Light					
Fire					

Key skills

The skills developed in RE overlap with some of those from other areas of learning. In RE children learn to name, describe, research, select, analyse and interpret as they might in science or geography or history. The purpose of developing these skills is, however, different from other subjects. In RE these skills are directed towards positive responses to the beliefs, feelings and lives of others. Reflecting on the detail of others' lives may be the first step towards the ability to feel and show compassion. In RE children are asked to identify and relate aspects of felt, emotional, non-material, religious or spiritual world. Through this it is hoped that they will develop more sensitive responses to different worldviews. When considering religious stories they may be led towards the skills of interpreting and retelling them, thereby developing the skill of empathy. As they develop the ability to express and communicate meaning, children will learn that these things can be done in non-verbal as well as verbal ways, through dance, drama, painting, sculpture, photography, music and video. Comparing the beliefs of different religions and philosophies can lead children to develop the skill of synthesising disparate ideas and discerning between good and bad, positive and negative.

Dominant attitudes

The dominant attitude sought through RE rests on positivity. Positive regard for the self and the lives and cares of others regardless of religion and culture. Positivity towards the self begins with self-awareness and a willingness to be still and reflect. Positivity towards others involves respect for all, and an open-mindedness that avoids automatic judgements. Positivity towards the world around us involves an attitude of appreciation for nature and human relationships and the time and space to wonder or stand in awe at the inexplicable.

The search for the meaning of life is probably common to all people religious or not. Meaning is found in countless ways but may involve questions of things bigger than ourselves such as: beauty, peace, kindness, care, justice and the whole range of inclusive values. Talking about, sharing and prolonging states of meaningful activity can be a powerful part of RE sessions and result in positive attitudes that last a lifetime (see, for example, Manchester Church Schools, 2017).

Citizenship

Key concepts

Citizenship is not a compulsory subject for children in the Early Years or Key Stages 1 and 2 in the countries of the United Kingdom though curriculum guidance exists. In Scotland, Northern Ireland and Wales it forms part of cross-curricular themes such as becoming an eco-school, taking part in community projects, having mock elections and involvement in charitable activities (see, for example, East Lothian Council website). In

England, guidance is provided for primary schools that wish to teach citizenship as either a separate subject or integrate it into the teaching of other subjects (DfE, 2015). Citizenship became prominent after the Crick Report of 1998 which strongly recommended that developing a '...common citizenship with democratic values' was essential for every 21st-century citizen. The report introduced the key concept of active citizenship where children and young people were equipped, willing and able to participate in public life and were from an early age taught about likes and dislikes, fairness and unfairness, right and wrong. From Early Years onwards children should be encouraged to share and explain their opinions, recognise their and others' feelings in a positive way, recognise their own strengths and set simple goals.

Democracy, a key concept, is the first of the five 'British values' taught across British schools (Gov.UK, 2014). In the context of citizenship, democracy involves understandings of social and moral responsibility, community involvement (see Association of Citizenship Teaching website). By Key Stage 2, schools may introduce beginnings of 'political literacy' involving early understandings of political decisions, human rights, the rule of law and ideas of justice. As with every humanities subject, knowledge and understanding of these complex, ever-developing concepts is incremental and begins with simple notions like: good and bad, friendship, questioning, reflection, practical engagement, responsibility, self-confidence and understanding of money and economics.

Key vocabulary

The core language of citizenship comprises of words that describe how we should live together. Citizenship approaches use values words like care, kindness, compassion, respect and words to describe social organisations like family, school, library, office, club, locality, county, city, town, village, council, government, country, ally. Active citizenship will entail an understanding of words such as gift, help, volunteer, charity, participation, organisation, practical, environment, culture, refugee, carer and guide. Concepts of democracy of course require the words vote, election and rules, but also the language of debate and enquiry – discussion, honesty, equality, courage, connection, listening, sustainability, respect, improvement, harm, choice, opinion, argument, justice, fairness, rights, responsibilities and trust.

Key skills

In the Early Years and at Key Stages 1 and 2 citizenship experience can involve many kinds of practical activity. Participation in active citizenship includes developing the skills of empathy, careful listening to the concerns and cares of others and an appreciation of other points of view. Children and young people should be made aware of local, national and international issues in which they might play a part and know of case studies where their peers have already done so. They also need to develop the skills of critical thinking and discrimination especially with regard to social and other media, how they present information and how we can judge the accuracy of statements. Skills involved in assessing risks to health, morality, friendship and community, and skills in understanding change in their bodies and lives are rightly developed in citizenship sessions. In our diverse society citizenship is the place for young people to be given skills to challenge stereotypes, resist racism, deal with bullying and understand cultural, ethnic and religious differences and similarities.

Dominant attitudes

Clearly, the dominant attitudes put forward in citizenship education across the UK are those of positive regard to other people. The word positive occurs throughout the guidance to apply to self and others. It relates also to individual rights and responsibilities and the citizen's role in sustaining a meaningful democracy. The attitudes of active participation, full awareness of human rights and the importance of law and order are central to notions of democracy. Affirmative attitudes to the self are equally important. Self-confidence, balanced by a willingness to understand the different views of others, is seen as essential to the developing identity. The positive responses to times of failure, disappointment or setback and the positive attitudes towards *forgiveness* advanced in citizenship guidance may well be instrumental in generating mindsets that are open for growth and fulfilment.

SMSC and PSHE

The social, moral, spiritual and cultural aspects of education (SMSC) and its personal, social, health and economic (PSHE) implications represent overlapping cross-curricular themes. Primary school Ofsted inspections (Ofsted, 2022) focus on aspects of health and relationships education, but the combined priorities of PSHE and SMSC are major functions of schooling itself. The Royal Society of Arts reminds us of the centrality of such themes:

> [SMSC is]...quite clearly a descriptor of not just a core purpose of schooling but of the core dimensions of our existence as social animals. In this respect, creating the time and space to reflect on, and design approaches to, meeting the statutory requirement to promote SMSC development may also be a path to re-envisioning our schools as first and foremost human places. (RSA, 2014, p. 30)

Schools are institutions built by, around and for people. In schools, therefore, the human soul, human differences, needs, similarities, the societies they live in, the cultures and the communities they form and choose should always be central to curriculum and pedagogy. Ideas about identity, community, responsibility, rights and attitudes, philosophy and philanthropy can be developed in mathematics as well as citizenship, history as well as RE. Approaches such as Philosophy for Children (SAPERE website) seek to help develop, from the Early Years onward, their moral understanding within an enquiry-based approach. For example, allowing children to discuss and question the charities they support encourages them to think together and carefully about issues of social justice, change and inequalities. When children participate in decisions about their rights it gives agency and the beginnings of authentic experience of decision-making (Equality and Human Rights Commission, 2020).

While PSHE (Gov.UK, 2021e) is not statutory, and therefore has no compulsory course of study, primary schools are expected to deliver the groundwork to the knowledge and skills needed for informed personal, social, health and economic decisions and to understand potential risks in those areas. Sex education though not compulsory in primary schools is nonetheless recommended for children in Key Stages 1 and 2 and since 2020 there has been a requirement for schools to teach Relationships. Relationships education covers personal well-being, families, caring friendships, respectful relationships and online relationships as well as helping children recognise and report sexual, emotional and physical abuse.

Putting the humanities to work

Education has multiple functions. If, as Martin Luther King suggested, it exists to teach students to 'think intensively and critically – intelligence plus character', then a balance between different kinds of thinking should be evident in all curricula, every classroom. We know that the human brain has evolved to facilitate the strongly contrasting modes of thought required for such activities as hunting, childcare, emoting, building, shaping, collaborating, inventing, and adapting to extreme climatic conditions. Recent analysis (McGilchrist, 2021) suggests that the brain's left hemisphere strengths in knowledge based on narrow focus, categorisation, simplification, emotional neutrality and measurement, tend to be moderated by the right brain's tendency towards the broad, embodied, flexible, subtle, expressive, emotional, wordless and meaning-seeking. The humanities as a group of disciplines are well placed to use and develop these different kinds of knowing. Geography balances the classifications and simplified processes of physical geography with the emotional values involved in pattern-seeking, identity, sustainability, locality and geo-politics. History teaching involves the sharp detail of dates and events but also interests itself in the softer skills of context, role play, empathy and current relevance. Attempted neutrality and dispassionate analysis in RE is often modified by discussion and investigation of broad feelings and deeply personal, emotional issues. Citizenship clearly combines both narrow focus on the self and personal relationships with 'big picture' issues like democracy, charity and the rule of law.

The humanities work well together too. When combined, the approaches of each separate subject provides a more rounded view of knowledge; offers an epistemologically different perspective. While each subject throws a different analytical light on children's personal experience, in cross-curricular application more balanced appreciations of the big issues confronting our world become possible. It is important, however, for children to know which discipline is being used to elucidate certain aspects of the big themes. Since awareness of the progressive growth of knowledge and skills offer a strong sense of personal development, specific and ever-more challenging learning targets should be provided in each Humanities project. In Case Study 4.1, for example, the targets for geography included the ability to devise and use five symbols on a sketch map and to collect using tally, tables and photos, valid information on the biodiversity of one area of the school grounds. In history, the targets were to be able to apply two visual data collection techniques to the school building to provide evidence for discussion on social change in the last 120 years and to compare conclusions with two other forms of evidence.

Case Study 4.1

Children in a Year 3 class in Leicester, humanities case study that introduced the theme of diversity

Year 3 children were given a short introduction to data gathering in geography fieldwork. They were shown how to use sketch maps, symbols, tally, use grids, graphs, samples, make collections and photos. They were reminded to take great care of any living creatures, not to handle but to collect photographic evidence. In groups of 5 or 6, children were allocated different parts of their school grounds and used grids, tallies and double-sided tape to collect or count examples of biodiversity in the mosses, lichens, plants, leaves and creatures they found. They were asked to locate their position on a base map of the school grounds and measure exact temperature in their place. On their return to class, groups were given guidance and new knowledge on how to make their own sketch maps (complete with compass directions, scale and key) of the biodiversity to be found in each area. They constructed maps that showed some surprisingly high biodiversity on the walls on one side of the school field and debated which areas of the grounds were the most biodiverse and why. They noticed the impact that buildings made on temperature measurements. Their teacher reminded them that because this exercise was about place and the effects that humans had made on that place they were using some key questions of geography. They were reminded that maps and data collection were key skills of geography too.

Later in the week the class teacher built on children's awakened interest in their Victorian school building and asked them to look for evidence of change over time and the different experiences of people in the past. Each group, armed with an iPad, looked carefully inside and outside the building using an 'evidence collection' sheet with headings for alterations, architecture, boundaries, materials, photos, words and writing and space for drawing features that caught their attention. After a 30-minute search the groups returned to combine their findings. They noticed blocked doors and windows, chimneys, antique ventilation systems, formerly overlooked signs for 'Boys' entrance' and 'Girls' entrance', railings around the present school yard that were already there in 1895, additions in different brick, a missing belfry, a repurposed caretaker's lodge building and an old air raid shelter. Their teacher told the class that this focus on change through time and the collection of different forms of evidence were classic skills and approaches of history.

Case Study 4.1 uses a multi-disciplinary approach to cross-curricular learning. Learning in and through both geography and history were motivated by the personally engaging experience of a simple trip outside the classroom into the grounds of the school. Children developed separate skills in each subject despite the fact that the stimulus was essentially the same. It was clear to their teachers that significant new learning occurred in a third subject, English (oracy, reading and writing). Since the overall theme was diversity, the children were helped to appreciate that thinking about diversity involved valuing both the variety of natural things and different ways of living. Practical experience of diversity in their own 'back yard' helped provide a range of meaningful mental representations of the concept in the minds of many children.

One way to assess the achievement of targets and test the transferability of new knowledge and skills is to give children the opportunity to 'perform' their understanding (Blythe, 1998) (see Table 4.4).

Table 4.4 A Performance of Understanding approach to assessing cross-curricular work on the school campus

Year 3 (7-year-olds)	
Big Issue: Diversity	
Unit of work theme in the form of a question:	How is diversity represented in our school building and school grounds?
Powerful shared experience:	A collecting walk in the school grounds followed by group investigations of details of the school building

Subject 1 Geography

Skills: Map reading and making, collecting data, using symbols, making tallies and using photos

Knowledge: Geographical vocabulary: map, plan, symbol, density, place, micro-climate, direction, north, east south, west

Understanding: Relationship between human habitation and biodiversity, impact of buildings on outside temperatures

Subject 2 History

Skills: Drawing, using photographs, finding evidence in architecture, chronology

Knowledge: Victorian architecture, changing attitudes to gender, evidence of change in buildings, boundaries and community

Understanding: Change and continuity

Sessions 1–6	Activities	Assessments
Introduction sessions	Class engage in a collecting walk in school grounds. Each group of 5 is allocated one area of the grounds and asked to seek and collect examples of biodiversity. Groups take a tour of their Victorian school to collect evidence of change and diverse usage of the buildings over time.	**General Assessment:** **Introductory performance:** individuals show they are involved in making appropriate collections **Formative Assessment:** teacher encourages and highlights inquisitiveness, collaboration, original responses

(Continued)

Table 4.4 A Performance of Understanding approach to assessing cross-curricular work on the school campus *(Continued)*

Sessions 1–6	Activities	Assessments
Guided enquiry (4 sessions) –	Whole class is taught how to make a sketch map using a base map of the school grounds. Terms scale, key, symbol, compass direction, North, South, East, West are introduced. Groups of young geographers map human features, parts of building, outbuildings, boundaries, and gardens on 'their' part of sketch map. They discuss ways of presenting data from their area onto map inventing their own symbols and making graphs of the diverse environments and the bio-diversity within them. Groups now renamed young historians are sent to various areas inside and outside the school. With a history checklist and brief explanations they record signs of change, decoration, Victorian lettering, heating and ventilation systems, architectural features. Back in class they look at old logbooks and historic photo's of the school and its pupils from 1900–2000, noting changes in ethnic diversity and school life.	**Formative Assessment: guided performances of understanding in geography:** teacher guides with vocabulary, examples and questions. Teacher supports the application of correct geographical language and skills in the use of symbols, simple sketch map making and bar graph construction. Teacher encourages and notes examples of observation, comparison, judgements of change, guesses about function, differences and similarities.
Culminating Performance of Understanding (sessions 5 and 6) – A culminating performance that demonstrates the new learning that has taken place	Whole class shown how to make simple 3D scale models to represent the school building and various outbuildings. Children learn how to locate models on to a large sketch map. Each group then decides how to present their findings in an exhibition on the geographical and historical diversity they discovered in their part of the site. Children designed and made posters explaining 120 years of change at the school and curated labelled exhibitions of photographs, drawings and artefacts to illustrate the changes witnessed since the school was built.	**Teacher supports by** encouraging neat, clear presentation, imaginative methods and assesses originality, imagination, collaboration in the groups, usefulness of the presentations. **Performances of understanding:** Teacher uses observations and each group contribution to assess degree to which individuals have achieved the target skills, knowledge and understandings. **Teacher assesses** qualities that demonstrate the use of historical and geographical language and confidence in skills of map making and using and the presentation of data.

The Early Years framework for England does not separately identify geography, history, RE and citizenship, but the foundations of these subjects are evident. The learning Goals for *Personal, Social and Emotional Development* and *Understanding the World* introduce children to see and understand aspects of the personal and physical world around them including the seasons and other changes, exploring natural things, their community and different roles people play, past and present, far and near, likes and dislikes. The activities outlined in Case Study 4.2 show how such goals can be met and how they provide a secure base for later learning.

Case Study 4.2

Children in a London Nursery School investigate awe and wonder in their 'Identity' topic on the Caribbean

In a nursery school in east London, Groundswell Arts work with light boxes, objects and X-ray images to generate fascination, curiosity and wonder in children under 4. In one session children investigated the shapes of unfamiliar but natural objects. Their teacher helped them capture what they saw by introducing the geographical language of a *plan* (a bird's eye view) and an *elevation* (the human eye-level view from the front), *above* and *below*. In the process children handled and drew images of large shells and corals from the Caribbean and looked at X-ray images of creatures, and were encouraged to speak about these aspects of the natural world (see Figure 4.2). They observed intricate patterns, links and designs they'd never seen before and shared their observations excitedly using words like: wow, beautiful, amazing, wonderful, mega, humungous to describe their amazement at the beauties of nature. The precise nature of the geographical language learned as part of their Understanding the World curriculum was balanced by their use of a more general language of appreciation and the facial/body language of involvement and wordless sounds of wonder at what they saw. In conversation, the adults with them were able to help children understand that there are some things that are so interesting and lovely that words are not always enough.

Using stories, maps and aerial views of islands in the Caribbean just after they had explored the artefacts and images, children discussed similarities and differences between their life and life in other places.

This short project with 3- and 4-year-olds laid the foundations of some concepts in geography, RE and citizenship. Maps, aerial views, plans and elevations were introduced for the first time to many in the group. The idea that some things were difficult to describe in words was encouraged as part of their experience and prepared them for thinking about ineffable experiences of awe or wonder. They understood through physical and emotional engagement with objects, images and stories that people

Figure 4.2 A nursery child using light boxes to learn about the geographical concept of a plan experience and the RE concept of wonder

have different conditions of living, dependent upon the climate, but that all people live in communities that support each other. Other big issues related to how we describe beauty, what we share with others, including other creatures and for some, personal identity, were also addressed in this work. In terms of cross-curricular learning, the activities described in Case Study 4.2 fall within the category of *Theme-based* cross-curricular learning. The theme of identity (a high percentage of the class had relatives in the Caribbean) was developed in the activities described above, but also developed in the construction of 'identity baskets' in which children placed their own collection of photos and small objects that had something precious to do with themselves and their family. These baskets were used as a framework for discussion between teacher and parents/carers on open days.

Case Study 4.3

Year 5 and 6 students construct their own Bronze Age dwelling on Eastbourne marshes and think about sustainability

A few years ago, an Eastbourne junior school consulted with a team of archaeologists and local historians to find that their modern building stood just a few hundred metres away from the site of one of Europe's biggest Bronze Age settlements. The imaginative headteacher changed the curriculum to respond to this unexpected and invisible resource. The decision was made to spend at least one-third of lesson time on the marsh and most of the rest in responding to it. Over the next few years five water buffalos were purchased (they were the nearest creature to the bovine inhabitants of the marsh 3,000 years ago), leather coracles were made to row across the shallow ponds and wetlands, hives of black bees were established (children examined drawings of excavated beehives) and the children learned from experts how to make bronze. The learning in science, technology, mathematics and English obviously skyrocketed! Several years of Bronze Age excitement culminated in the construction of a wooden causeway and several round, thatched dwellings based on evidence from archaeological digs in the area (see Figure 4.3). Governors, parents, friends and teachers supported the young people in this building project that lasted a term. History, geography and RE came together powerfully to help the children make sense of these unique experiences. Working with archaeologists and using their findings, visiting a museum to find the artefacts their historical neighbours had once used, imagining the difficulties and joys of life in the marsh they shared with ancestors, gave the children authentic experience of being historians.

The experience did not just involve history. Children learned directly from a local shaman about the likely approach to religion in Bronze Age, nature-dependent society and responded with their own spiritual reflections on what bees can teach us about community. They sensitively investigated the habitats of grass snakes, rabbits, rats, frogs and newts and made stories about what they and their continued occupation of the area symbolised. Geography skills and knowledge was developed in their response to the marsh – how deep was the water? How could the area be protected from the encroachment of urbanisation? What damage had pollution done to the area? How could what they had learned be mapped? The children enthusiastically learned new knowledge in each Humanities subject. Their varied perspectives on sustaining the beauty and natural life of the area were brought together in a series of information posters designed, produced and erected around the marsh.

Figure 4.3 A replica causeway and Bronze Age dwelling based on archaeological evidence and built by 10 year olds and adult helpers

The activities outlined in Case Study 4.3 combined highly focused learning in three subjects. Their work was unified under the general heading of sustainability – how the techniques and materials of Bronze Age builders were sustainable, how the mapping, fieldwork and fine descriptions of place can help in sustaining its unique characteristics and why certain approaches to the spirit of place may have survived. Children demonstrated the detail of their learning in the ways they performed their understanding. The buildings were built, reflective, 'spiritual' poems and stories written, and the area was measured, mapped and recorded. This project went further, however. Children were asked what they could *do* with their new historical, geography and RE knowledge. In teams they decided on a number of *Performances of Understanding*, that required the fusion of the different skills, knowledge and attitudes learned in this project through the humanities subjects. Information posters, a dramatic performance and exhibition of the years' work for parents and governors, an animation of causeway and round house building, a loop of photographic illustrations of the project for the school entrance video, reflections and maps capturing developments were all proposed and produced by the children. This process of combining separate subject learning within new, valued, original, imaginative, creative outcomes illustrates what I have called inter-disciplinary cross-curricular learning (Barnes, 2015).

Summary

In this chapter you were introduced to the educational concept of the humanities. You learned that in a primary school setting the humanities involved citizenship, geography, history and RE. The distinctive contributions of each subject were introduced by summarising the unique set of concepts, vocabulary, skills and attitudes that characterise each. Each humanities subject was argued to provide a different lens through which to see the world around us.

In combination the humanities can provide a rounded and comprehensive method of understanding the local environment of the school and its catchment area. The global reach of each of the subjects will also help children appreciate the many links between their experience and the experience of others living far away.

The chapter ended with three case studies where cross-curricular and creative 'big issue' themes of diversity, sustainability and identity were investigated using the combined but distinct tools of geography, history, RE and citizenship. The suggestion was made that cross-curricular themes, issues and questions should provide insights into the epistemological qualities of each of the subjects (Epistemic Insight, website) – what each subject contributes to knowledge and what their combination adds. Assessment by means of Performances of Understanding was recommended for humanities cross-curricular projects. This approach allows young people progressively to demonstrate and apply their new knowledge in real situations, events and contexts with increasing independence throughout their learning within a topic.

5
CONNECTING THE WORDLESS DISCIPLINES – ART AND DESIGN, DRAMA, MUSIC, DANCE AND PE

Objectives

In this chapter you will be introduced to:

- The special contributions of the arts and Physical Education (PE) to learning and motivation
- The ways that the arts use often non-verbal but emotional and physical means to build understanding in a child's internal and external worlds
- How the arts and PE can be used to approach difficult subjects in non-confrontational ways
- How the arts and adventure-based learning can be and often are connected with each other to address controversial issues

Introduction

Why arts, design and PE? The arts, design and PE are essentially wordless disciplines. Of course, these subjects of the primary curriculum use words, some indeed are fundamental to understanding their unique contributions to knowledge, but they exist because they express concepts and feelings beyond words.

As far as we know, art, music, dance, drama and design have existed as long as the human race. The range and complexity with which humans have developed these activities sets us apart from other animals. The arts along with our complex language, versatile hands and big brains arguably define us as a species. Hand-sized stone tools, shaped with three or four deliberate chips, provide the earliest evidence of the human-like dexterity and intelligence in east and south Africa. These first pieces of design were fashioned at least three million years ago by *australopithicus*, and predate early humans, like *homo erectus*, who subsequently dominated Africa and later travelled and settled across south Asia. *Homo erectus* and *homo neanderthalis* created much more carefully crafted, tear-drop shaped hand-axes, the first of which were made around 500,000 years ago. Geometric scratchings and carvings on shell, stone and red ochre stencilled hand-prints have been found in Indonesia, the Middle East, throughout Africa and parts of southern Europe, dating back 100,000 years, and before the dominance of modern human beings – *homo sapiens*.

Evidence of music-making such as resonating stones, bones, horns and flutes, exists from around the same period, possibly even before homo sapiens developed complex language. Indeed, there are theories that suggest humans sang before they could speak (Mithen, 2005). Certain musical intervals, cadences and melodies appear to communicate and provoke similar emotions regardless of culture (Egermann et al., 2015). It is more difficult to discover convincing evidence of ancient drama, dance and spoken poetry, but observations of traditional societies and analysis of their language strongly suggest that music, and accompanying dance/drama, have existed across human time (Blacking, 1974; Brown, 1992). While music and dance doubtless existed in times of war and peace, famine and plenty, physical games and sports are more likely to have developed in periods of peace and abundance.

Since their early genesis, the arts, design, adventurous play and entertaining physical games must have been important to humans. These activities, however, exist outside specific value systems. We know, for example, that sport, arts and design have been, and are, powerfully used by dictators and war criminals as well as humanitarians and peace activists. These wordless, often emotionally charged activities move and influence us personally and collectively for good or evil. Their ability to unify and express have played fundamental roles in building and sustaining all types of human community (Malloch and Trevarthen, 2019); affirmative and inclusive communities place the arts within a positive moral context.

Throughout the chapter the arts, design and many of the physical activities in PE are treated as languages of aesthetic awareness and discourse, '… in which our ideas of beauty, grace, harmony, balance, harshness, stridency and ugliness are conceived, formulated and expressed' (Robinson, 1989, p. 18). Consciousness that we are expressive, creative, inventive, problem-solving creatures often confers feelings of pleasure, fulfilment and meaning (Csikszentmihalyi, 1997; Panksepp, 2004).

The subjects examined in this chapter share common processes, in contrasting physical and sensory ways of exploring aspects of the physical, emotional, social or imagined world. Each focuses on presenting and performing, but their methods of demonstrating an understanding differ. Art, music, drama, dance, and aspects of PE involve various processes of responding, making, designing, forming and finishing. These common processes, identified by Robinson (1990), will be referred to throughout the chapter.

Art and Design

The first art was body centred. Abalone shell containers, used to hold red ochre for body markings or spattered to make hand-prints, indicated *neanderthal* presence well before their species extinction. Pierced shell or stone body ornaments and hand-held amulets found in prehistoric caves across the world are still used in traditional communities today. The representational cave painting of *homo sapiens* hunters is found from Sulawezi to Spain, Cape Town to southern France, Australia's Northern Territory to the *Cueva De Los Manos* in Argentina. We can never know the precise meaning of these art works but assume they *had* meaning because they were protected, revered, carefully added to and copied over the millennia.

The high importance of visual art remains. Art in advertising, information, decoration, attention-gaining, status-enhancing, entertainment, cultural or political statement is surely as prolific now as any time in history. For centuries, humans have been prepared to invest significant amounts of time and money on works of art. Only relatively recently have researchers begun to recognise the therapeutic and health-giving aspects of art making and sharing (Scott, 2021). In this chapter, art is defined as a visual expression of imagination and creative skill, valued for its beauty and/or ingenuity but also for its ability to communicate on emotional and intellectual levels usually without the use of words. Even at 6 months old, babies divert their attention towards predictable shapes and patterns in the natural and made environment. It seems humans like many other animals are programmed to discern and interpret patterns, similarities and subtle differences from a very young age (Tummeltshammer and Kirkham, 2013). Art, a powerful alternative mode of thinking and 'speaking', is able to communicate ideas and feelings beyond spoken language (see Figure 5.1).

Like every discipline, the visual arts use a progression of skills, concepts and attitudes.

Skills and concepts

Beginnings

The long period of childhood in the human species means that play is a major route towards knowing and understanding. Children need time and relaxed, playful opportunities to experiment with ways of forming with paper, scissors, brushes, pencils, pens, crayons,

Figure 5.1 татои TA and Year 1 drawing on location

charcoal, markers, paints, digital art software, clay and other modelling, printing and mark-making materials. The teacher's role is to allow and encourage such play but also model and help refine skills of handling and controlling the tools of the artist. The first art tools are those that support drawing, a skill that underpins much visual art and almost always provokes more careful looking and longer engagement. Teachers should encourage confidence in drawing whether with sticks in the sand, pencils, markers or fingers on a steamed-up window. Mark-making allows every child quickly to manifest the art within them (see Figure 5.2).

All children need confidence. At nursery and Key Stage 1 children are helped towards self-assurance in art-making, through frequent opportunities to handle and carefully examine interesting objects and being given related drawing experience. Drawing,

Figure 5.2 Bella's drawing from life. Note the toes and the skin of the elephant

painting and other early art skills develop most richly in places where artistic imagination is liberated (Manera, 2022). Acceptance, openness to investigation and the planned gradual introduction of skills and challenges, characterise such environments. Teachers help shape this atmosphere by planning activities to exercise new skills: drawing the family or an angel, making a coil pot or computer monster, designing a monochrome poster for a class play or carefully capturing the subtle colours of a primrose. Offering quite young children possibilities that may add to their visual literacy, like investigating the properties of different papers and processes or the effects of combining water with gouache, crayon, pastel, ink or PVA glue, will build both confidence and imagination.

Evaluating the work of other artists adds to children's understanding of art as an established, serious discipline. Positive teachers will encourage frequent opportunities for focused, positive responses and thoughtful questions about the work of others. You should strive to help children develop an emotional, personal vocabulary of evaluation quite different to that of other subjects, by talking with others about subjective responses to art and articulating the multiple ways that art creates meaning.

Group art marking strongly supports artistic development for most. When children co-construct large murals, collages, structures, sculptures, group presentations, sales or exhibitions, they begin to appreciate the concept of collaborative creativity and notions of finish, fitness for purpose, criticality, durability, function that link to design technology (see Chapter 6).

New concepts

Concepts such as line, colour and pattern generally develop early. Ideas of tone, form and texture should be introduced gradually through Key Stage 1 and into Key Stage 2 (see Figure 5.2). Plentiful occasions for open-ended investigation help children deepen a personal understanding of these concepts. Art's inclusive nature should be stressed from the beginning – encourage original interpretations in line and colour, congratulate unusual uses of texture, pattern or tone. Individual responses to a common brief, for example, representing emotion on a clay face or constructing a portrait gallery of friends, will begin to build lasting models of the numberless languages of art.

You will help children develop a sense of form and shape, space and perspective through exposure to the work of older artists, designers, photographers and architects (DfEE, 1999a, pp. 16 and 18). Support the growth of new skills by setting increasingly challenging first-hand observation tasks that exercise the skills as soon as they have been taught. Stress the importance of constructive criticism through frequent peer-led evaluation: what worked? what could be developed? what is missing? Encourage the identification of creative ideas (see Table 5.1).

Creativity and personal development

Creativity is often generated when newly learned skills are applied to new challenges. Creative action need not wait until a vast body of extra knowledge is taught, it develops alongside others and responds to authentic and relevant problems. Creativity develops

Figure 5.3 Pencil self-portrait by 9-year-old Isaac using a range of drawing techniques

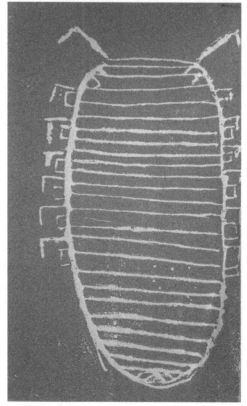

Figure 5.4 Polystyrene print from close observation of woodlouse, made by 6-year-old Naomi

Table 5.1 Some art and design skills, techniques and concepts

Art skills, techniques and concepts	Examples
Experimenting with different mark-making media	*Opportunities to play, experiment and practise with pencil (different qualities), charcoal, crayon, marker pen, pen and ink, paint, tracing, digital media*
Exploring different techniques, tools and modes of manipulation	*Line drawing, shading, colouring, tone, texture, printing, silhouette, collage, pottery, construction, resist, mixed media, digital art software, animation*
Understanding concepts of tone, colour, texture and contrast, and eventually, of more complicated ideas like balance, focus and proportion	*The techniques above and the artistic concepts used in practical application. Increasing emphasis on the detail of proportion, perspective and composition*
Responding to a variety of styles and forms of visual art, including differences between cultural forms (e.g. Western, Eastern, African, Traditional) and historical periods (e.g. primitive, ancient, medieval, modern)	*Introducing the work of artists from other times and cultures and linking these with aspects of geography, language, English, history, PSHE and citizenship*
Progressive awareness of the use and potential of visual symbols to convey ideas and feelings	*Symbols in Egyptian, Greek or Chinese art. Invention of own symbols for big concepts like love, pain, fear, sorrow*
Developing sensitivity to design — relationships between materials, forms and functions of objects and constructions over time and culture	*Looking at changes in the design of buildings, clothing, furniture, fabrics 1700–2023*
Demonstrating progressively greater powers of observation and description	*Life-drawing, drawing and painting out of doors and from observation. Looking at the observational drawing and painting of others*
Increasing expertise in using three-dimensional skills	*Experience making sculpture and vessels in clay. Making and using plaster casts, modelling in card, recycled or found materials, wax, fabrics, paper maché*

best in conditions of positive emotion and often has the effect of generating additional positive effects as Fredrickson (2010) has shown.

The expansion of your own personal interests will also enrich the experience of children. Staff development that includes virtual and actual visits to art galleries, sculpture gardens, exhibitions, arts workshops, museums, great houses and zoos will not only grow your own enthusiasm and knowledge but impact strongly on well-being. The enhanced experience will add to the range of historical/cultural standpoints and the drawing, painting, printing, collage and digital media techniques you can offer children.

Sketchbooks and digital media

We all respond positively to encouragement. Personal sketchbooks can quickly become the focus of such reassurance. When regularly used, cared for, and with each page dated, they provide chronological evidence of skill development, style and individuality in every individual. Treat these unique records of observation, design and analysis as places of celebration and personalised prompts for discussion between child and supportive adult.

A sketchbook is required by the national curriculum in England for children in Key Stage 2, but otherwise the Art curriculum has relatively few expectations (DfEa, 2013). Knowing about and linking work to famous artists and designers is important, but so too is making personal, artistic responses to diversity, culture, society and identity. The seminal *Arts in Schools Project* (Robinson, 1990) recognised this. It saw the arts as ways of recognising and celebrating cultural diversity and acknowledged diverse interpretations of 'quality'. It suggested that primary school children should practically integrate art and design skills and concepts with their social/cultural world:

> The arts are not a separate domain of cultural life. The forms they take and the ideas and perceptions they express are woven deeply into the fabric of social culture, stimulating and interacting with developments in all areas of social life. Consequently an effective and coherent programme of arts education is an essential part of cultural education. (Robinson, 1990, p. 6)

Digital media are increasingly important in art and design. Most young people are familiar with modifying and editing photographic images, but schools can now provide classroom-based opportunities to present and manipulate images, animations and sequences in different formats, create new images, import and layer them using graphics packages. A digital personal library of images, notes and source material is now within the reach of most primary school children.

The positive pedagogue in primary school:

- strives to make art and design knowledge, skills and attitudes inclusive
- chooses art projects that communicate personal stories and respect for diversity
- demonstrates how art can exemplify beliefs in positive values
- shows that styles, symbols, relationships and functions differ individually culturally and over time
- accepts there is no single 'right' answer to questions of beauty, description, form, feeling or style
- encourages constructive criticism and positive responses to failure

Drama

Although drama is subsumed into the discipline of English in the English national curriculum, the other UK education administrations separate it as an expressive art (Northern Ireland Council, 2020; Education Wales, 2022a). The Scottish 'Curriculum for Excellence', states that through drama traditions like improvisation, plays, comedies, pantomime, mime, voice-over or freeze frame:

> … learners have rich opportunities to be creative and to experience inspiration and enjoyment. Creating and presenting are prominent activities for all learners. Their acting and presenting skills are developed through participating in scripted or improvised

drama. Exploring real and imaginary situations helps learners to understand and share their world. (Curriculum for Excellence, Expressive Arts: Experiences and Outcomes, Education Scotland, 2022b, p. 7)

Drama generally uses words. Poetic or prose words are gathered into compositions that use a character or characters to perform some kind of story to an audience, usually involving movement and action. There are many kinds of drama. Some use words and music as in opera, operetta and musicals, others combine them with dance in ballet or dance-drama or present dialogue or story as a play. Role play, puppet plays, drama games, storytelling and improvised theatre-making, brings drama to education, training or therapy. Like drawing and painting, drama is an ancient, probably universal art. It has the emotional power artificially to construct authentic feelings of joy, sadness, anger or fear in both audience and player. Drama is not just entertainment, but can effectively be used to build empathy, hypothesise and model or manage emotion. Drama is much underused in formal education.

Drama skills, techniques and concepts

Many positive pedagogues will use drama liberally across the curriculum because of its power to communicate. The dominant concepts of drama include: actors, a stage, scenery, props, movement, script and dialogue used to tell a story or plot to an audience. Drama skills involve communicating through bodily and facial expression, movement, tone and prosody in addition to words, props and scenery (see Table 5.2).

School drama School drama generally involves working in groups or as a class, but each individual will offer different ways of communicating meaning and feeling through key skills and techniques.

Drama in the primary years can experiment with all the skills above but generally in the context of text or plot. After modelling by a teacher, improvisation games often become satisfying points of growth (Barnes, 2015). Pairs of children might practise bodily and expressive responses to provocations or try out ways of gaining and holding

Table 5.2 Some key skills to develop in school drama – how to use:

Eye contact	Prosody (the melody of speech)
Rehearsal	Gait (the ways people walk or get around)
Narrative	Movement
Dialogue	Gesture
Pause	Characterisation
Pace	Mood
Silence	Body language
Rhythm	Facial expression
Tone and volume of voice	Soliloquy
Coming 'out of role'	Special effects

attention. By Key Stage 2, classes should be introduced to the skills of devising and writing scripts. Text must be interpreted, ways of moving and gesturing improvised and evaluated and ways of grabbing attention trialled. Children should also have experienced the work of dramatists from their own culture and others.

Theatre-making also needs that special space we call a stage. Teachers and children should agree on how they want to use this space that may simply involve rearranging the seating or tracing out a story square on the floor. The empowering teacher will lead children to warm up outside that space with exercises that play with different tones of voice, distance and proximity, movement and stillness, tension and release, anger and empathy (see Figure 5.5). Actively developing these skills is fun, but within drama they should be quickly transferred to theatre-making on stage.

Across the curriculum

Drama skills are transferable. They can enlighten aspects of every subject. Its standard techniques offer alternative (often emotional) modes of understanding, enliven lessons, deepen thinking and establish novel connections across the curriculum. Playing a role can be a highly effective route towards understanding the feelings and actions of others – a central skill in the humanities. Use Table 5.3 to think about how some of the following techniques might be used in a subject in which you feel confident.

Table 5.3 Your ideas about using some drama techniques

Technique	Activity	Where and how I/we might use it
Mime	Group or individual acts out a scene using gesture, body language, eye contact and gait, but no words at all	
Freeze frame	Group uses body shapes and poses to turn a story or poem into three or more 'frozen' scenes	
Tableaux	Group use their bodies to represent a single complex scene and hold it very still for a set amount of time (possibly for a photo)	
Hot seating	Individual teacher or child adopts a role and is questioned while in that role	
Soundscape	Group constructs and performs sounds to provide background to a dramatic happening	
Living pictures	A painting is brought to life by reconstructing it with real people and props	
Forum theatre	Written play is stopped in the middle and an audience member takes over and improvises a role from then on	
Improvisation	Group or individual makes up and communicates a response or story on the spot	
Shadow puppet theatre	Uses voices and the shadows of cut-out figures, shapes or objects to tell a story	

(Continued)

Table 5.3 Your ideas about using some drama techniques *(Continued)*

Technique	Activity	Where and how I/we might use it
Thought tracking	Different members of a freeze frame are asked (in role) what they're thinking	
Narrative	One narrator reads out a story or description while others silently act it out	
Mirroring	Pairs work with one being the mirror and the other a person standing in front of it – the mirror copies the gestures and faces of the person	
Choreography	A story is told in a series of planned dance-like, often abstract movements	
Flashback	Present action stops while a significant past episode is recalled through the dramatic representation of a memory	

Drama and mental health

Through drama we can enter the world of others, feel their emotions, face their dilemmas. Drama offers a safe place within which to play with our feelings and responses and imagine alternative outcomes to problems. An enduring role of drama is that it provides opportunities playfully to work through issues that in real life would be too distressing or difficult to deal with in actuality. It can also develop imagination in observable ways. A

Figure 5.5 A simple drama warm-up where each child unfurls their fingers in turn (Photo: Adam Annand)

recent research study among teaching assistants (TAs) working on a drama intervention for children with communication and language difficulties, elicited the following summary of the effect of drama on those with difficulties at school:

> I have noticed a growth in imagination – It's all to do with play isn't it? And using enjoyment. Yesterday I saw five Year 1 children [from the drama project] turning a pile of crates into a bus – that would not have happened before. I also notice the different use of language – they use the language of emotion, of theatre or imagination more. (Barnes, 2023)

The positive pedagogue:

- helps children communicate meaning and feeling through the use of dialogue and expression
- ephasises empathy in acting out a story
- models drama skills and helps children refine them
- encourages playful experimentation with emotion and spoken narrative
- highlights imagination
- uses the concept of the stage to create a safe space for exploring feelings and alternatives

Music

Music, especially singing, is probably older than *homo sapiens*. Several research studies suggest singing evolved in the lives of archaic humans some 500,000 years ago (Aiello and Dunbar, 1993). Some researchers see song as having developed as a tool of sexual and social selection, and that singing together fulfilled a similar role to the grooming which serves to keep other primate groups together. Oxford Psychology Professor Robin Dunbar suggests for example:

> Music arose originally because it allows individuals to become more group oriented. Music seems to achieve this through capacity to produce endorphins which have a positive effect on our attitudes towards others. (Dunbar et al., 2012)

The release of endorphins – pain-relieving hormones that also produce feelings of euphoria and enable bonding in many animal communities – is measurable in the systems of members of choirs during and immediately after singing together (Goldsmiths, 2015). Singing also generates oxytocin, another hormone that creates feelings of security, trust and relaxation. These 'feel good' hormones are released alongside measurable reductions of the stress-related hormone cortisol, which in high concentrations compromises the immune system (Fancourt et al., 2016).

Music is clearly a way in which we express, moderate and call-up emotions (Justlin and Sloboda, 2011). The developmental importance of song sharing, melodic greetings, or sung vocables (for example, humming and 'la'-ing), between carer and child has been well-researched (Trevarthen, 2008, 2020). These songs have a powerful effect on feelings of security and preserving mental health of both infant and parent/carer, but researchers such as Trevarthen and Malloch also claim that shared musical moments are the foundation of secure language development, the growth of consciousness, communication and narrative. Outside family influences, experience of music in Early Years education offers a vital chance to develop these essential life skills.

Music also expresses key aspects of culture, emotion and identity. Every nursery and primary teacher should use this fundamental human ability daily, but many lack confidence. The examples in Table 5.4 are really basic, and as you grow in confidence make up your own songs, first by using two notes (for example the first notes, *Swing Low,* in 'Swing low sweet chariot').

Table 5.4 Some simple musical activities for 3–7-year-olds

Musical activity	Example
Singing the register	Hello Ahmad how are you? Hello Ismail how are you? Hello Charlie how are you? How are you today? (Ahmad, Ismail and Charlie reply together to the same tune – *'Skip to my Lou'*) Clapping music to bring class together
Clapping music to bring class together	Teacher (clapping, tapping, etc.) Children copying X x x x X x x x x x x X x x x X Xx X xx X Xx X xx X
Regular music for change of activity	When the music for *'Let it go!'* or some other popular song plays, children stop what they are doing and listen for instructions
Just before lunch song	*We're going to eat our dinner yes we are x 2* *We are going to eat our dinner, going to eat our dinner, going to eat our dinner yes we are!* (To the tune of *'She'll be coming round the mountain'.*)
After lunch	*Together with friends* *I like to sing I like to sing (x2)* *Until it's time to play*
Providing background music for the class story	One group is given classroom musical instruments and they improvise sound effects to illustrate a section of the class story
End-of-day song	*Goodbye Cherryanne* *Goodbye Nadia* *Goodbye Isaac* *we're going home right now!* (to the tune of *'Row, row, row your boat'*)

The language of music

Music has a specific vocabulary to capture its basic concepts. Sung, played, improvised and historical music from every culture have common and inter-related elements, these are called the *dimensions of music* in the English national curriculum (Gov.UK, 2021f). Music everywhere has:

- pitch (a range of high and low sounds)
- dynamics (its louds and softs)
- tempo (how fast or slow it is)
- timbre (the quality of sound, booming, scraping, metallic, hollow, brassy, resonant, etc.)
- silence (that builds tension or marks the beginning of new section or idea)

Most music has:

- texture (different layers of sound like a duet or the different instruments in a band)
- duration (a regular pulse, patterns of rhythm, accents or sounds against the beat)
- structure (the bigger building blocks of a musical piece like verse and chorus or a repeated riff)
- notation (written, drawn or painted means of recording a composition so others can play it)

Music is often played or sung from memory. It can, however, be 'written' for others to play. It can be captured in a series of shapes or patterns, painted in colours, recorded as a set of numbers, described in words or written in 'standard notation' – the specialist language of western music. This language of staves, bars, crochets, minims and breves, annotated with Italian words, results from the history of western music. So, *largo* means to play slowly; *allegro*, quickly; *presto*, really fast; *prestissimo*, really, really fast. The word *crescendo* is used to mean getting gradually louder. *Forte* or *fortissimo* might be used to guide the players or singers to play loudly. *Piano* or *pianissimo* written on a piece of music means it should be quiet or very quiet. Introducing such words to children in the primary school can give them a sense that they are learning something new and special which perhaps even their parents don't know about.

Standard notation also calls upon words to suggest the mood or emotion of a musical piece. Traditionally, Italian words were used, for example: *cantabile* – to be played like a song; *furioso*, furiously; *misterioso*, mysteriously; or *tranquillo*, calmly. However, descriptive English words are more common in music education today. Help children use language to express the feelings engendered by music, by offering a range of descriptive words to choose from (see Wheway et al., 2018).

Skills and concepts in music

Music is in our bones and bodies. Blood pumps around our body in regular pulses, we speak in musical phrases and tones, walk and run rhythmically, recognise each other's voices by pitch and timbre, use dynamics and duration to create meaning in conversation and communicate using prosody with babies (Trainor et al., 2000). Yet many primary teachers worry about teaching music and don't feel 'musical', partly because community music-making in the UK has involved progressively fewer people. Teachers also often fear the 'noise' the music makes and the potential for disturbing others – this is partly why teaching children to control the sounds they make is an important starting point for music. Primary music teaching does not need established skills on a musical instrument or existing ability to read and speak an exclusive musical language – a sense of pulse and a willingness to play with sound are already enough. The strong expectations we put upon ourselves in regard to music are not made in traditional societies outside the west (see Blacking, 1976; Mann, 2015). Your involvement in music-making, music appreciation and music sharing is as a member of the human race that sees music as the birth right of every child. Show children you enjoy playing with sound as much as they do.

Playing with sound

At its simplest, music can be described as 'controlled sound'. Playing with everyday sounds and silences may be your first steps in making music with your class. You might build awareness of these concepts by using furniture, body percussion, paper, plastic pots and introducing a manual sign – for silence perhaps hands together and hands apart for sound – and playing with this idea for a while. Follow this introduction with widening or narrowing hand movements to indicate that sounds should get louder or softer. After a while, ask children to take over conducting.

Establishing a steady beat or pulse is fundamental. Practise it at home by tapping or clapping out your resting pulse rate – perhaps around 1 beat per second. Many simple exercises can help build on this skill (see Table 5.5). Using silences, changing timbre, making rhythmic patterns against an underlying pulse, controlling loudness, softness, harshness, gentleness and tempo all need practice and you can make it fun and include all.

Using just the sound of repeated words of a sentence or haiku, you can introduce dynamics, pattern and texture and give experience of musical improvisation and composition. Control sound further by adding structure by chanting repeated words, making worded riffs, rhymes, raps, or layering sounds in patterns.

History and culture

Music has a history; it is evident in every culture, therefore the diversity of musical genres and styles is huge. This diversity should influence the range of music heard, used and created in school. Through exposure to many types of music, concepts of melody, harmony and musical form will help children appreciate the ways that music is different from other curriculum subjects. Use medieval, baroque, classical, romantic, nationalistic/ traditional, minimalist and atonal music to link with historical periods. Give children daily experience of modern popular music from Africa, Asia and South America as well as Europe. This sonic environment in your classroom will add to the lively and inclusive atmosphere that marks out the excellent school. Introduce classes to the polyrhythms of Burundian or Ghanaian drumming, the different percussive instruments in a Brazilian *samba* or the plethora of metallic sounds in Balinese *gamelan* so they are familiar with

Table 5.5 Starter activities to develop skills of controlling sound

Musical skill	Starter activities to develop skills of controlling sound
Pulse	• Sitting in a circle establish a regular 1,2,3,4,1,2,3,4,1,2,3,4 pulse with clapping or tapping. Teacher always starts off with a regular 1,2,3,4 count before the children join in • Repeat the tapping or clapping quietly, then loudly, then with a louder emphasis on 1 (or 2 or 3 or 4) • Repeat with a silence (x) for the second and fourth group of four 1,2,3,4, x,x,x,x, 1,2,3,4, x,x,x,x, 1,2,3,4, x,x,x,x,1,2,3,4, etc. • Keeping the pulse very regular, each child says their name in the *1 2 3 4 1 2* • silent, four beat gap: 1,2,3,4, Jonathan Barrrrnes, x,x,x,x Katie *3 4 1 2 3 4* Hankir, x,x,x x Barnaby Morris x,x,x,x, etc.
Silence	• Teacher uses closed hands to indicate silence and open hands to denote sound, class responds with silence and verbal sounds • Using simple class percussion instruments teacher leads class in wordless sound and silence instructions • Teacher widens the gap between hands as an instruction for getting louder (*crescendo*) and closing the hands together (*diminuendo*) for softer • Groups of 5 or 6 children practise sound, silence, crescendo, diminuendo led by a child volunteer
Duration	• Against a regular 4-beat pulse teacher chants (not sings) a well-known nursery rhyme like: '*Row, row, row your boat gently down the stream*' • Children chant it too against the tapped regular pulse 1,2,3,4,1,2,3,4 • Half the class chants the words of the song while the other half clap the regular beat. They will note that the rhythm of the words is different to the regular rhythm of the beats • As teacher keeps the clapped pulse going, half the class chants just the first line of the song (*row, row, row your boat*) repeatedly. The other half repeatedly chants the second line (*gently down the stream*) – a different rhythm • The four separate lines of the song are chanted simultaneously by four groups of 7 or 8 children to make a four-layered texture of chanted sounds
Timbre	• Teacher places groups of wooden, metal, skin (drum), shaker instruments in different parts of the room • Each child is assigned one type of instrument • Each type of sound is signified by a different symbol: ● for drum; ▲ for metal; ■ for wood; and ✲ for shaker. • Teacher makes a pattern of symbols like: ■ ■ ● ▲ ✲ ✲ ● ▲, children respond by playing 'their' sound when the teacher points to the appropriate symbol.
Pitch	• Start a 'call and response' pattern with two notes (the first two notes of '*Swing low sweet chariot*') *1 2 3 4* • Begin with a 1,2,3,4 lead-in, then Hel lo_ x,x,x,x, *1 2 3 4* after which the children answer Hel lo_ (keeping the same *1 2 3 4 1 2* pulse throughout) then x,x,x,x How are you_? x,x,x,x, How are *3 4* you_? • Sing simple sentences, greetings, registers, instructions using just those two notes and then graduate to a third note just one step above the note for the word 'low'

musical expertise and concepts well beyond the standard western repertoire. Providing a vocabulary with which to evaluate music of all kinds will deepen your own and children's listening skills.

The positive pedagogue:

- provides opportunities for children to play with sound
- uses music as a means of communication
- allows children safely to use sound to express emotion
- models and encourages careful listening
- recognises the therapeutic qualities of group singing and music-making
- expresses cultural and personal diversity in music listening and creating
- builds collaborative communities through shared music

Dance

Dance, another wordless art, is part of the physical education (PE) curriculum in English schools, but counted as an expressive art in Scotland (Gov.Scot, 2017), Wales and Northern Ireland. Like drama, dance uses gesture, space, movement and facial expression to communicate emotion. Dance, however, is distinguished by its largely unspoken nature, its association with music and emphasis on expressive body movements. Like music, it depends on rhythm, pauses, repetition, pulse and variations of intensity. As with music, dance might have a structure, repeated sequences, variations, aim at a climax and an appropriate conclusion. Dance utilises these elements in bodily movement rather than sound. It aims to use and increase physical, mental, expressive control over movement. Using a range of different styles dancers embody emotion; they *become* through movement – playful, serious, confrontational or questioning. Dance 'says' things that cannot be expressed easily in words.

Dance easily links with subjects across the curriculum. In geography, it might illustrate the longshore drift of pebbles on a beach. In science, dance can capture the movement of molecules as liquid water changes to steam or ice. Dynamic action can be frozen in drawing; the energy of a dance may be expressed in colour and line. Dance can silently express aspects of big issues like: automation, equality, exclusion, discrimination, change or nationality.

Skills and concepts in dance

The central concept of dance is movement. What distinguishes it from the other expressive arts is its focus on the careful, intelligent and often musical coordination of movement (see Table 5.6). Dance choreographs the body and groups of bodies to make synchronised, rhythmic, controlled, angular or graceful movements. Balance, both physical and aesthetic, characterises the excellent dancer. Timing and embodied understanding of pulse and phrasing are essential aspects of the aim to communicate feeling. Copying and using jumps, falls, twists, turns, links, lifts, movement at different levels, in angles, shapes or lines, dancers communicate feelings of joy or sadness, anger, fear or a range of subsidiary emotions experienced across gender and cultural divides. Well-taught, the safety aspects and the physical and psychological elements of dance can be used positively to help young and old control, express and regulate such emotions.

Developing dance skills, especially amongst reluctant boys, needs confident modelling by teachers. Work with male dancers and male teachers prepared to lead sessions is one response to hesitancy, but videos of joyful, rhythmic, contemporary dance from other cultural settings will powerfully illustrate its importance across genders. In the crowded primary curriculum dance is omitted from PE or expressive arts sessions, but short periods of well-framed dance or movement interruptions can punctuate the week and add embodied alternatives to worded thought. Some starter ideas are outlined in Table 5.6.

Table 5.6 Some basic starter ideas for dance

Dance skills	Detail
Strength	*Embodied emotion:* Move into *and hold* (first for 30 seconds then longer – up to 2 minutes) a stationary bodily position and expression of anger, joy, sadness or fear. Classmates draw a simplified version of this pose with pastels or charcoal.
Posture	*Big ideas:* Choose two emotion words representing big concepts like joy, kindness, jealousy or loss. Groups work to express these words in two different body sculptures. They design and perform a way of moving from one emotional body sculpture to the next in smooth, balanced and coordinated movement. Did they learn anything about these concepts while they were embodying them? Did they think anything about the relationship between the two concepts?
Alignment	*Keep to the beat:* Groups devise a synchronised dance sequence in response to hip hop or other music with a strong, clear beat. *Baroque hand jive:* Sitting in a circle class copy a leader as they respond, with arm and hand movements, to music with a clear pulse (for example Bach's *Air on a G string*). After 15 seconds, the leadership passes to a neighbour who responds to the music with another hand/arm movement and all copy them. The leadership passes around the class, everyone tries to avoid duplicating movements.
Balance	*Dance fight:* Groups stage a stylised, very slow - motion, no-physical-contact fight, in which one person is apparently beaten but then recovers to win the day.
Coordination	*Deportment dance:* Children balance books on their heads and move imaginatively around the room to slow dreamy music. They must keep the book well-balanced on their head. If they drop the book, they pick it up and re-join the group. *Dances for pieces of wood:* Each child has two drumsticks or claves. They move rhythmically around the room to Samba music hitting the sticks together on every *second* beat: 1 2 3 4, 1 2 3 4, 1,2 3 4. Keeping in time. Ask for ideas for different rhythms for the second or fourth beat: for example: 1223 4, 1223 4, 1223 4; 12223 4, 12223 4, 12223 4; 123 444, 123 444,

(Continued)

Table 5.6 Some basic starter ideas for dance *(Continued)*

Dance skills	Detail
Control	*Body-part dancing:* Stand in a circle for a strongly pulsed trance, reggae, hip hop/rap music. A leader dances to the middle of the circle in a series of movements that make creative use of just one part of their body – arms, legs, torso, head and neck, hands, etc. The rest of the class copies the leader who time passes the leadership to another person who dances to the centre activating another body part. https://education.gov.scot/education-scotland/scottish-education-system/policy-for-scottish-education/policy-drivers/cfe-building-from-the-statement-appendix-incl-btc1-5/what-is-curriculum-for-excellence
Flexibility	*Emoji dance:* Teacher chooses five pieces of music: sad, happy, angry, scary and peaceful. The class listens to the first piece and responds in movement to what they hear until the music changes to another emotion and they change styles.
Mobility	*Animal dances:* Teacher prepares six laminated photos of animals and distributes them privately to six groups of children. Each group talks about, researches, rehearses and eventually performs a dance that expresses the way they think their animal moves.

The positive pedagogue:

- introduces and helps develop dance as a means of communication and expression
- models and supports a progression of dance skills to support greater control of movement
- opens minds to the global significance of dance as an art
- uses dance to enhance listening, trust, collaboration and creativity
- generates enthusiasm for dance across genders, cultures and personalities
- encourages experience of the diversity of dance around the world

Other aspects of PE

PE also involves other imaginative, stretching and balancing activities. Outdoor and adventurous activity, exercise, orienteering, safe and careful extension of the physical possibilities of the body are essential to healthy development. Collaborative and competitive games, following trails, meeting physical challenges and coordinating movement using parachutes, balls, hoops, bean bags, markers or cones, all add to the joy and inclusiveness of PE (Gov.UK, 2013e). Activities that develop the physical confidence, essential to dance, drama and music, are equally fundamental to PE with the added context of bodily health and strength. The positive pedagogue makes teamwork in competitive and collaborative physical settings a guiding value in primary PE, but also helps children see disappointment and difficulty as opportunities for growth.

In contrast to other subjects discussed in this chapter, there is an expectation that some PE will happen outdoors. Being outside the classroom is a vital ingredient of positive pedagogy for many reasons. Outdoor work helps children:

- recognise and respond to seasons, terrain, weather and other unchangeable aspects of the world
- benefit from the positive physical and psychological aspects of fresh air
- identify and address common environmental risks and dangers
- improve their spatial awareness, sense of direction and physical coordination in contrasting terrain
- develop interests in and care for nature
- discover enjoyment and adventure in 'real life' settings in contrast to virtual environments
- collaborate and communicate with peers and teachers in informal contexts

Case studies across the arts

The disciplines discussed in this chapter are readily combined. Each are practical, embodied and capable of expressing emotion. Think of film, musicals, TV, dance or pop videos, advertising and local/national cultural 'events' – almost all fuse several arts. Pick out the different arts involved in familiar adverts, videos or events – children will readily offer examples of arts fusions from their home viewing repertoire. A positive approach to pedagogy suggests that every child's school experience should contain frequent occasions that are affirmative, involving, including and exciting for children, but also presents them with new challenges, constructive criticism and opportunities to deal positively with lack of immediate success. Successfully dealing with difficult tasks through the arts will help create the positive mental associations that build resilience.

What constitutes a new and fulfilling experience varies for every child, but certain commonalities have guided the choice of the following two or three session case studies. Each example:

- addresses a 'big idea'
- has an emotional focus
- involves communication
- uses a stimulus outside the classroom
- has collaborative aspects
- aims to generate creative outcomes such as a performance or exhibition
- uses combinations of at least two disciplines
- requires the application of specific knowledge and skills from two or more disciplines
- can be assessed for new learning and/or deeper understanding

The assessment ideas after each two- or three-session case study suggest subject-based learning outcomes. A 1–10 scale could be used, age-appropriately to record levels of subject skill for each child or group within the mini project.

Case Study 5.1

A written haiku becomes music and freeze-frame dance

Search information on the Japanese poetic tradition of haiku – a miniature poem, typically with a structure of 17 syllables arranged in the pattern 5, 7, 5. These delicate poems often refer to the season or weather and attempt to capture a single thought.

___ ___ ___ ___ ___

___ ___ ___ ___ ___ ___ ___

___ ___ ___ ___ ___

Year 5 children at a Manchester primary school were given the following brief:

Make a haiku inspired by a very small and insignificant object found near you (e.g. a leaf, hair, button, paper clip, old sweet wrapper, pen top, tiny stone, as in Figure 5.6) and turn it into a 15-second, six-part piece of music *or* three linked body sculptures.

In pairs they made very simple five syllable descriptions of their small object for the first line, worked harder to agree on just seven syllables to describe their object more poetically, perhaps mentioning the season, and decided upon a deep philosophical question to address to their object for the third. After ten minutes the pairs shared their haiku with two other pairs. Each group then agreed on one haiku they would turn into six-part music or six-person freeze-frame body sculptures.

Each member of the *haiku to music* group chose an appropriate sound, pattern or repeated word to capture the detail of each line of the chosen haiku. They had to combine and extend these sounds so that their piece lasted at least 15 seconds and used all six people. The *haiku to freeze-frame* groups arranged themselves into three tableaux representing the three lines and invented smooth ways to move from one to the next. Their sequences lasted between 15 and 30 seconds.

The class evaluated the presentations, collectively itemising their most successful and attractive aspects. Class members were also encouraged to ask positive questions that pinpointed some weaknesses, such as, 'Did you think of some other ideas to end your piece of music?' or 'We liked the ending of your dance, we wonder if it could be even more sudden'. Each group of six then returned to polish their presentations into finished performances – addressing the questions and enhancing the good points. The session finished with polished performances of the haikus that included narrators, musicians and dancers combining their arts in an example of *inter-disciplinary cross-curricular learning*.

Figure 5.6 Tess wrote a haiku about a fuchsia flower she found in the school garden (Photo: Barnes)

- **Assessment 1**

Music

Combining musical sounds to make expressive sense	1 2 3 4 5 6 7 8 9 10
Composing and performing music with independent parts	1 2 3 4 5 6 7 8 9 10
Making improvements to compositions	1 2 3 4 5 6 7 8 9 10
Improvising melodic and rhythmic lines in musical structures	1 2 3 4 5 6 7 8 9 10

Dance/PE

Coordination and control of movement and stillness	1 2 3 4 5 6 7 8 9 10
Responding to a visual stimulus in movement	1 2 3 4 5 6 7 8 9 10
Making fluid links between dance movements	1 2 3 4 5 6 7 8 9 10
Inventing variations within movement ideas	1 2 3 4 5 6 7 8 9 10

Case Study 5.2

Biodiversity in drama, dance and art

Children love nature. Teachers in a Shropshire school helped children deepen their natural abilities to distinguish living from inanimate things (Tomkins and Tunnicliffe, 2015) by constructing opportunities to think about the biodiversity evident in their school wild area.

Year 2 children were taken into the school wild area. In groups of four, wearing thin plastic gloves, and carrying metre measuring sticks and double-sided tape for samples, children marked off wild areas roughly one metre square. Each group had two minutes to view and tally the different kinds of natural life discovered in 'their' square. What looked like 'just grass' contained several of the plants their teacher had taught them about previously. Their metre squares also contained a number of insects, other creatures, leaves, roots and seeds. Using double-sided tape adhered to card strips, groups collected samples (no living things) to bring back to class for drawing, discussion and detailed labelling.

After the collections groups were asked to decide how to share their findings (see Figure 5.7). Using skills acquired in separate subject sessions children were asked to represent their biodiverse discoveries in three different ways: art, dance and drama. They carefully observed and painted and drew greatly enlarged versions of their wild area findings and made invented dance/drama showing different textures and movements discovered in their metre square. The groups had ten minutes to plan and rehearse an initial 'work in progress' response for the whole class to evaluate. The metre-square collecting exercise generated separate developments in art and dance/drama and this could be seen as *multi-disciplinary learning*. This might be assessed as in Assessment 2 below.

- **Assessment 2**

Drama

Collaborating creatively with a group	1 2 3 4 5 6 7 8 9 10
Showing awareness of audience	1 2 3 4 5 6 7 8 9 10

Dance/PE

Transforming natural patterns into movement	1 2 3 4 5 6 7 8 9 10
Use of repetition to show multiples	1 2 3 4 5 6 7 8 9 10
Coordination and physical control	1 2 3 4 5 6 7 8 9 10
Ability to select and combine movement ideas	1 2 3 4 5 6 7 8 9 10

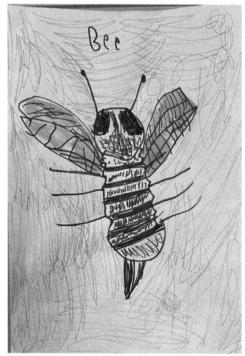

Figure 5.7 Daisy found a dead bee in her square metre. See the sting? The teacher told the children not to touch it but took a close-up photo. Daisy (5) carefully drew it from the photo (Photo: Barnes)

Art

Using a variety of materials	1 2 3 4 5 6 7 8 9 10
Collecting visual materials for art work	1 2 3 4 5 6 7 8 9 10
Using a variety of mark-making techniques	1 2 3 4 5 6 7 8 9 10
Showing awareness of design	1 2 3 4 5 6 7 8 9 10

Case Study 5.3

Talking about war and peace through dance, drama and music

Talk is probably 'the true foundation of learning' (Alexander, 2004). Authentic talk, however, requires stimulus for dialogue and debate and, in 2022, the war in Ukraine generated near-universal provocation for meaningful discourse. A school in Glasgow decided it was necessary to give children opportunity to talk about their worries.

After intense class discussions on the war in Ukraine, a Year 6 teacher planned an arts-based unit of work based on war and peace. The unit began with multiple images painted by war artists Paul Nash and Henry Moore and discussions on how they created atmosphere. This was followed by a challenging listening exercise using two pieces of music. The class first listened to *Libera Me* an evocative section of Benjamin Britten's *War Requiem* (1962), that mimics the sounds of distant explosions, rattle of guns and in a rising wave of discordant sound conjures up the horrors of war. To support listening the teacher laid out a wide range of descriptive words on cards in the centre of a circle of listeners, with an empty PE hoop in the centre. During the seven-minute listening children were asked to pick words that matched feelings generated by the music and place them into a hoop. In the dying moments of the piece children had selected 70 different words to describe its message. They listened to the piece again. This time the class was divided into seven groups of four, surrounding A1 sheets of sugar paper. Using fibre-tipped markers, crayons and pastels each group made abstract marks on their paper to express in colour, line and form what they were hearing, as they were hearing it. In the next lesson they followed the same process but with a very slow, peaceful, lyrical piece – the *Adagio* from Ravel's *Piano Concerto in G*. The A1 abstract art pieces were mounted and photographed and used to form a projected backdrop for dance and drama performances later.

Children responded to the listening exercises with enthusiasm and serious, philosophical talk. Dividing into groups the class decided to express one of the pieces in dance or mime using skills they had developed in earlier sessions. After responding, forming, evaluating and presenting 'work in progress' for further peer evaluation, the groups planned full performances to share their reflections on War and Peace with the rest of Key Stage 2. Assessment 3 offers a simple way of assessing such creative and artistic activity.

- **Assessment 3**

Drama

Sustaining atmosphere and tension	1 2 3 4 5 6 7 8 9 10
Collaborating creatively with a group	1 2 3 4 5 6 7 8 9 10
Choosing appropriate language and actions to convey a situation	1 2 3 4 5 6 7 8 9 10
Consistently expressing feelings in role	1 2 3 4 5 6 7 8 9 10

Dance/PE

Precise control of bodily movement	1 2 3 4 5 6 7 8 9 10
Composing movements to express ideas	1 2 3 4 5 6 7 8 9 10
Expressing different modes of travel through movement	1 2 3 4 5 6 7 8 9 10
Ability to adapt rhythm and speed appropriately	1 2 3 4 5 6 7 8 9 10

Art

Using abstract images to communicate meanings	1 2 3 4 5 6 7 8 9 10
Creatively manipulating visual and tactile qualities to interpret an event	1 2 3 4 5 6 7 8 9 10
Evaluating personal or collaborative art work	1 2 3 4 5 6 7 8 9 10
Ability to analyse the work of other artists	1 2 3 4 5 6 7 8 9 10

Music

Ability to make and use graphic notations	1 2 3 4 5 6 7 8 9 10
Evaluating the music of others	1 2 3 4 5 6 7 8 9 10
Evaluate different kinds of music	1 2 3 4 5 6 7 8 9 10
Ability to use a range of musical devices to create desired effect	1 2 3 4 5 6 7 8 9 10

Summary

This chapter has brought together arguments for the importance of the arts and physical activity in the primary curriculum. It has shown how each art and activity holds different ways of communicating emotion and develops different kinds of intelligence (see for example Gardner, 2000a): specifically, bodily-kinaesthetic, musical, intra and interpersonal ways of understanding the world, but also logical, naturalist, spiritual and linguistic approaches. The specific language, skills and concepts of each separate discipline of the arts have been outlined and ways of integrating them discussed. Illustrative transdisciplinary case studies demonstrated what integration could look like in the primary classroom and how it might be assessed.

6
SCIENCE, TECHNOLOGY, ENGLISH AND MATHS IN CROSS-CURRICULAR CONTEXTS

Objectives

This chapter introduces cross-curricular aspects of science, technology, English and mathematics (STEM). It will:

- Support and challenge the primacy of STEM subjects
- Show how concepts, skills and attitudes in STEM help us to develop and thrive
- Balance the importance of STEM with arguments that other ways of thinking are equally important to human development
- Emphasise the increasing economic and social need to treat all disciplines equally
- Use case studies to show how STEM connects with skills in the arts and humanities

Introduction

The STEM subjects are, of course, important. The absolute supremacy of mathematics and English in British education has endured since the 1870 Education Act. These two subjects dominate entry to universities, colleges, teacher education and most jobs. The need for good reading and communication skills and basic understanding of number remains vital to most occupations, but the unique issues and needs of 21st-century life demand more. A post-modern, secular, 'post-truth' society can be argued to require a sense of meaning, criticality, purpose and emotional truth as much as it requires the empirical truths of mathematics and science. Educationalists and researchers make the case for an education with broader definitions of knowledge, wider experience of the world, creativity and 'softer' skills (see Barnes, 2018; Lucas and Spencer, 2018; Alexander, 2021; Cremin, 2022; Robinson, 2022).

The development of soft skills can and should be part of the delivery of STEM and every other primary school subject. Collaboration, compassion, perceiving and understanding emotions, using them to enhance thinking and managing others' and our own emotions are part of Mayer and Salovey's concept of 'Emotional Intelligence' (1990). The related idea of 'Social Intelligence' arising from Gardner's work on inter-personal and intra-personal 'intelligences' (1999) has had major impacts in the worlds of business and administration, but surprisingly little on national education policy in England.

Another characteristic often absent from the STEM subjects in primary education is creativity. Past definitions of 'creative' that apply to artist or just a few specially gifted people, are unhelpful in rapidly developing and interdependent societies aiming at inclusivity and innovation at every level of human life. In these times of constant change and challenge, countries and communities need to raise populations aware of and confident in their personal creative strengths in order to sustain development and well-being. Creativity, as defined in Chapter 1, should be nurtured from the earliest years and is discoverable in every child. Robinson's subsequent definition of creativity as, 'the process of having original ideas that are of value' (2022, p. 5) makes this ubiquity and the importance of values even clearer. Creativity can be seen in children's imaginative responses to scientific observation, their original take on the application of mathematics or technologies and their values-conscious and culturally aware uses of English. Robinson argued in the NACCCE Report (1999) that we should seek creativity and promote it across the curriculum in every subject and expressed the same views in one of the most viewed of TED talks seven years later (Robinson, 2006). Applying cross-curricular links between the STEM subjects and the humanities or Arts encourages what psychologist Sternberg (2003) saw as the integrative mode of creativity where two formerly diverse ways of thinking are combined and interact to provoke and produce new thinking.

You might ask, 'How do ideas like compassion and community fit with STEM?' The answer is that they are fundamental human values that should affect understanding of every discipline. Like it or not science, technology, English and maths like all the disciplines and activities of a school, are presented, understood and applied within a system of values. No education occurs outside of values – it is for teachers and schools to ensure that the values they communicate, consistently affirm what is good in humanity. Science can look at human and animal life, for example, compassionately or cruelly, mathematics can be used to deepen appreciation of or disparage community, technology might centre around designing objects that support those in need or improve a neighbourhood. In a positive pedagogy it seems reasonable to argue that the STEM subjects should play their part in building a values-based society. This chapter will illustrate what this might look like when some of the subjects of the curriculum are integrated.

Science

Science concerns pattern-seeking in the natural and physical world. It asks questions about that world, seeking answers through observation, the collection of evidence and experimentation. Its most influential concepts include: classification, fair testing, detailed observation, hypothesis, cause and effect, change, variation and diversity, structure and function, and the model. Each of this sample of fundamental science concepts is also usefully applied to other subjects (see Table 6.1).

Table 6.1 Science concepts across the primary curriculum

Science concept	Also used in…
Pattern	Geography, art, history, languages, English, Music, dance, PE
Classification	Geography, history, languages
Fair test	Design & Technology
Detailed observation	Art, English, dance
Experiment	Music, art, dance, drama, poetry, mathematics, design & technology
Hypothesis	History, geography, English
Cause and effect	Technology, geography, English, citizenship, PSHE
Change	Geography, history, mathematics, drama
Variation	Music, geography, mathematics, drama, dance, art
Diversity	RE, history, geography, music, drama
Structure	Design & Technology, art, PE, music, dance
Function	Technology, music, PE, geography
Model	Geography, mathematics, history, RE
Questioning	English, geography, history, RE, PSHE, citizenship, design & technology, languages
Evidence	History, geography
Systems	Design & Technology, geography, citizenship
Collecting/presenting data	History, geography, mathematics

Science in cross-curricular contexts

Science can be combined with other subjects in multiple ways. In some cross-curricular approaches, science knowledge and skills take a subsidiary, supportive role, in what I have called hierarchical cross-curricular learning (Barnes, 2015), (see Chapter 5, Case Study 5.2). The case studies in this chapter will place science as an equal in combination with another subject in multi-disciplinary or inter-disciplinary approaches to cross-curricular learning. The example activities will have specific learning objectives for both science knowledge and skills.

Case Study 6.1

Mapping atmospheric pollution

Overarching objective

To understand some of the actions humans can take to address pollution

Science learning objectives

- Know that trees contribute to cleaner air quality
- Know that a fair test is a central science concept
- Collect evidence of differential pollution
- Make and test hypotheses on causes and effects of different concentrations of Particulate Matter (PM) deposited on leaves
- Construct and use a fair test

Geography learning objectives

- To be able to use maps to gather information beyond location and scale
- Know how to present information on a map
- Know how to use a map for direction-finding
- Make a map to show information

A Year 5 class had been studying air pollutants using a science website and a comprehensive data set on air quality in 2020 from Belfast. They knew what air pollution was and the different kinds of pollution common in the air around their town. They had also learned new knowledge about the effects of air pollution on health. They had used spreadsheets and comprehensive data for their own city and already combined knowledge from science with techniques from mathematics. Their teacher wanted to take their understanding further and make it directly relevant to the students' own lives. Not far from the school there was a large country house with mature grounds and many large trees. The teacher planned a visit there.

Before the visit the class was taken to the school playground. They were shown how to use tissues to gently wipe low hanging leaves of trees to collect and eventually measure the amount of Particulate Matter (PM) (carbon, dust, some trace metals like lead, cadmium, zinc, chromium, manganese and aluminium) in the air. In this introduction the children found big differences between the PM found on leaves that were near the main road and those further away in the school wild area. They discussed in class how to make the collection of PM part of a fair test, by standardising the size of tissue pad and the number of seconds spent on wiping the leaves.

On their class visit to the country house grounds, groups of 4 or 5 were allocated to a beech tree at different locations in the gardens. Groups had to locate 'their' tree on a plan, draw a profile of the tree and wipe sample leaves from different sides of the tree. They placed the tissues into bags labelled with the precise location of the wiped leaf.

Back in class they graded the PM residue on their tissue wipes from 1–10 using a PM density grid devised in the previous lesson. Using a prepared base plan of the gardens they marked the location and detailed evidence of PM on specific trees around the garden. Groups decorated their maps with the profile drawings and worked to propose a hypothesis that explained why different parts of the tree and garden had different PM ratings (see Primary Science website).

Case Study 6.2

Drawing for understanding

Overarching objective

To appreciate and understand how and why simple structures are made

Science learning objectives

- To know and understand the forces of compression and tension work in an arch
- To know and understand structural terms: buttress, key stone, voussoir, arch and pier
- To make a diagram to show compression and tension using a real-world example

Art learning objectives

- To observe and carefully record shape and relationship in a building by drawing
- To use shading and repetition to create pleasing effects in drawing

A Year 3 class in Dover visited the nearby castle to understand the science of 'forces'. In class they had been learning practically about compression and tension forces by making toy bridges with card and wooden bricks. Having been shown a short video about the construction of Roman semi-circular arches, they learned the words voussoir, key stone, pier, abutment and buttress. On their visit they were led to different kinds of arch that showed these features. Groups of students were directed to each type of arch (flat, semi-circular, pointed and parabolic) and asked to make careful drawings to show every (easily distinguished) stone (see Figure 6.1). Students had to use their previous knowledge to label their drawings with arrows to show the compression and tension forces and the words: key stone, voussoir, buttress, arch and pier.

Figure 6.1 10-year-old child's drawing of arches in Dover castle (She noticed that these arches did not have a key stone but addressed compression in a different way.) (Photo: Barnes)

Design and Technology

The word 'design' appears alongside art and technology in the English national curriculum. In the Scottish curriculum, the subject appears as simply 'technologies' and with a greater emphasis on creativity, innovation and interactions. In Wales, technology is firmly linked with science and in Northern Ireland a cross-curricular approach links science, technology, history and geography. The education administrations outside England clearly connect design and technology to the bigger issues of sustainability, creativity and collaboration.

The imagination and dexterity to design increasingly complex tools, dwellings, artefacts, arts, movements and sound worlds is a distinctive feature of humanity. Our ability to shape the world around us and respond to change and challenge by planning and inventing new things is a continuing source of hope for the future. Any positive pedagogy should celebrate and nurture human ingenuity at every level of ability. Children should know about key technologies and technologists of the past and from all cultures. They should understand the technological advances that have made today's world. Nurturing design and technology (D&T) today in our schools is tantamount to cultivating hope for a future that will inevitably depend upon populations confident in their own imaginations and technical skills to face the enormous technological challenges the 21st century will bring.

Skills and concepts of D&T

Teaching D&T at primary level involves giving children the knowledge and skills to develop confidence in their own designing and making abilities. Cooking, building, mending, constructing, assembling, adapting, inventing and the ability to use information and communications technology (ICT) are the basic skills children will need to develop. At the same time they need knowledge. Young people should learn from teaching, discussion and evaluation how to recognise beautiful, operative and useful artefacts made by others and emulate some of the key principles of design in their own work. They also need to be given confidence to use their own imaginations. The language of D&T (see Table 6.2) indicates some of its priorities towards aspects such as fitness-for-purpose, finish, practicality, function and technical skills. Building a lesson around three or four of these key concepts will keep an appropriate D&T focus and help in objective-forming and assessment.

Table 6.2 Some D&T language

Design	Make	Evaluate	Technical knowledge
Annotate	Add	Accurate	Axel
Appealing	Balance	Apply	Bulbs
Appropriate	Biscuit	Communicate	Buzzer
Beautiful	Cake	Compare	Cam
Computer-aided	Card	Consider	Circuit
Criteria	Combine	Control	Communications-Technology
Cross-section	Construct	Discuss	Cooking
Digital	Cook	Evaluate	Cut
Effective	Dish	Existing products	Finish
Efficient	Generate	Explore	Gear
Exploded diagram	Ingredient	Improve	Glue
Fit-for-purpose	Material	Monitor	Information-Technology
Function/al	Meal	Polish	Join
Graphic media	Mend	Principles	Lever
Healthy	Mix	Range	Link
Mock-up	Model	Shape	Mechanism
Pattern piece	Product	Talk	Motor
Practical	Recipe	Understand	Pulley
Product	Recycle	Variation	Reinforce
Prototype	Repair	View	Shaping
Purpose	Savoury		Slider
Remote	Shape		Stick
Retrieve	Textile		Stiffen
Safe	Variety		Strengthen
Search			Switch
Sketch			System
Software			Wheel
Sustainability			
Template			
Useful			

D&T across the curriculum

Since D&T involves planning, making and mending 'things' it can be paired with subjects across the curriculum. Games, art objects, dance moves and exhibitions are either enhanced or enabled by design; technologies can be involved in modelling religious stories, mathematics, history, geography, or science concepts. Any subject can be presented in a designed presentation in ICT or use other technologies. The two case studies below exemplify the fusion of D&T with another curriculum subject.

Case Study 6.3

D&T and History in a concentric castle

Overarching objective

To be able carefully to assess and appreciate significant details of a contrasting environment

D&T learning objectives

- To know three different ways of joining different slab-built clay components
- To know how to evaluate functional features and fitness for purpose in a gift shop article
- To design and make a prototype of a small souvenir that reflects a specific location

History objectives

- To know, recognise and record the following features: moat, gatehouse, outer ward, inner ward, arrow slit, murder hole, turret, chapel
- To use visual evidence to make four propositions about life in a 13th-century castle

Castles, stately homes, museums and country houses are not just collections of the design and technology skills of former ages culturally important to particular groups of people. They are exciting, unusual places to be; places where new cultures can be born and built by young visitors of any and many cultures. The positive pedagogue is able to help young people see such places as theirs. One such teacher took his Year 4 class to a concentrically walled castle in Anglesey, Wales. The class had been learning about the castles built by Edward I, about castle design and everyday life in medieval Welsh towns. In D&T they had been working on joining materials, fitness for purpose and some principles of good design – functionality and innovation. The young people in the class had experience of joining using clay pieces, fabrics, card and plastics.

In preparation for their visit, the teacher told children they were to work on designing and making prototypes of articles for the castle gift shop. They agreed that to be saleable their designed gift articles had to be small, attractive, strong, useful and related closely to observable characteristics of the castle. Their teacher brought items from other gift shops to give them ideas: mugs, wrapping paper, scarfs and ties, medals and decorative plates. Groups of youngsters examined these artefacts looking at practicality, finish, attractiveness and faithfulness to the place.

On their two-hour visit to the castle the class collected information to complete their history project on medieval life in Wales, but also collected ideas for use in planning their D&T unit of work on castle souvenirs. Groups were directed to make detailed drawings of doorways, turrets, walling materials and the ground plan of the castle for inspiration.

Back in school the groups used their on-site drawings to provide authentic detail to the finished plans for their gift shop products. Their planned proposals for a range of saleable ideas included:

- A 'castle wall headscarf' with printed images of the distinctive irregular stone patterns from the curtain walls of the castle
- A 'turret mug' that used the profile, plan and materials of the gatehouses as inspiration
- A 'castle-plan platter' that impressed the plan of the castle's concentric walls into a raised ceramic platter for the presentation of 'castle food'
- Three types of wrapping paper inspired by the repeated pattern of arrow slits, fireplaces and windows found at the castle

The initial drawings, finished plans and final, finished and evaluated products were assembled to become a special exhibition in the school and judged by the custodian of the castle. This combined history and D&T project demonstrates an *interdisciplinary* cross-curricular learning – where two sets of subject skills and knowledge are combined to produce a creative outcome (the exhibition).

Case Study 6.4

Food technology and the geography of food

Overarching objective

To understand our global interdependence and how it affects our life

D&T learning objectives

- Know how to wash, peel, slice and/or grate vegetables
- Know the basic principles of a healthy and varied diet
- To consider and suggest ways in which a recipe could be adapted to be made healthier (e.g. adapt and improve recipes involving white flour/salt/sugar)
- Knowing where relevant ingredients come from

Geography learning objectives
- Know the location of … on a world map
- Know the climatic conditions necessary to grow…
- Know the transport implications of …

As part of their course on geography a Year 3 class was asked to consider the journey of a banana and a mango. At the same time in the D&T lesson, groups of three children shared the making of a fair-trade banana and mango spicy crumble. Their teacher shared information on the mineral and vitamin content on mangoes and bananas. Children peeled and prepared the fruits, some decided to add passion fruit for an additional tropical flavour. They made the spicy crumble mix, poured it over the prepared fruits and cooked for 30 minutes or more. They took samples of their dessert home for eating.

The next day the geographical sources of the crumble mix of brown sugar, oats, flour, butter, cardamom and cinnamon were traced as well as the origins of the mango, banana, passion fruit and lemon used in the filling. The total of the miles travelled by all the ingredients were calculated. The class then discussed the cost of such a meal to the environment in terms of fuel, atmospheric pollution and time. After discussion their teacher asked if the class could think of any fruits and other ingredients that could be used to make a more planet-friendly dessert.

It was September, so children volunteered that pears, apples, gooseberries, blackcurrants and raspberries were locally available. The groups of three planned, trialled and tested recipes that used local fruits. After advice about the crumble mix from a chef/parent they chose: British sugar made from sugar beet, local oats and flour flavoured with fennel, carraway or rosemary and thyme to replace oriental spices. Again, they researched the miles these ingredients would have travelled. Class discussion on the labour, transport costs and damage to the air quickly demonstrated the differences in cost between imported and locally sourced ingredients. In their geography session they marked on maps of the world and the British Isles the sources of each ingredient.

This activity illustrates *multi-disciplinary* cross-curricular learning, in that the same stimulus (making a dessert) was used to address objectives belonging to two separate subjects.

English

Communication is an essential to all animals. Communication through language must be, always has been, a priority in schools. While Welsh, Scots, Scottish or Irish Gaelic continue to be taught, across the UK politics and history has ensured that English language is dominant. Like every other language, English has its own developmental expectations, history, rules, symbol systems, standard and non-standard usage, heroes and heroines. British schools, along with the compilers of dictionaries, lexicons and grammars, are among the gatekeepers of language, classifying and standardising the English we use.

Written and read language has facilitated many of the creative, inter-personal, logical, spiritual, spatial, scientific, mathematical, design, arts and humanities ideas discussed in earlier chapters. But there is more to English. The oracy skills of fluent speaking, careful listening and achieving interpersonal understanding through dialogue are equally important and highlighted in the case studies outlined in this chapter. The word oracy does not appear in the national curriculum of England. Despite the fact that 'spoken language' is emphasised, its association with conversation, classroom dialogue and listening is often confined to non-statutory guidance and limited to a particular version of the English language. The Scottish and other UK curricula have larger sections on speaking and listening. Drama too is seen as non-statutory in the English curriculum but as we have seen, it is part of statutory expressive arts in Scotland, Wales and Northern Ireland. In practice, in each of the administrations, the skills of active speaking and listening are relatively low in the English language hierarchy. In a world both divided and united by technology, dominated by images, with contested views on knowledge, multiple narratives and perhaps declining emotional intelligence, confidence and proficiency in speaking, listening and dialogue are of increasing importance.

English is a central form of communication in almost every school activity outside foreign languages. The case studies in English language in this chapter address standard English learning objectives, but also rely on many levels of spoken interaction between teacher and child, child and child. Indeed, the case studies throughout this book include multiple opportunities to develop oracy beyond the stated objectives. Each case study below focuses on the positive, creative and trans-disciplinary uses of spoken language in association with other forms of knowledge. The first example links speaking/listening from the English, Scottish, Welsh and Northern Irish curricula applied within the expressive arts discipline of drama.

Case Study 6.5

Telling my story

Overarching objective

To be confident communicators in language and movement

English (oracy) learning objectives

- Know how to articulate and explain a story
- Know how to adjust their story so others can understand them
- Show ability to listen and respond to the stories of other people

English (drama) learning objectives

- Improvise or act out a story
- Developing ideas through acting them out
- Communicating in movement, pose, gesture and facial expression

A group of ten Year 1 students from a Manchester primary school walk into an empty room with a teaching assistant (TA). There they meet the drama practitioner (DP) who worked with them last week. Each child blows up and climbs into an imaginary bubble and floats out of the classroom window, rises over the school, up and over the city and looks down. None of the bubbles bump into each other but each bubble occupant can 'see' the school, the playground, and the park below, floating higher they can see the shopping street, their home, the flats. After bursting their imagined bubbles and a few other warm-ups the children form a circle and two children carry an imaginary, heavy purple and orange spotted bucket to the middle and put it down. Each child in turn verbally 'throws' their name into the invisible bucket. 'As loud, as soft or as silly as you like – just make sure it gets into the bucket,' says the DP. After these introductions the children sit around a masking tape 'story square' on the classroom floor and chant:

In Speech Bubbles we do gooooood listening,
In Speech Bubbles we are gentle with each other,
In Speech Bubbles we take turns,
In Speech Bubbles we do gooooood acting.

The DP then introduces the day's story. 'I've got Meena's story from last week here, it's got five characters in it, Meena, a tiny dragon, a princess and Meena's dad and mum.' 'Who wants to be Meena?' – three children want to be Meena, so they all stand in the story square.

The DP begins to read the story slowly and meaningfully, 'Meena was feeling sad and lonely…' The DP asks the three Meenas to look and move in a sad and lonely way and as they do so whispers, 'There is a tiny dragon in this story, could Eric and Hanzah go into the circle and be the tiny dragon, breathe little bits of fire quietly and flap your baby wings, swing those baby tails.' The boys join in behind the sad Meena.

'Suddenly Meena saw a tiny baby dragon,' – ('look surprised Meena', says the DP), 'What do you think you would do if you saw a little tiny sweet dragon?' (the Meenas stroked it and give it some sweets).

Meena's story progressed within the story square brought to life by all ten children, some taking multiple parts, most including the TA, swapping parts. The story ended as the TA grew into a (friendly) giant dragon and Meena's parents put it on a lead and led it back to the woods where it lived in a cave, made from the body shapes of six children. Meena was thrilled with the telling of her story and the admiration she received from her peers. When the group was asked about the best bit of the session several individuals remarked that they liked 'the bit where the dragon didn't want to go into the cave and kept running away'.

As the children left the room one child remained behind to relate a story to the DP and a TA for next week's session.

This case study formed part of a weekly drama intervention designed to support children with speech, language and communication difficulties delivered by Speech Bubbles (Website). It combines story telling with drama in a way that generates confidence, well-being, the ability to speak out, invent narratives, make friends and enjoy communication (see Barnes, 2015; Barnes, 2020).

Case Study 6.6

Talking about and to refugees

Overarching objective

To know what it means to have respect for other cultures

Citizenship learning objectives

- Ask questions about a different group in their community
- Have informed opinions on an issue important to their community
- Know some causes and consequences of global displacements

English (oracy) learning objectives

- Participate freely as active speakers and listeners
- Use more complex sentences
- Speak and listen confidently and carefully in two different contexts
- Know how to ask appropriate questions

A Year 6 class were from a community where strong, often negative views about refugees were expressed. Their teacher wanted to help the class develop more critical and informed thinking and in their citizenship lesson presented a series of figures and facts about asylum seekers and refugees in the UK. Children were taught about the international agreements related to those fleeing war, persecution and natural disaster, the language that distinguished asylum seekers from immigrants or refugees and about the contribution refugees currently make to the British economy and culture. The class used maps to locate the countries of origin, and the causes of displacement across the world in 2022.

The following week, five people who had been granted refugee status by the UK Home Office were invited to the class. Each refugee was in their twenties and had lived in the

UK for more than two years. They had been trained as 'young ambassadors' by a refugee charity and were used to answering questions and talking to young people. Class members were arranged around five large tables each of which hosted one refugee ambassador. The refugees were from Ukraine, Syria, Afghanistan, Congo and Sudan and each introduced themselves using an artefact, like a flag or photo, and gave a brief statement of their name, where they came from and how they got to the UK. Students had been told to be sensitive and to avoid questions about family and friends and to adapt their language appropriately for people with English as a second or third language. Left to chat among themselves the questions and conversations between the young people soon became relaxed, friendly, lively, detailed and difficult to stop. Almost every answer from a refugee generated a supplementary question. The children were disappointed to be stopped after 40 minutes of intense dialogue.

The next day the teacher planned to develop a different kind of oracy. They arranged a whole class debrief and open debate/discussion on refugees and asylum seekers. Two children were asked to prepare a short talk on what they had learned from the previous day's conversations. There followed a lively, well-focused debate on what these conversations meant to rest of the class. The authentic, interpersonal contact and careful listening to the real stories of refugees had had a transformative effect on the oracy of the vast majority of children. Many shared finely detailed information they had gained from their dialogue with their refugee guest. Speaking was animated, sentences noticeably longer and more complex than children's habitual utterances; arguments were richly illustrated, more balanced and nuanced. The many stories retold by their classmates were intensely listened to. Their teacher recognised evidence of the broadening of children's experience through this encounter:

> ...from just this one genuine conversation about something real and relevant, language became energised, rich, emotionally powerful and meaningful for large numbers of usually reluctant speakers. (Year 6 teacher, Dover)

Case Study 6.6 reminds us of the importance of oracy in establishing meaning and purpose in education. Exercising it increases confidence and fluency and often enhances perception by extending vocabulary. Alexander's (2019) emphasis on dialogic education is well illustrated here. The study also highlights the importance of the subjective in learning. Informed, well-resourced class discussions on matters of community importance, have a high chance of being personally and emotionally meaningful to children. The work of Gert Biesta (2011, 2016) supports a view of education where such subjectification is used to emancipate young learners from the oppression of a curriculum that may otherwise feel irrelevant. Clearly, an education where relevance and values matter is likely to provoke involvement critical thinking, but it also involves risk, uncertainty and a degree of messiness. Embracing such risks is not always appropriate, but education without risk quickly becomes pallid, uncreative and excluding for high numbers of students. The positive pedagogue will seek to use dialogue to broaden students' outlook, to find an appropriate balance between risk and predictability, fact and opinion, knowledge and creativity.

Mathematics

The programmes of study within the mathematics curriculum for Key Stages 1 and 2 in England offer a detailed path through the skills and knowledge of number, measurement, geometry and statistics. Similarly, the other devolved education administrations place mathematics in core position because of the importance of numeracy and logic skills across the curriculum. Mathematics allows us to make sense of our world and manage many aspects of our lives: money, weights and measures, timetables, distances, predictions, plans for the future and the analysis of information. Most of the mathematics we use in everyday life is practical and relatively straightforward involving adding, subtracting, multiplying and dividing, simple fractions, area, volume and perimeter. Fundamental numeracy skills help us solve problems, record data, store and present information, assess risk and make informed decisions. The knowledge and attitudinal groundwork for the more complex numberwork needed for careers and interests in science, design engineering, computer science, medicine and finance is laid in the final years of Key Stage 2.

Numeracy is without doubt essential to everyday life. The case studies below illustrate ways in which practical experience might be used to teach, motivate and consolidate the learning of mathematics skills and knowledge alongside those of another subject.

Case Study 6.7

Year 2, Three bowls for three bears

Overarching objective

To know that measurement and number helps us make sense of our world

Mathematics learning objectives

- Accurately weigh unfired clay into 50, 100 and 150 gram lumps
- Know how to measure in millimetres
- Know, find and use the word 'diameter'
- Know, find and use the word 'circumference'

Design and technology learning objectives

- Plan three pottery bowls to illustrate a 'three bears' story
- Know how to make three thumb pot bowls in ascending sizes
- Know how to finish a clay vessel, by smoothing, flattening its base and making rim and side walls regular
- Understand that as it dries the volume and weight of clay decreases

The positive pedagogue strives to make links between the child, their world and their education. For many, fairy stories are part of that world. A Year 2 class had been reintroduced to the story of 'Goldilocks and the three bears' because their teacher wanted them to invent their own stories to read to children in the school Reception class. After revising the structure of the traditional story, small groups of children were asked to take photos with the class iPads that might illustrate a modernised story starring their own big, middle-sized and tiny soft toys as characters. They needed props for the story too – variations on the characters and the three different sized chairs, three bowls for the porridge and three beds. The three porridge bowls provided an opportunity for new teaching and learning in mathematics and D&T.

Children were asked to weigh three different amounts of clay: the first bowl needed 50 grams of clay, the second 100 and the third 150 grams. Groups of children were asked to use scales to weigh out these three accurately weighed lumps. Each group was shown how to make thumb pots from the clay. Group members were asked to make their bowls as regular and strong as possible and pay special attention to the rims. Bowls had to have a neat hemispherical shape, with walls not too thin, not too thick and a tapped base that would allow it to sit securely on a table. The children were asked to use their rulers and pencils to plan their three bowls estimating their dimensions, shape and size before actually making them (see Figure 6.2 and 6.3). They made the 50-gram (tiny) bowl first, smoothed it and flattened its base and compared it with their plan.

Before placing their tiny bowl on a drying rack, children were shown how to use a small ruler laid gently across the widest part of the rim to measure its diameter. They made a label for each bowl to record its measurement. The groups of children went through the same process to make the middle-sized and big bowls. The bowls dried over a few days, after which the children measured the diameters again – they noticed they had shrunk. Using a tape measure to measure the circumference of their now dry bowls, the children added this information to their label. Finally, the dry pots were fired in the school kiln and a few days later children were able to measure the diameter and circumference again. Again, they noticed the pots had decreased in size and their teacher helped them understand that the very high temperatures in the kiln had driven out all the water as it turned clay to ceramic.

Figure 6.2 Measuring the smallest porridge bowl

Figure 6.3 Preparing for illustrations to enliven a modernised three bears story (Photo: Barnes)

Case Study 6.8

Year 4/5 maths in a Forest School

Overarching objective
To develop an appreciation of and sensitivity towards the contribution of the natural world to human well-being

Mathematics learning objectives
- Know and understand the terms isosceles and equilateral triangles
- Know and understand the concept lateral symmetry
- Be able to construct a symmetrical sculpture from natural objects
- To accurately complete a laterally symmetrical image from half a leaf

Art learning objectives
- Know and understand the work of environmental sculptor Andy Goldsworthy
- Make artwork arising from a knowledge of Goldsworthy's work
- Use a digital camera to present and preserve artwork

Forest schools (website) have become very popular in the UK over the last 30 years. The idea of child-led learning in forests or other wild environments has, however, existed in traditional societies all over the world throughout human history. The educational philosopher Rousseau wrote about this approach in the 18th century and forest schools are its latest Western iteration. Since the lockdowns of 2020 and 2021 there has been a surge of interest from both parents and schools in forest schools, recognising the well-being benefits alongside the educational value of hands-on experience outdoors.

A village primary school in the Southwest of England used its timetabled forest school sessions as a motivator for learning in mathematics. The school reports that work on number, repeating patterns, size, distance, graphing, estimation, place value, fractions, shapes and division at different levels are all initiated in forest school sessions. A Year 4/5 session on symmetry provides a helpful example of quality learning in both mathematics and art.

In April the class teacher planned to begin a maths topic on symmetry in the forest. As they walked with children through the woodland, parents, the TA and other helpers were asked to point out and examine examples of symmetrical leaves, flowers, seeds, berries, branches and insects and birds. The idea of lateral symmetry was introduced, discussed and illustrated in small groups led by the TA and the teacher. The children were encouraged to make collections of natural items that showed left/right symmetry to bring back to school for a class exhibition on symmetry. As preparation for this, some leaves were cut in half from top to bottom and stuck to pieces of paper. Children were asked to draw the symmetrical missing half (see Figure 6.4).

SCIENCE, TECHNOLOGY, ENGLISH AND MATHS IN CROSS-CURRICULAR CONTEXTS

Figure 6.4 Drawing to complete the symmetry of a leaf involved unusually careful observation (Photo: Barnes)

The main practical activity in the forest that day was for individuals or pairs to make something beautiful from natural materials. Children were asked to construct and leave behind some symmetrical natural sculptures made from stones, twigs, leaves, grasses, flowers or seeds in the manner of environmental artist Andy Goldsworthy whose work they had already seen in class. They were encouraged to use circles, squares, rectangles and equilateral or isosceles triangles at any scale to provide a guiding structure for their ephemeral sculptures. Within the basic geometric shapes they had chosen, everyone was given freedom to find and use natural objects from the forest floor to develop appealing, symmetrical patterns. The teacher and all helpers made their own sculptures alongside the children. Class cameras were used to make a series of photographic images of the sculptures to enliven their symmetry exhibition back at school.

The illustrated Three Bears story in Case Study 6.7 and the culminating symmetry exhibition in Case Study 6.8 addressed mathematics learning objectives within what I have called *inter-disciplinary cross-curricular learning*. The aim of interdisciplinary learning is to synthesise learning across several subjects within some kind of performance that captures and applies what has been learned. Often that synthesis involves creative thinking: imaginative plans, decisions about relative value and original approaches and solutions.

Throughout this chapter it has been argued that a positive curriculum is one that makes authentic, practical and meaningful connections with the lives and interests of the learners.

The positive pedagogue supports the young people in their class to become deeply involved in those connections and build on them. During the authentic experiences planned for children, teachers deliberately highlight and name good examples of collaboration, friendship, sensory engagement, wonder and achievement by naming or highlighting them. These often powerful personal experiences will for some, endure in the memory as occasions of deep learning and times of happiness in school.

Summary

This chapter has striven to link the STEM subjects to others in the primary curriculum. It has revived Robinson's radical suggestion that all subjects of the curriculum should be treated with parity and that existing distinctions between the status of STEM and the rest of the curriculum should be removed. The chapter has reaffirmed that language and literacy, mathematics and numeracy, science and technological education are vital to economic and personal progress in today's world, but suggested that so too are other well-established ways of making sense of experience. It has argued that the world and every individual life is potentially enhanced by the widened horizons brought by knowledge and understanding of the arts, the humanities and physical education. The case studies in this chapter therefore combined learning in a single STEM subject with objectives from an arts or humanities discipline. Both were treated as equal in status. Both subjects threw a different light on an overarching issue wider than an individual discipline.

Regardless of the specific subjects exercised in the case studies it is evident that oracy – speaking and listening – is developed in every one of the eight activities summarised. In action and specifically through exercising values such as respect for diversity, sustainability, compassion and beauty, social and personal engagement are promoted. In each of these sessions observed in real classrooms, such engagement was abundantly evident, in the conversations, body language, facial expressions and relationships shared between class members and the adults working and learning with them.

7
THINKING CAREFULLY ABOUT THE WHOLE CURRICULUM

Objectives

This chapter will focus on curriculum as a whole and concentrate on planning and implementing a motivating, broad and rich curriculum with '…appropriate coverage, content, structure and sequencing' (Ofsted, 2022). It will discuss a curriculum and learning end points designed to:

- Engage hard-to-reach and poorly motivated children, through relevance, activity, sequencing and progression
- Ensure the development of transferable, deep and memorable knowledge
- Link with quality and motivating staff development for teachers and other school staff

Introduction

Human commonalities: our connectedness, diversity, creativity and inclusion are big themes throughout this book. Its content so far has rested on discussion of principles directly related to these themes. The ability to develop deeper understandings of these features shared by all humanity can be an aim of education itself. But many other big issues and questions also demand progressive curriculum support.

Curriculum

Curriculum matters. The curriculum is not just the subjects taught and the order in which knowledge will be presented, it is the totality of all the learning experiences students will have in school. In other words, there is a 'hidden curriculum' (Snyder, 1971) that often carries as much weight as the official one. For a school successfully to support children in reaching their potential, all managers, teachers and support staff should understand and agree on purposes and approaches of the explicit school curriculum but must also be aware of a hidden or tacit one. To develop what I have called a positive curriculum, every teacher and assistant (TA) should of course be knowledgeable in the school subjects and be able to see connections between them and progression within them. They should also be conscious of their reflex responses, attitudes and the emotional/social climate they create in their classrooms.

The child

The child should be central to curriculum. Their flourishing should be its aim and a positive ethos will do much to ensure it. From the Early Years, a curriculum to build children's confidence, experience and knowledge involves nurturing an increasing awareness of their physical and social environment, discovering their innate strengths and developing trust in each other. As confidence and collaboration grows acquiring an ever-broadening raft of relevant knowledge and skills becomes a general aim of that curriculum, but educational neuroscience also tells us that successful learning requires children to feel a sense of emotional security and involvement (Immordino-Yang and Gottlieg, 2020). Psychology research (Fredrickson and Joiner, 2018) with adults has shown that experiences that nurture opportunities to observe, imagine, reflect, question and enjoy mental or physical activity generate an upward spiral of positive emotional, physical and social change in individuals and groups. It is reasonable to suggest that generating positive emotions in children result in similar physiological, intellectual, creative, social and mental health gains. Psychologists such as Vygotsky, Bruner, Seligman and Booth have reminded us that lasting learning thrives in settings that support inclusive values like: mutual trust, collaboration, compassion and friendship. The ability to nurture these 'soft skills' in children and self, marks out the positive pedagogue.

The learning environment

Environments shape our thinking and learning. Secure environments are more likely to make that learning a positive experience. The school campus and neighbourhood, whether city centre, suburb or rural idyll, should therefore be seen as the chief curriculum resource and reference. The curriculum cannot be wholly locally based, however, because we live in a richly interconnected world and through digital technologies children are increasingly in contact with the world beyond home. Applying inclusive attitudes to learning about other places, people and cultures is equally important. There is no conflict between these soft-skilled, values-based aims and a curriculum focus on the rigour of disciplinary knowledge. Every curriculum example shared below will link values with learning in both disciplinary and transdisciplinary contexts.

Disciplined knowledge

The subject disciplines are among the greatest inventions of human cultures. Gardner (2000) argued this decades ago and as global crises multiply his claim seems ever more apposite. Every discipline offers potential answers in a world of multifarious problems. Each branch of learning from architecture and computing to zoology, offers unique and creative ways of making sense of our internal or external worlds, but the combination of disciplines often multiplies their usefulness through provoking new thinking and creative responses. A broad, rich and integrated curriculum is primed to foster an atmosphere where everyday creativities become commonplace (Burnard and Loughrey, 2021). When different kinds of knowledge are brought together to solve shared, authentic, meaningful challenges, children's imagination is fired, novelty results and value is generated (Barnes, 2018). But creativity alone is not enough.

The basics *are* important. A growing confidence and ability in reading opens the world of other people's minds to children. Ease with speaking and writing build a greater sense of agency and the ability to express personal feelings and collaborative responses increasingly persuasively. 'Mathematical knowledge, ideas and operations' (Ofsted, 2022, para. 204) provide accurate tools to ease everyday life and offer models of logic and analysis. All children need this vital knowledge and ability to be firmed up, committed to long-term memory and ready to be built upon. Knowledge appears to be retained when it has become emotionally significant and is somehow involved or necessary in everyday life. Involvement happens, for example, when new knowledge is put to work in real and novel situations. The most effective subject teachers have always worked in this way, but engaging all young people in a curriculum may be more difficult in today's diverse, technology dominated, anxious and more unequal society. Teachers may need to work harder on connecting youngsters to a curriculum that motivates them.

Sequencing knowledge

Knowledge also must be sequenced to be useful and committed to long-term memory. Sequencing involves:

- organising thoughts
- planning movements and actions
- seeing patterns
- understanding cause and effect
- building one aspect of knowledge upon another

Sequencing makes learning and living more efficient, controllable and predictable. Children with dyslexic and dyspraxic tendencies may have particular difficulties planning and organising their thoughts in this way. Teachers need to know and understand this, their sympathy and support should be balanced by an appreciation that children facing these barriers also have original and creatively provoking ways of seeing the world.

The examples of sequencing of knowledge and skills in geography and history in this chapter will remind you of the importance of the progressive introduction of new information and activity. This will inform curriculum planning as well as smaller-scale lesson preparation, and is implicit in the themes, sub-themes and projects suggested below.

Making the curriculum relevant

It has been argued that every school curriculum should be a connecting curriculum. At times connections to children's lives are appropriately made via the separate subjects and at times pairs or groups of subjects will link personal experience to collective, local and global issues. The problem with linking subjects is that it is more difficult to plan and track single subject progression and coverage. In the sections below and in the next chapter you will be guided towards ways of establishing clear progression and effective assessment within activities that connect the perspectives of two subjects to answer a question or tackle an issue relevant to the lives of children. Positive pedagogy should confirm the importance of specific and agreed subject knowledge or skills 'end points', plan them collaboratively and agree on their value. In addition to clear subject objectives every proposed educational activity will involve values objectives such as: inclusive action, sustainable living, creative thought, positive dispositions toward self, and teamwork. This chapter will also highlight the ongoing need for teachers to be sustained by continually developing their own expertise and outline a curriculum closely connected with the real world of children, in the following sections:

- Connecting through expert teachers
- Connecting with self

- Connecting with others
- Connecting with the locality
- Connecting with culture
- Connecting with the world
- Connecting the disciplines

A connecting curriculum

The concept of a connecting curriculum was introduced in *Applying Cross-Curricular Approaches Creatively* (Barnes, 2018). This notion was motivated by observations throughout a long career that many children showed signs of being disconnected with education in schools. This perception has been reinforced by research and bare figures relating to absent, disaffected, disengaged, disruptive or unhappy young people. The 2,000 English school children excluded each day in 2018 (Timpson, 2019) represents the very tip of an iceberg of disconnection. WHO figures in 2020 show that the proportion of English young people (11–16) feeling safe at school has decreased over the last 10 years, that 44% could not say they felt they 'belonged in school' and around 25% considered themselves pressured 'a lot' by school work (WHO, 2020). These figures on British, especially English, child well-being compare poorly with other European countries. Symptoms of unhappiness at school, like mild disruption, isolation, distraction, poor relationships or lack of interest, often first show in the primary years and we know that unhappiness results in poorer health as well as educational outcomes (Marmot, 2020). Every teacher knows the effect on others of having two or three disaffected children in class, from current figures it may be quite common to have eight or nine.

Children's general happiness has shown a significant decline in the last ten years (Children's Society, 2021). About 1 in 8 say they are unhappy with their lives and there is plenty to be unhappy about. About 30% of England's children now live in poverty (End Child Poverty Website) and poverty overlaps closely with other types of disadvantage unequally affecting some Black and ethnic minority communities, lone parent families and in pockets of poverty in city centres and the north (Children's Society, 2021). The pandemic appears to have exacerbated the sense of alienation in many young people. Figures for children not in school rose dramatically during the 2020 and 2021 pandemic, and absence figures have remained high. Though these figures are higher for secondary-aged young people, the effects of their disaffection easily passes down to younger children. Numbers of children identified as needing Special Educational Needs and Disabilities (SEND) support have also risen, as have those on Education, Health and Care (EHC) plans and with statements of SEN. Taken together, those disadvantaged through absence, illness, mental ill-health, lack of support or guidance, speech, language or communication difficulties, poverty, discrimination or social deprivation, represent significant percentages of the school population. Too many children show poor development. Too many feel unconnected to what used to be called British culture and need a curriculum that helps them find meaning, raise their horizons and links with their identity and experience.

A relevant, interconnected curriculum is not just for the unenamoured. For children who thrive within existing provision, a curriculum that excites and inspires beyond simple examination success, will enrich and extend learning. The 30+% (Communication Trust, 2017) who experience barriers to their learning are more likely to overcome them if the curriculum involves them at emotional, social and physical levels. Such a curriculum requires inspired, knowledgeable and inspiring teachers.

The curriculum must also be connected in more standard ways. Knowledge should be continually built upon and broadened. Earlier versions of the national curriculum in England recognised the need for guidance how to build this progression in each subject. The last pages of the 1999 national curriculum for England contained a sequence of eight, levelled 'attainment targets' that for each subject charted an appropriate trajectory of knowledge and skills from Key Stage 1 to 4 (see for example the attainment targets for geography and history taken from the archived national curriculum (DfEE, 1999b & c) below). Though no longer law, the abandoned attainment targets for each subject provide helpful guidance to teachers seeking a workable sequence of objectives or end points for each subject.

In Table 7.1, a suggested sequence of geography skills for Key Stage 1 is summarised in the following phrases:

At a beginner level (and in relation to their locality), children should be able to:

- recognise human and physical features
- make observations about places
- express views about places
- answer questions about places
- use resources like simple maps or images

Table 7.1 Sample of Key Stage 1 skills and knowledge progression in geography

Level 1 Pupils show their knowledge, skills and understanding in studies at a local scale. They *recognise and make observations* about physical and human features of localities. They *express their views* on features of the environment of a locality. They *use resources* that are given to them, and their own observations, to *ask and respond to questions about places and environments*.

Level 2 Pupils show their knowledge, skills and understanding in studies at a local scale. They *describe physical and human features of places*, and recognise and make observations about those features that give places their character. They show an *awareness of places beyond their own locality*. They *express views on the environment* of a locality and *recognise how people affect the environment*. They carry out simple tasks and *select information using resources* that are given to them. They use this information and their own observations to help them ask and respond to questions about places and environments. They begin to *use appropriate geographical vocabulary*.

Level 3 Pupils show their knowledge, skills and understanding in studies at a local scale. They *describe and compare* the physical and human features of different localities and *offer explanations* for the locations of some of those features. They are aware that *different places may have both similar and different* characteristics. They *offer reasons* for some of their observations and *for their views and judgements* about places and environments. They *recognise how people seek to improve and sustain environments*. They use skills and sources of evidence to respond to a range of geographical questions, and begin to *use appropriate vocabulary to communicate their findings*.

Later, perhaps at 6 or 7 years of age, children should be able to build upon their observations in their locality by:

- describing specific aspects in more detail
- making observations about the character of the place
- showing awareness of places beyond it
- recognising how people affect their environment
- begin to use appropriate geographical language (e.g. compass directions, street, house, field, boundary, weather words)

By 7 or 8 years of age, most children should be able to show their understanding about a range of several places by:

- demonstrating their knowledge and observation of similarities and differences
- offering knowledgeable reasons for differences
- recognise how people have tried to improve or sustain environments
- accurately using a range of geographical terms (e.g.: hill, valley, river, lake, urban, rural, country, county, continent, ocean, town, city, village)

The abandoned 1999 history curriculum for Key Stage 2 also suggested how new knowledge could be built upon earlier understandings. Although this guidance is now archived, it still offers a logical progression of skills that teachers could use as a guide.

By the time children were 7 or 8, the 1999 history curriculum expected them to:

Table 7.2 Sample of progression in history skills and knowledge at Key Stage 2

Level 3 Pupils show their developing *understanding* of chronology by their realisation that the *past can be divided into different periods of time*, their recognition of some of the similarities and differences between these periods, and their use of dates and terms. They show knowledge and understanding of some of the main events, people and changes studied. They are beginning to *give a few reasons for, and results of, the main events and changes*. They identify some of the *different ways in which the past is represented*. They use sources of information in ways that *go beyond simple observations to answer questions about the past*.

Level 4 Pupils *show factual knowledge* and understanding of aspects of the history of Britain and the wider world. They use this to describe *characteristic features of past societies* and periods, and to *identify changes* within and across different periods. They show some understanding that *aspects of the past have been represented and interpreted in different ways*. They are beginning to *select and combine information* from *different sources*. They are beginning to produce structured work, *making appropriate use of dates and terms*.

Level 5 Pupils show increasing depth of factual knowledge and understanding of aspects of the history of Britain and the wider world. They use this to *describe features of past societies and periods and to begin to make links between them*. They describe events, people and changes. They describe and make links between events and changes and give reasons for, and results of, these events and changes. They know that *some events, people and changes have been interpreted in* different ways and suggest possible reasons for this. Using their knowledge and understanding, pupils are beginning to *evaluate sources of information* and *identify those that are useful* for particular tasks. They *select and organise information* to produce structured work, making *appropriate use of dates and terms*.

- know that the past can be divided into different periods of time
- show their understanding of similarities and differences between historic periods
- use relevant dates and terms to show their understanding of different periods
- give a few reasons for, and results of, major events and changes in a particular period
- identify some of the different ways in which the past is represented
- answer questions about the past that use more than one source of information

As they progressed through Key Stage 2 children were expected to add to their existing knowledge of the past, for example by:

- understanding that aspects of the past have been represented and interpreted in different ways
- selecting and combining information from different sources
- presenting information about a period by selecting and combining information from different sources

Towards the end of primary school children should be able to:

- describe distinctive features of past societies
- make links between past societies and their features
- give reasons for changes in a certain period
- evaluate different sources of information and choose the most useful
- know that event, people and changes may be interpreted in different ways
- select and organise information using appropriate historical terms and dates

With good subject knowledge and thought, a logically connected progression of skills and knowledge like those above can be constructed for every subject and successfully steer teaching and learning.

Connecting through expert teachers

Teachers are a school's most important resource. They are the most effective means of ensuring sustained positive contact with children and organising learning across the curriculum. Good teachers do this by tapping into children's emotional responses, sharing their own interests, providing models of good behaviour and establishing a positive environment. But these contributions are not enough – the positive pedagogue must be a continual learner themself. They will grow their knowledge and experience throughout their life in education and aim to become the kind of enthusiasts that inspire children.

Primary school teachers usually teach all 12 subjects of the primary curriculum. They have to ensure that cross-curricular themes like relationships, social, moral, spiritual and cultural education are part of the experience of all children in their class. It is a tall order along with implementing behaviour policies, planning, assessing, meeting with parents and addressing school targets. Retaining them in education is a major issue. Around 1 in 3 teachers plan to leave in the next first five years (Schoolsweek, 2022), often citing problems with discipline, administration or mistrust of government and media (Guardian, 2021). Maintaining enthusiasm is difficult, despite the fact that many owe cherished attitudes, skills, values, passions, even career choices to their own inspirational teachers. How then do we create more inspiring teachers?

Research-informed reports (Education Development Trust, 2014; Sammons et al., 2014) identify a number of features shared by 'inspiring' teachers. They are remembered as constructing positive, empathic relationships with children and colleagues and creating secure, supportive atmospheres conducive to learning. Inspiring teachers are also seen as having good classroom and behaviour management though the style of that management varies from relaxed to strict. When they give feedback it is kind, formative and helpful. They teach from a position of deep and passionate subject knowledge and construct what Ofsted might recognise as 'high quality learning experiences'. They appear to enjoy their job. They smile a lot.

Evaluations of attempts to retain such teachers highlight similar qualities. The RETAIN project in Cornwall, for example, attempted to keep young teachers in the profession through coaching, workshops, collaborative learning, new and enhancing skills using high-quality research into pedagogy and practice. It found that the sustained intervention improved the '…self-efficacy, confidence and quality of teaching of Early Career Teachers (ECT) in differing but complementary ways' (Ovenden-Hope et al., 2018, p. 1). They noted that all teachers supported by the project had remained in the profession.

The positive pedagogue might expect more than a staff development programme on self-efficacy, however. To make a positive difference to curriculum they need inspiring staff development throughout their careers. The teacher who enthuses others does so through enhanced and expert personal knowledge as well as empathy. Often the best sources of single subject enthusiasm come from the world outside formal education. Many tourist attractions, civic museums, libraries, art galleries, theatres, field study centres, historic monuments, science parks, zoos or big industries have education officers, expert volunteers or public relations staff. Most have enormous and current knowledge in their specialist areas. If individuals have worked for a while in their institutions they will also have experience in effectively communicating their knowledge. Schools should make full use of this eager and often free resource for staff training and know that enthusiasm is more often caught than taught.

Since the 2020/21 pandemic much staff training has gone and stayed online or been reduced to distance learning resource packs. There is little doubt, however, that face-to-face interaction between teacher and enthusiast – whether bird watcher, steam train devotee, librarian, actor, musician or artist – is the most effective way to pass on enthusiasm. Schools should seek in-person and practical development for subject specialists. Table 7.3 lists some examples where interpersonal or online staff development may be negotiated, but every locality has a host of ardent enthusiasts willing to share their passion.

Table 7.3 Some organisations offering staff development for teachers

Subject	Links
Art	Wakefield: https://hepworthwakefield.org/your-visit/for-schools-colleges-and-universities/ Scotland: https://www.nationalgalleries.org/learn London: https://www.nationalgallery.org.uk/learning/take-one-picture/take-one-picture-cpd-sessions
Music	https://www.musicmark.org.uk/resources/resource-category/courses-and-workshops/page/2/ https://www.drakemusic.org/learning/training/ London and national: https://groundswellarts.com/training/
History	Warkworth, Northumberland: https://www.english-heritage.org.uk/learn/teaching-resources/local-learning/warkworth-castle-and-hermitage/ Stonehenge, Wiltshire: https://www.english-heritage.org.uk/visit/places/stonehenge/schools/stonehenge-education-partnerships/ Chichester: https://www.wealddown.co.uk/courses/cpd-courses/
Geography	London: https://www.rgs.org/schools/teacher-cpd/ West Wales: https://naturesbaseeducation.co.uk/inset/ National: https://www.geography.org.uk/Training-and-events
Design and Technology	https://designmuseum.org/the-design-museum-campus/schools-and-colleges Belfast/Holywood: https://www.nmni.com/learn/For-schools-teachers/Education.aspx Chichester: https://www.wealddown.co.uk/courses/cpd-courses/
Computing	Northern Ireland: https://swgfl.org.uk/magazine/primary-school-teachers-in-northern-ireland-are-set-to-benefit-from-a-new-barefoot-partnership/
English/Literature/drama	Bristol: https://www.oldvic.ac.uk/ Swansea: https://www.lighthouse-theatre.co.uk/education-outreach/ Belfast: https://lyrictheatre.co.uk/creative-learning London, Manchester, Rochdale, Salford, Oldham: https://www.speechbubbles.org.uk/for-schools National Libraries: https://www.sla.org.uk/
Mathematics	Nationwide: https://www.atm.org.uk/?gclid=CjwKCAjw7vuUBhBUEiwAEdu2pONaTeREBwEump0UQyEw7uk6nMXqqKCqPvlGA5d26lopqALNzVeZPBoCosEQAvD_BwE
Science	Edinburgh: https://www.dynamicearth.co.uk/learning Winchester: https://www.winchestersciencecentre.org/learning/in-school/ Belfast: https://www.nmni.com/learn/For-schools-teachers/Education.aspx
Foreign Languages	Reading: https://pdcinmfl.com/ National: https://www.futurelearn.com/courses/teaching-languages-in-primary-schools-putting-research-into-practice
RE	York: https://www.visityork.org/business-directory/york-minster-learning-centre England and Scotland: https://hinduismre.co.uk/our-centres/
PE	Manchester: https://www.british-study.com/uk/learners/sports-education/manchester-city-football-school-development Liverpool: https://www.liverpoolfc.com/education Sandbach, Cheshire: https://www.sportscoachinggroup.co.uk/cpd
General	https://educationendowmentfoundation.org.uk/support-for-schools/eef-regional-support https://pshe-association.org.uk/training-and-events/trainees-and-ects

Effective schools make contact with local community partners for teacher development part of their character. Teachers working with non-teacher experts say they are sustained and given new resilience by such opportunities. Non-teacher subject experts often have more straightforward agendas and higher expectations for their subject. They understand key concepts and address misconceptions more easily, use more up-to-date knowledge and are often closer to the gatekeepers of their discipline. For example, teachers and TAs observing drama practitioners leading theatre-making with 7-year-olds (Barnes, 2015) or watching how musicians composed original songs with nursery children (Barnes, 2018), said they returned to the classroom with new energy, ideas and attitudes. The same teachers reported gaining both professionally and personally as newly experienced insights become a valuable part of their lives and practice. The children in their classes benefited twice from such interventions, first from the outside expert and then from inspired teachers.

Connecting with self

Children are interested in themselves. Their rapidly changing body, mind and life offers a rich seam of motivation that should run throughout a primary curriculum. A curriculum on self, however, should also help children seek and find their passion (Robinson and Aronica, 2014). If a child is to discover what they will love doing for the rest of their lives, school must offer a broad and varied diet of experiences; a palette with many colours to choose from. That same curriculum should lead children to nurture, with ever-increasing knowledge and skills, the interests they have discovered. But following one's passion is not always a positive experience, it involves disappointments, doubts and difficulties. Developing the mindset that uses such negative experiences as growth points also needs teaching and exemplifying (Dweck,

Figure 7.1 Self portrait of a 9-year-old (Photo: Barnes)

2017a). Finally, learning how to act with wisdom and respond with resilience are transferable, self-management skills that need to be taught from the very earliest ages. Table 7.4 lists some themes focused on the self and the curriculum subjects that can be used to guide learning objectives and end points.

The ideas in Table 7.4 offer curriculum thoughts on the theme of 'myself'. The overarching issues of such a theme involve questions like:

- How do I find out and record information about myself?
- What makes me, me?
- What am I interested in and how can I find it? How can I develop it?
- How do I deal with problems and disappointments?
- Where can I get new knowledge about the things I like?
- How can I use my knowledge wisely?
- How can I get stronger intellectually? physically? mentally?
- What have I to give to others?
- How can I make people trust me?
- What do I want to do with my gifts and talents?

Table 7.4 A sample of themes and subjects with some possible end points

Theme	Subjects	Sample of possible end points
My measurements/my growing	Mathematics, science	SCIENCE: Able to gather and record data to help answer questions about my breathing.
My body/how do I protect it?	Science, mathematics	SCIENCE: Able to perform simple tests to find out about my senses.
My gifts and talents/what I like to play/where I like to explore	Any curriculum subject, plus	MUSIC: I can respond to music by describing my thoughts and feelings about my own and others' work.
My friends/being a friend/how do I deal with disappointment/sadness?	Relationships, English, foreign languages	ENGLISH: Able to ask relevant questions to extend understanding and knowledge. RELATIONSHIPS: How can I be a good friend?
My likes and dislikes/toys/what scares me and how I can overcome it/what are my ambitions?	Any curriculum subject, plus	ENGLISH: Able to plan what they are going to write about by writing out key words and ideas. RELATIONSHIPS: what do I want to be when I am older and why?
My feelings/happy/favourite places/how do I deal with obstacles to my happiness?	RE, English	MUSIC: Able to experiment with, create, select and combine sounds using the interrelated dimensions of music. PSHE: How do I develop resilience?

(Continued)

Table 7.4 A sample of themes and subjects with some possible end points *(Continued)*

Theme	Subjects	Sample of possible end points
My family/important people/who do I really need to make me happy?	Relationships, English, science, history	ENGLISH: Able to write about others and about real events. RE/PSHE: what do I really need? How is that different to what I want?
My pets and favourite animals/how do animals help me?	Science, mathematics, art	SCIENCE: Able to ask simple questions about three different species of animal and recognise that they can be answered in different ways.
My diary/favourite story/what would be a happy end to my story?	English, computing	ENGLISH: Able to write narrative about personal experiences. REL/CIT: What is my ambition? What would I like to do with my life?
My gratitude book/favourite people/how should I act?	RE, English	RE: Able to be aware that people's beliefs and values affect their actions.
My imagination/what I like to pretend	Art, music, drama, dance, English	ART: Able to use drawing, painting and sculpture to develop and share their ideas, experiences and imagination.
My favourite things/happy memories	Design and technology	ENGLISH: Able to give well-structured descriptions, explanations and express feelings about favourite things.
My response to….	History, geography, art, music, PE, English	ENGLISH: Able to articulate and justify answers, arguments and opinions.
My garden/house/locality/street/country/how can I find out more?	Geography, citizenship, PSHE, relationships, design and technology, mathematics	MATHS: Able to compare: lengths and heights, long/short, longer/shorter, tall/short, double/half mass/weight measure and begin to record the following: lengths and heights mass/weight
My health/how can I protect it?	Science, PSHE, RE, PE	SCIENCE: Able to observe my breathing closely, and use simple equipment to measure aspects of it.
My food/my resources/what do I really need? What else makes me strong/brave?	Science, design and technology, geography	DESIGN/TECHNOLOGY: Able to select from and use a wide range of ingredients, according to their characteristics to make a savoury meal.

Such questions are arguably universal and can be answered at an appropriate level by children of all primary age groups. To answer them in any depth they require attitudes, knowledge and skills from the subject disciplines, usually more than one. For example, to answer the first question, children would need the knowledge and skills of mathematics (measurement of height, circumference, width, weight, volume; addition, subtraction, conversion, simple decimals, fractions or graphs) and some from science (perhaps knowledge about breathing, lungs, heart, digestion, experiments and records related to sight, hearing, touch, smell, taste). The second question involves English language to a much higher degree (the language of likes and dislikes, or comparatives and superlatives, past, present and future tenses), but might equally call on the visual language of art (self-portraiture, symbolism, colour, texture, setting, style, abstraction), PSHE knowledge (aspects of physical and mental health, growing and changing, personal safety and the self in relationships and sex education) or citizenship (How do people see me? How do I see myself? Feeling positive about the self; making good choices; developing relationships).

Question 3 might be asked after children have shared a broad introduction to the many ways of representing self. We might understand ourselves through music that expresses our emotions, geography that examines our impact on place, or maps detail of places we love to be in. Children might find fascination in a personal history that identifies family roots generations back, special objects or discover that food technology gives them a chance to design and make their own recipes. After exposure to a range of subject options related to self, the question, 'What am I interested in?' potentially makes much more sense.

Connecting with others

Relationships education has been highlighted in both primary and secondary education in recent years. It is an important focus of Ofsted inspections and fundamental to the development of social intelligence (Goleman, 2007) implicit in optional PSHE and citizenship teaching or the cross-curricular threads of SMSC. Social intelligence is a concept that has existed for over a century and can be defined as the ability to act wisely in human relations and to understand and inclusively manage social situations. Concepts like wisdom may vary between cultures, but in the context of positive pedagogy the wise child or adult responds within an agreed values system that believes certain actions, for example inclusive ones, are good. So, affirming the wise child, able to put their personal interests aside and make decisions that serve a common good, establishes a model of good community behaviour.

The ability to build, maintain and generate relationships inclusively is learned. It is best learned when modelled in community and school life presents plentiful opportunities to demonstrate healthy, inclusive relationships and the characteristics we share. How should this affect curriculum?

The theme of connecting with others could involve any curriculum subject. In order to plan successful subject progression, however, it is best to sub-divide a theme like 'Connecting with others', into sub-themes and employ two curriculum subjects at a time to investigate them. Table 7.5 suggests some possible sub-divisions and pairs of subjects for a Year 3 group.

Table 7.5 Connecting with others: sub-themes and subjects for a Year 3 class

Sub-theme	Subject focus	Subject end points
Connecting through friendships	PSHE/Citizenship Relationships Art	PSHE: To know what constitutes a positive healthy friendship (e.g. mutual respect, trust, truthfulness, loyalty, kindness, generosity, sharing interests and experiences, support with problems and difficulties); that the same principles apply to online friendships as to face-to-face relationships. ART/DESIGN: Improving art and design techniques by using clay to create a 3D representation of the idea of friendship showing ability to make robust connections between linked sections.
Embodied connections	PE (Dance) Drama	PE(DANCE): Able to respond to stimulus like friendship by selecting composing and performing a set of physical actions coordination and control. DRAMA: Know and demonstrate a range of drama techniques (such as hot seating and flashback) that explore character and any issues.
Connections on the web	Computing English	COMPUTING: Able to share and exchange ideas and information with students in another locality or country. ENGLISH: Able to communicate confident, organised, clear descriptions and questions showing awareness of the needs of a school contact in another locality. LANGUAGES: Communicating in another language.
Connections in the community	History Computing Geography	HISTORY: Know how to use a census and local directories to answer questions about the past in their locality. COMPUTING: Able to retrieve useful information from online census or street directories. GEOGRAPHY: Know how people in their community have worked to improve and sustain aspects of the local environment.
Similarities that connect us	Science Mathematics	SCIENCE: Know how to respond scientifically to questions (e.g. about average height, handspan, foot size, head circumference). Know why it is important to collect data and how to interpret it. MATHS: Know how to measure the height in centimetres of class colleagues and find an average and a median. Know how to make graphs to present the information found.

Connecting with the locality

Our locality offers an almost limitless resource for learning across the curriculum. We can add to our understanding of the place where we live through the eyes of any subject. Frequent opportunities throughout the year to get outside the classroom into the streets and open areas around the school provide an invaluable motivator for learning – but learning aims must be carefully planned and part of a well-understood and shared school philosophy. A quick search through primary school websites reveals that many schools choose curriculum focuses important to their community. They include curricula founded on themes like:

- Sustainability
- The natural world
- The locality
- Links with another school in a distant place
- The arts
- Diversity
- Culture
- Science
- Community action
- The religious
- Adventure
- Internationalism
- Global links
- The developing child
- The humanities
- Respect for rights
- Sports
- Communication

Every example above suggests local starting points but also implies many links across the curriculum and globe. If sustainability is the big curriculum focus then this can obviously be approached through language, mathematics, science and geography, but with thought and advice from subject specialists, any other subject could contribute creatively to the theme. The essence of an effective curriculum is that it is agreed and understood by all and represents a rounded view of what quality in education should be. It is not difficult to get agreement from managers, classroom teachers, TAs, governors and parents on the importance of a curriculum centred on the locality, because of its instant relevance and flexibility. It is also relatively easy to make work in the local environment relevant and meaningful. A 'sustainability' school, for example, would choose local as well as distant, perhaps historical examples of sustainable living. It might look critically at the design of its building, suggesting sustainable changes, children will make and view art pieces on sustainability themes, make musical instruments from recycled materials, consider sustainability principles enshrined in religions or dance to a sustainability theme. Similarly, beyond citizenship, relationships and sex education, a 'rights-respecting school' will look at children's rights, rights in other countries, through the ages, as expressed through the arts (including poetry and protest songs), rights in sports, languages and design technology perspectives. There are multiple opportunities for local applications of a rights education too, through parents meetings, exhibitions, displays, links with unaccompanied minor refugees and awareness-raising campaigns.

The locality is a major resource. Its rich, accessible and obviously multi-disciplinary character means that wherever you are, the locality should be your first choice of teaching material. Without leaving the school playground or field, free sources of illustration, issues, lesson setting, data, inspiration, provocation, subject focus and raw materials are quickly available.

Locality is even important for those whose Xbox and social media have become a significant part of the 'real world'. Describing and illustrating the details of one's own daily life and environment to an Xbox friend or gaming partner in California or Indonesia needs ever-increasing skills and knowledge in English, geography and history as well as computing. Internet links can, of course, also be quickly exploited to teach foreign languages and respect for other cultures.

Connecting with culture

The development of cultural literacy and/or cultural capital (Bourdieu, 1985) has become part of a critique of progressive education (see for example Social Market Foundation, 2013). A sociological concept, 'cultural capital' describes the key knowledge that will assist a person to rise up the social ladder in a hierarchical society. The idea of gaining access to privilege and power through a particular kind of knowledge rather than one's experience and strength of character, may sound rather undemocratic and discriminatory, but unfortunately it remains true that to enter certain professions or rise within them it still helps to have the kind of knowledge more common in white, male, middle-class people (see Parsons, 2020). Choosing a view of culture that is confined to what used to be called 'high culture' – western classical music, history and literature of mostly dead white mainly British males – is to dismiss the cultures of our richly diverse society.

This book has used a large number of examples to offer a wider view of culture. British culture, of course, includes an increasingly diverse representation of the great, good and worthy of history, but must also reflect a society positively enriched and transformed by invited and inevitable immigration from countries of the old English-speaking empire. Its culture has been further enhanced by a long tradition of welcome to those fleeing injustice from other parts of the world. We are a diverse society and our curriculum should demonstrate and celebrate it.

There is another kind of culture too. Defined by Robinson as: 'The shared values and patterns of behaviour that characterise different social groups and communities' (NACCCE, 1999, p. 47), this culture is more intimate and can endlessly be created and recreated. Each school and classroom can create its own culture as argued in Chapter 1 and this book has maintained throughout that a school culture should be a positive one. Hopefully, this chapter has filled out the concept of a school culture that reflects today's society more equitably and provides all children and teachers the attitudes and skills to build good things into it.

Global connections

The pandemic demonstrated quickly the reality of our global interconnections. Within two months of its discovery, Covid-19 had travelled from China to most countries in Europe and North America. By the end of 2020, there were outbreaks in almost every country in the world. Our world is inextricably connected by disease, pollution, warming and loss of biodiversity just as much as it is by communication technologies, trade, commerce, financial crises, travel, tourism and ideas. We cannot avoid being global citizens. Yet many primary school curricula fail to represent this reality. The current low priority of the global perspective follows from overlapping phenomena that include: nationalism, local and geo-political resistance to recognising global inter-relationships, inadequate teacher education, media and often cultural disinterest in global matters. As a consequence, the word 'global' occurs just three times in the whole of the primary curriculum for England. 'World', often in the sense of domain, is mentioned ten times in the geography and science curricula and six in both history and English. The languages curriculum refers to the world once and art, mathematics, music, PE and D&T don't mention it at all. The Global Learning Programme (website) attempts to address this lack.

When perspectives from other cultures are ignored, schools miss important, social and cross-curricular opportunities to:

- acknowledge global interdependence
- address the disadvantages of nationalism
- consider the experiences and thoughts of others living in very different situations
- broaden experience and thinking within the subject disciplines
- promote critical thinking by addressing contrasting perspectives
- think about the 'bigger picture' on a range of global issues
- understand inclusive principles in practice
- recognise the reality of children's online global links outside school life
- think about an increasingly globalised future
- confront global issues from a global perspective
- discuss global inequalities and solutions
- confirm the universality of some human values

Returning to values in the context of the global is intentional. Most inclusive values are recognisable across cultures (Barnes, 2019). Children of all ages understand values, in their age-appropriate ways, and can talk about them and apply them. Consider the inclusive values below identified by Booth in Figure 7.2.

THINKING CAREFULLY ABOUT THE WHOLE CURRICULUM | 143

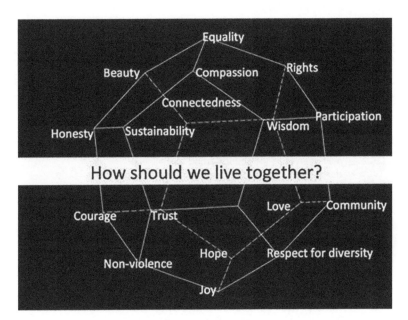

Figure 7.2 Inclusive values: How should we live together? (Booth, 2018)

Each of the values listed and linked in the diagram above, when explained, will have some level of meaning for even the youngest child. Every value has an example or its opposite in their lives (see also the 'Excluding values' diagram in Booth's 2018 paper). When I talk about a meaningful education it is about an education, a curriculum, founded upon such values that appear to have meaning across the globe. What can the application of such values look like in a global education context?

Table 7.6 Some examples of primary school projects that develop the idea of global connections

Subject	Global connections vignette	Some inclusive values introduced/developed
Art and Design	*Kintsugi in Japan:* A Japanese potter came and explained how in her tradition often the broken pot or an unplanned irregularity in its making or glazing was considered the most beautiful and natural thing – this approach of valuing imperfection is known as *wabi sabi*. Sometimes breakages and errors are highlighted by filling them with gold – this process is called *kintsugi*. Children followed this up by making their own pots more freely, keeping the imperfections, celebrating the mistakes and taking close-up photos of irregularities in nature and decaying things in the world around them.	*Beauty* *Respect for diversity*

(Continued)

Table 7.6 Some examples of primary school projects that develop the idea of global connections (Continued)

Subject	Global connections vignette	Some inclusive values introduced/developed
Music and dance	*Gamelan in Bali:* Gamelan (literally 'to hammer') is a type of percussive music from southeast Asia. A Gamelan ensemble is a highly collaborative group of often over 20 players playing different sized metallophones, gongs and drums. Gamelan music serves as the sound setting for Balinese dance-drama stories of the Hindu gods. The music is written down, not in western notation but in a series of number patterns. Children in a Year 4 class in Cardiff were introduced to this music and dance by a member of the local Indonesian community and shown how the music was constructed. Their teacher then took up the idea and showed children how to construct simple number patterns and turn these into music using a pentatonic scale similar to the traditional Balinese scale. Children developed the idea by combining into xylophone or metallophone groups and performing their own 'question and answer' musical performances using number notation.	Community Beauty Participation
Science and geography	*Conserving Orangutan in Sabah, Malaysia:* A primary school in Chester worked on a project with Chester Zoo on conserving Orangutan – a seriously endangered species. They found that the deforestation of large parts of the Sabah forest where orangutans live, were being replaced by huge oil palm plantations. The school made links with a primary school in Sabah that had taken part in a government-sponsored environmental education project. Now the Chester and the Malaysian school are working on conservation awareness and Chester has become the world's first 'Sustainable Palm Oil city'.	Sustainability Rights Hope
Geography and oracy	*Way finding in the DRC:* In Hastings a Congolese resident told a Year 3 class about his life as a cattle herder in the Democratic Republic of Congo. He told them how as an 8-year-old he was in charge of a whole herd of family cattle and had to take them to fresh grazing. His parents trusted him completely to do this. With no maps or broadband he had to find his way to grazing and find his way back home. He only had trees and hills and rivers to guide him. Later in their geography lesson children were taken to the local park to construct verbal way-finding instructions for their classmates to find a hidden treasure using only descriptions of trees and small variations in the landscape to guide them.	Trust Courage

(Continued)

Table 7.6 Some examples of primary school projects that develop the idea of global connections *(Continued)*

Subject	Global connections vignette	Some inclusive values introduced/developed
RE and English	*Sacred groves in India:* The parent of a Year 1 child in a Glasgow infant school came to tell the pupils a story about a sacred grove near her mother's home in Kerala, India. The grove of trees is highly protected along with about 100,000 other sacred groves. It cannot be destroyed or built upon and often contains small monuments and offerings to the deities and spirits that are believed to live there. Children in the class chose their own sacred grove of protected trees and bushes at the end of their school grounds. They decided to build some small gifts for the trees out of stones, branches and leaves and took their favourite toys to sit near them. They took photos of their special place, the gifts and their toy animals in the peaceful grove they had identified and used them as illustrations for a group story which they wrote and shared with the Year 2 class next door. They also learned about sacred spaces near their school.	*Sustainability* *Non-violence*
Computing and geography	*Class zoom links with Kakuma:* A Year 6 class in Norwich made links with a teacher in Kakuma refugee camp in Kenya – one of the largest refugee camps in the world. Each week the teacher collected different groups of 6 refugee children from different countries in Africa, took them to an office with a laptop and broadband and joined in a 40-minute Q and A Zoom call.	*Connectedness* *Equality*

Vignettes from a range of UK and world classrooms will give you an idea of what taking a global connections approach can look (and sound) like.

Connecting the disciplines

Throughout this chapter themes and classroom examples were chosen for their cross-curricular nature. The first chapters stressed that cross-curricular/transdisciplinary approaches are recommended as just one part of the curriculum experience of the primary school. It is important to avoid binaries. This book makes the suggestion that a motivating, rounded curriculum should be a mix of imaginative, creative, exciting subject-based teaching *and* cross-curricular opportunities to put new learning into practice as skills. This is the double-focus approach proposed in Barnes (2018) (see Figure 7.3).

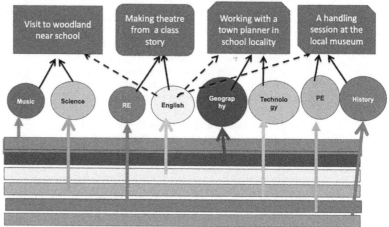

Aim: to balance subject knowledge with meaningful interdisciplinary experience.

Figure 7.3 Double focus cross-curricular learning

When we look around it is clear that the made world is a product of a coalition of many disciplines. The chair you are sitting on, the room you live in, your mode of transport, your laptop, mobile and the platforms you use and the medicines you take were all created by the coming together of cross-disciplinary teams. We only get close to fully understanding the natural environment if we consider it through several lenses. Seeing the trees outside our window through the eyes of poetry, geography and history helps us appreciate them more. Better understanding of our bicycle or car requires knowledge of science and design/technology. We might use a fusion of ideas from PE, PSHE, citizenship and perhaps RE as guidance to keep our bodies and minds healthy. All of these examples will be enhanced by the application of English, mathematics and science and computing. Trans-disciplinarity will need to increase as humanity faces the global crises listed at the beginning of this book. Indeed, the human race as a species has no hope unless we and the subjects collaborate much, much more to solve the world's problems.

Rising social disadvantage and inequality is a particular problem for the UK. Teachers and the curriculum they plan can be part of the solution to this. The socially and economically disadvantaged, those with special educational needs and disabilities, those that just think differently and the many who have delays and gaps in learning due to the pandemic must not receive a reduced curriculum. It needs to be significantly more inclusive to address both the world's and the nation's problems. To include and enthral more children, the curriculum must be:

- **positive** – aiming for each child to feel secure, safe and flourishing
- **broader** – offering a wide range of choices to help them find their passion
- **more relevant** – relating to their locality and world
- **meaningful** – offering them multiple chances to think about the meaning of life

- **an exciting experience** – providing frequent opportunities to apply and deepen new learning
- **collaborative** – building their social intelligence
- **confidence-building** – recognising that an uncertain future requires them to be confident individuals
- **compassionate** – maximising upon skills that distinguish humans from AI
- **creative** – building mindsets and approaches to cope with an unpredictable future
- **memorable** – the knowledge for a successful life is seated in the long-term memory

Bringing the disciplines together is one way of addressing the need for breadth, relevance and experience described above. Experience of over 50 years in education tells me clearly, however, that cross-curricular learning is not the only way to make the curriculum more inclusive, effective and memorable, but it is a way. Neither are traditional methods, silent corridors, smart uniforms or a relentless focus on teacher as the fount of all knowledge, exclusive routes to educational success, despite working for some. As teachers, we know children well enough to avoid the 'one size fits all' mentality that so easily creeps into education debates and policy. We should resist the temptation to think in binaries like traditional versus progressive, experience versus facts, establishment versus common-sense, child versus teacher-centred, because children are demonstrably individuals. Different children respond to different approaches and respond differently at different times. They always have, regardless of the dominant education philosophy. A curriculum should accommodate these variables and be multi-faceted.

The cross-curricular approaches I have outlined in other books take account of these differences. The more formal double-focus approach has already been mentioned, but some children, some*times,* respond positively to opportunistic approaches (see Figure 7.4) where they are free to focus on what strikes them as interesting.

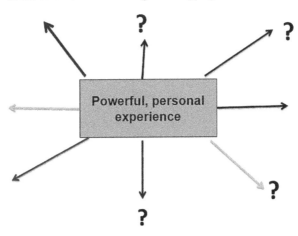

Figure 7.4 Opportunistic cross-curricular learning

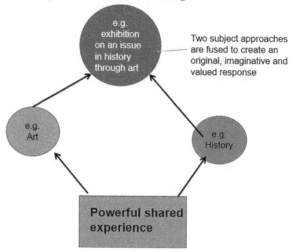

Figure 7.5 Inter-disciplinary cross-curricular learning

Others are excited and learn from a more focused creative approach where specific learning in two or three subject perspectives combine to make something demonstrably original, as in inter-disciplinary cross-curricular learning (see Figure 7.5).

There are those for whom the stimulus is more important. They may feel happier to interpret one emotionally powerful experience in two different ways, as in multi-disciplinary cross-curricular learning (see Figure 7.6).

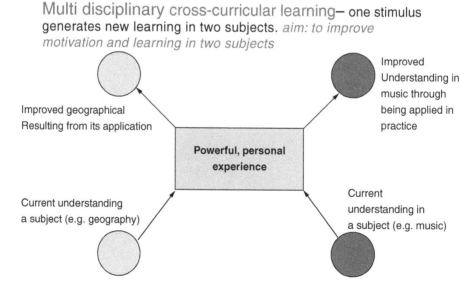

Figure 7.6 Multi-disciplinary cross-curricular learning

Sometimes a bigger theme is so rich and varied that two subject perspectives are not enough to fully appreciate its significance. In these times it may be necessary to take time and energy to interpret that powerful experience in a larger number of ways in what I have called theme-based cross-curricular learning (see Figure 7.7).

Theme-based *cross-curricular learning* — a significant theme is explored through the eyes of several different subjects *aim: to allow the widest range of learners to enter into a powerful experience*

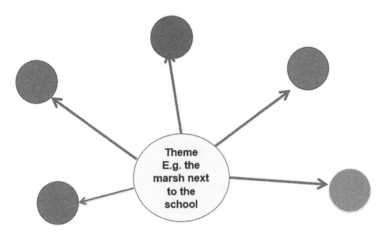

Figure 7.7 Theme-based cross-curricular learning

On other occasions you may wish to emphasise the importance of one particular subject. To deepen understanding of its significance you may ask children to look at it from the perspective of several other subjects (see Figure 7.8). How do historians use English language and how is English different when geographers use it? Are there ways of using words

Single Transferable Subject cross-curricular learning – one subject is developed in its relationship to other subjects in turn *aim: to deepen single subject learning from many angles*

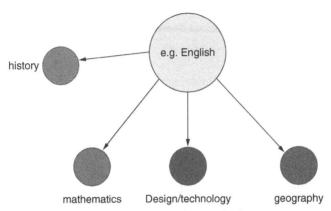

Figure 7.8 Single transferable subject cross-curricular learning

that make English more like art? How do we use English differently in Design Technology or maths? To answer such questions, we may use the Single transferable subject mode of cross-curricular learning.

For those children that like a safe and motivating route into a subject they are more uncertain of, a hierarchical approach where one subject provides a 'way in' to another may be appropriate (see Figure 7.9). In hierarchical cross-curricular learning, science for example, may be used as an entry point to a bigger art project, or an English idea like a poem or piece of descriptive writing might take children into a music composition exercise.

Hierarchical cross-curricular learning – one subject used to support learning in another discipline, aim: to deepen learning in one subject by using another as an entry point

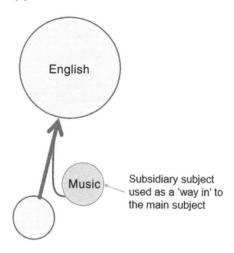

Figure 7.9 Hierarchical cross-curricular learning

Traditional and progressive approaches to learning are easily combined. The double-focus approach introduced earlier (Figure 7.3) depends upon traditional subject-based learning throughout the year. However, this teaching is interrupted roughly every six weeks by opportunities practically and creatively to apply new knowledge and skills from two or three subjects to planned authentic, relevant experiences or problems. In this method traditional and progressive methods are ever-present, both with equal weight. Their combination offers a more holistic inclusive experience of education. This approach will be illustrated in Chapter 8.

There is a time for formality and rote learning, a time for freedom and open-endedness. Paying more attention to cross-curricular approaches does not imply lack of structure or rigour – indeed, the best cross-curricular learning has to be even more carefully planned. It will include big, overarching questions, the development of new knowledge as well as the application of newly learned skills and very clear learning objectives or end points. You as a teacher need to decide on the balance between the freedoms and creativities of cross-curricular learning and sometimes more formal approaches common in separate subject teaching. The balance will be different for each teacher and possibly each class. Try out some of the ideas and see what suits you.

Summary

The curriculum is the totality of learning experience a child has in a school. This chapter has attempted to make you aware of the paramount importance of well-planned, well-sequenced, knowledge-rich curricula in making that experience positive. It has also argued that an effective primary curriculum should enable and excite all children and include the many that currently experience barriers to their learning. It reminds you that most curriculum decisions are controlled by teachers and adults, but some unplanned aspects are generated by other children, the attitudes and mood of teachers, the general atmosphere and ethos of the school and a host of accidental, unexpressed aspects of the hidden curriculum. Sometimes these learning environments coherently and positively sit together; sometimes they are in conflict or inconsistent with each another. A curriculum only becomes truly successful when philosophy and values are shared, held and understood by all in and with the school. This book has argued those values should be inclusive and positive and that as far as possible teachers should embody positivity.

The chapter developed the concept of a 'connecting curriculum'. It argued that connections inspired by excellent and expert teachers help children link their own lives to the curriculum. It suggested a range of attributes that mark out a connecting primary school curriculum, including:

- keeping the palette of subjects as broad as possible to allow children maximum opportunity to discover their passions
- teaching approaches that enhance children's mental and physical well-being
- connecting all subject teaching to humanising characteristics like confidence, compassion, creativity and care
- teaching attitudes such as tenacity and a growth mindset to develop greater resilience
- ensuring a logical progression of knowledge, skills and end points in each subject
- combining pairs of subjects to address particular issues and questions
- setting out to create a school culture unique to its locality, community and chosen values
- connecting all subjects and questions to aspects of identity, community, locality and the interconnected world upon which we depend

Connection through the disciplines brought the chapter to its end. It offered examples of seven ways in which subjects might be combined and asserted that combining subjects to interpret powerfully engaging experiences, effectively motivates new, deeper and more easily retained learning. Teachers and student teachers are encouraged to try out some of the ideas and gauge the balance right for them.

8
EMBODYING POSITIVE PEDAGOGY IN A DIVERSE UK

Objectives

In this chapter we will dwell on sensory, social, physical and emotional experiences for children, that draw on aspects of humanity that are shared regardless of perceived ability or cultural or linguistic diversity. It will:

- Examine concepts of human diversity
- Stress aspects of commonality that can form the basis of a truly inclusive curriculum
- Offer 11 case studies that use embodied experience to generate meaningful links between subject disciplines
- Outline essentials for the effective assessment of cross-curricular projects
- Demonstrate the importance of social, moral, spiritual and cultural (SMSC) education in bringing the curriculum together
- Value the contribution of other languages

Introduction

Human diversity and the creativity it engenders is closely linked to human survival. There are many kinds of diversity. Differences in language, religion, tradition, history, attitude, physique, neurology, gifts, talent, skin colour, facial features, sexual orientation, gender expression, family or social class and structure and personal experience, both divide and define us. The concept of cultural diversity brings together some of these differences, yet the same variables also describe the variations in character between twins brought up in the same family. My autoethnographic research (Barnes, 2012) suggested some diversities may also be *within* us, in that we may hold sometimes conflicting views and responses in different settings or different times of our lives. Despite being a feature of our human-ness, diversity remains a central cause of tension between communities. While the importance of biodiversity has increasingly been seen as vital to human survival, views about cultural diversity remain sharply divided in the UK and USA (Dempster et al., 2020). Even within 'British culture', children with a linguistic code at variance with notions of 'received pronunciation', 'good' grammar and vocabulary are commonly excluded and disadvantaged – their lived experience is treated as a deficit (Cushing, 2022). Throughout this book, ideas and approaches that celebrate the beauties of human diversity have been presented, but it has not examined the concept of cultural diversity itself, which in the UK is still seen by many as a threat to social, political and economic stability (Migration Observatory, 2022). Schools are charged through their responsibility to teach 'British values' to help build more positive public responses to human diversity; therefore, modelling community harmony, integration and justice is a major educational duty. Developing harmony involves illuminating human commonalities as well as respecting and benefiting from our differences. The teacher that cares about justice will seek to counter inequality and discrimination in their personal attitudes as well as their curriculum planning. Positive pedagogues embrace cultural and personal diversity at the same time as celebrating the many things we share.

The case studies will illustrate how our commonalities can be used to involve and include. They will also show how in an affirmative educational environment the child's voice and experience can become an integral part of lesson planning, delivery and assessment.

Cultural diversity

British attitudes to cultural diversity have deep historical roots. An ongoing narrative of the 'never-invaded' island nation has existed since 1066. The legacy of Empire and relentless export of English language over the past 400 years has meant that the United Kingdom is often considered to have become one of the most diverse countries in the world. Some have even coined the term 'superdiversity' to describe UK society (Economist, 2021). Neither perception is wholly accurate; Britain is not as diverse as many think. Although the majority estimate that immigrants form 24% of the UK population, the actual number is 13%. Many countries of the world are much more diverse than the UK (Goren, 2013; World Population Review, 2022). The 20 most ethnically diverse countries of the world are all in Africa. Measures of linguistic diversity place Papua New Guinea as the world leader with 840 separate languages, each with its own way of understanding reality (World Economic Forum, 2021). Singapore ranks highest in religious diversity (Pew, 2013). If we define culture as involving shared religion, language, values and behaviours, Chad with its vast spaces and widely spaced tribal groups is the most culturally diverse country in the world. In comparison with 180 other nations in some measures the UK ranks 139th in cultural and ethnic diversity.

There is little scientific basis for defining diversity along racial or ethnic lines. The largely 19th-century beliefs in ethnic difference were strongly contradicted by the Human Genome Project (see National Human Genome Research Institute website). The genetic diversity of races or ethnicities is now seen to be largely a social construct. There is very little genetic difference between the DNA of an African, an Asian, a Polynesian, a Native American or a European. Indeed, two individuals taken randomly from two different places in the world are more likely to have genetic similarities than two taken from the same country and ethnicity (Witherspoon et al., 2007). The boom in private DNA testing to explore individual ancestry confirms a wide genetic mix amongst most Europeans and Americans.

Overlapping concepts of racial and cultural diversity partly explain beliefs in the UK's superdiversity. Certainly, the nationals of many countries live there, but culturally the UK population is not exceptionally diverse. Observable differences like skin colour tell us little about beliefs, values, behaviours, religion or language, yet many assume skin colour is a prime indicator of diversity. The 90 million population of the Democratic Republic of Congo (DRC) may not *look* culturally diverse to white Europeans, but the DRC is one of the most linguistically and culturally diverse countries of the world, with over 200 languages and distinctive cultures. On the other hand, we might expect Brazil, with its visible mix of native, African and immigrant European populations, to have a high degree of cultural diversity, but it ranks among the least culturally diverse nations (World Population Review, 2022). Positive pedagogues should not be distracted by colour; indeed, it appears they may be much less likely to see it (Johnson and Fredrickson, 2005).

Commonality

The idea of community cohesion underlies the responsibility of schools to deliver the values of democracy, the rule of law, individual liberty, mutual respect and tolerance of those with different faiths and beliefs (DfE, 2014). Building a tolerant, respectful, democratic society should affect the teaching of every subject but also the lives and attitudes of every teacher outside school. Social as well as personal well-being must, therefore, be at the centre of positive approaches to teacher recruitment and retention as well as their pedagogy and curriculum in school. Well-being should not be a surprising theme – at interview most prospective teachers express in some way, their desire to make the world a better place through education. Well-being in education starts with that of the teacher and should continue in settings that appreciate and continually make use of the infinitely varied mix of similarities and differences between us. Basing a curriculum and pedagogy on human diversity and commonality should be a fundamental expectation for the 21st-century teacher, yet initial and in-service training spends little time on them.

When education begins with what unites us, all can feel included, but many feel, and are, excluded. Despite central government policies over the last 20 years, high degrees of educational inequality in British society have remained (Nuffield, 2022a). Left without external interference, educationalists, teachers and schools are well equipped through research and daily experience, to address the inequity so evident in the country. They might begin by reducing tendencies to favour one accent, language code or social class over another. They could make their classrooms and schools models of a society where the divisions between children are minimised and the gap between the adult and child's world is diminished. Tackling educational inequality begins by seeking, honouring and using human common human traits in the curricula we devise and the teaching styles we adopt. From early years to adolescence these commonalities are more often expressed through our bodies, senses, emotions and the powerful experiences that we share. An education heavily weighted towards the intellectual, linguistic and logical misses out on much that unites us and distinguishes us from machines (see Chapter 5).

Education policy in England is in danger of becoming more exclusive. Creativity, personal relevance, the child's voice, major global concerns, living in diverse communities and the spiritual/moral meaning or 'soul' of education, are words largely absent from official education guidance to primary schools and teacher education (Gov.UK, 2019b; Gov.UK, 2019c). More inclusive and positive approaches require a holistic approach that, of course, teaches and exercises 'the basics' but balances the three Rs with an equal focus on the mental, social, spiritual and physical characteristics we share:

- Our bodies
- Our senses
- Our physical needs
- Our values
- Our emotions
- Our experiences

Children are highly conscious of these developing and humanising aspects of self. Each characteristic develops rapidly as they grow and schooling can help children understand, manage and use them. Below are a few examples of how these shared attributes can form starting points for the development of knowledge and experience in and across the curriculum subjects.

Our bodies

In PE and games

Our bodies form an appropriate starting point to consider human commonalities. The vocabulary, workings and measurements of the human body are frequently the subject of Early Years and infant topics. We chart growth in weight and height, handspan and shoe size, senses, skills and the science of breathing. These are rightly captivating and highly relevant to children increasingly aware of their own uniqueness, but the body can form a theme throughout primary education. Balance, articulation, strength, safety, precision and exercise need equal attention as the child develops – PE, dance and sports take children further along this route.

Sports provide an international language of communication, cooperation and friendly competition. The rapid rise in popularity of women's football, the high international status of the Olympic, Commonwealth and European Games and worldwide televising of major sporting events greatly adds to the sense that sport represents a meeting place for all. Sensitively planned, communicated and evaluated in school, PE and games are a major force for inclusion. Energetic physical involvement contributes to our mental, physical and social health and should be an often revisited theme in science and PSHE since they powerfully connect active bodily experience with all-round health. Primary teachers with specialisms in science will help you identify and devise testable scientific hypotheses on the physical and mental impact of games and exercise throughout the primary years. PE specialists will share their expertise on the social benefits of sport and exercise.

Schools are in a good position to maximise on the popularity of sport when welcoming newcomers to their community. Even without new class members, PE and games offer countless opportunities to teach about globally understood values like fair play, teamwork, generosity and friendly competition. The global representation evident in our national teams effectively illustrates ways that its international language crosses national boundaries. Some schools, for example, are already using football, racquet sports and other games to help integrate newly arrived young refugees and other migrants – even before they are allocated school places. A quote from an online school magazine expresses sport's role in bringing people together (Gravesend Grammar, 2019).

> The [Naaz Coker] project … seeks to provide relaxed, 'down time' for local and newly arrived unaccompanied young people through Wednesday afternoon sport…. Relaxed because there is no agenda apart from friendship, 'down time' because the focus is on enjoying participation with other young people in the fun and largely wordless activity of games. Many of these children will have had traumatic journeys to the UK, having already escaped unimaginable violence and tension and they need space to be just normal young people. There is good research and convincing anecdotal evidence to suggest that the use of arts, sports and contact with local peers supports them to become more quickly and sustainably integrated into their host communities. (2019, p. 10)

The basic rules of most sports are quickly understood without the need for complex language. A full game of football, table tennis or basketball can be very successfully completed to fully include young people with no English, through the use of international gestures and sounds of beckoning, disappointment, triumph and joy. Full participation is relatively easy to generate, praise easily communicated and disappointment genuinely shared. Displays around school should make it possible for all to find recognisable models of excellence in the names and faces of diverse and international sporting heroes and heroines.

Safe movement, stretching, balancing, supporting and extending physical capabilities, are always part of PE teaching. The controlled but cooperative nature of exercise and physical development in PE again needs little language and when presented positively can quickly involve children of all abilities and backgrounds. Alongside their primary responsibility for safety and a good knowledge of children's physical development, the positive pedagogue is sensitive to the reality of different abilities, preferences and feelings. Positive teachers are continually open to learning different ways to involve, encourage and inspire learners. The teaching of movement and dance in PE in Case Study 8.1 offers pointers as to how it can be linked with other curriculum areas and life outside school. Dance and other kinds of rhythmic, symbolic movement are common to all cultures and form an essentially wordless and potentially inclusive medium of communication and enjoyment for all. The case study uses emotion, knowledge of the body and physical experience to generate skills and knowledge in each category.

Case Study 8.1

Thinking about home

A class of Year 5 children worked with an aerial theatre company to think about the feelings of those who have left home. The leader began by giving each child a key to hold. Children were asked to lie in a circle on the floor of the school hall, holding the key close to their heart. They had a soft cloth to cover their eyes. They were then guided to visualise their first home, imagining their key unlocking its door. What does it look like outside? Is it a house or a flat or a room? Does it have windows? How many? What is the door like, the entrance hall? Does it have shoes and coats in it? What sounds can you hear there, outside, inside? What smells? What can you feel? The temperature, is it cold or hot? What is your room like, its walls, its floor, the things inside?

After the visualisation exercise the drama practitioner asked the children to share their memories with a partner. Many discovered overlaps and similarities in their stories. They also spoke about the people in their community that had recently moved there from a different country and spoke about what they might feel.

The children then went on to use a range of theatre games and expert support to develop gestures and movements that expressed comfort, security, community. After this they thought of other movements in groups of three that described the feelings and fears of parting, leaving home and new beginnings.

The theatre company specialised in aerial theatre and had suspended a set of harnesses just a metre or so above the hall floor. Their experience was that thinking and acting silently but suspended a little above normal reality, helped children think and act differently and more creatively. After preparation games and movements the children were taught how to get into the harnesses, move gently within them and create 'cocoons' in which to make simple yoga-like movements to express home-feelings of security, peace and comfort, moving on to make movements of connection between one cocoon and another. These activities formed the beginnings of physical theatre that expressed friendship and community. The end point was to perform a simple aerial dance expressing home, moving away and making new friends.

Case Study 8.1 illustrates connections between guided storytelling and physical education with a social purpose. After this physical and emotional experience of embodied thinking and sharing about home and what it means, the children worked in class about the places of home for the migrant families that had moved to their area. They also learned greetings and food names in the languages of the migrant families. The wider intention was to encourage empathy, welcome and friendship in the community.

Our senses

The human senses of smell, taste, hearing, sight and touch are the first faculties to develop. All form in utero, indeed the sense of touch begins to develop around 8 weeks after gestation. Smell and taste are probably the 'oldest' of the senses (Sarafoleanu et al., 2009). The fine balance of the senses is again a distinctive human characteristic, yet touch, smell and taste rarely form part of our lesson planning or curriculum. Education of, about, and with the senses is largely absent from guidance on subject teaching beyond science. So much is missing from government guidance it is for teachers to agree, school by school on what will make statutory education requirements generate personal meaning for children. Consciousness of meaning through using the senses to secure individual 'buy in' for learning multiplies the chances of provoking motivation, engagement and deep, transferable learning. Case Study 8.2 illustrates how one school constructed sensory starting points among its Year 1 and 2 children.

Case Study 8.2

Sensory trails in Canary Wharf

The Infant department in a school near Canary Wharf decided to use its central location for a series of sensory trails. Mixed groups of Year 1 and Year 2 children were allocated two senses each and with their TA, a prepared parent or their teacher, followed two trails during a morning visit to the area near the underground station.

Those on the TOUCH walk had to take photos of different materials and choose from a set of adjectives to describe the textures, temperatures and vibrations found in seven distinct locations: cold, warm, smooth, rough, still, shaking, shiny, spiky, dusty, clean, soft, spongy, sharp, bumpy, and so on. They were also asked to add their own words to describe the trees, walls, floors, railings and building materials they came across.

The SMELL groups walked with their TA using a simple map. At each of six stopping places (waterside, shopping centre, office entrance, roadside, garden, café, etc.) they had to stop and gently smell and then discuss in pairs what they noticed. At the end of their walk they were asked to grade the smells from favourite to least favourite.

The two groups of six children considering TASTE had been invited to sample pizza ingredients at a small restaurant. They had to decide between bitter, sour, sweet, savoury, salty, strong and weak tastes and were surprised how different some of their decisions were. They shared the pizzas they made with the rest of their class.

Those investigating SIGHT had two jobs. Their TA had prepared colour swatches from a paint supplier, each with different strengths of green or grey or brown or blue. Each swatch, covered with double-sided transparent tape, was given to a pair of children. The children had to find stickable examples of exact matches for the colours on their swatch as they walked around pre-planned locations. The second task was to use the class iPad to take photos of six different objects in the area that shared the same colour.

SOUND groups were asked to walk to five contrasting areas on a simple map of the area. In each new place they had to stand still and silent for 2 minutes and capture in symbols or words the sounds they could hear to their left, their right, in front of them and behind them (see Figure 8.1).

The conversations between children and their adult helpers involved in Case Study 8.2 were revealing. Some children had not realised that sounds were directional, some had never described a taste or a touch before, many were surprised how accurate their colour discernment was. Their teachers were offered multiple aspects to follow up. Developing the sensory walks and information collected involved mounting an exhibition of findings illustrated with further research. Some Year 2 children also asked how the eye works and their teacher devised a lesson with models, diagrams and further practical experiments on the workings of the eye. Children themselves requested to do another 'smell walk', this time around the school and its playground and found their discrimination between smells had improved.

Our common physical needs

In Design/technology

All humans need warmth, shelter, safety, love, food and water. Each essential offers countless opportunities for development across the curriculum. Human needs have generated ingenious design technology solutions from adapting a cave to building high rise flats, hand axes to power drills. Our daily need for food has powered food technologies in every culture. Food's fundamental importance means that language use food as metaphor and subject of intense conversation across the world. For example, the English word 'companion' links the two Latin words *com* (meaning together) and *panis* (bread) to literally mean 'one who shares bread with you'. Linking food with friendship expresses something of its social role. Food obviously powers our bodies, but talking about it and sharing it builds community, cements relationships, establishes trust and expresses shared values, Case Study 8.3 illustrates one way in which food may be used in establishing a connecting and positive curriculum.

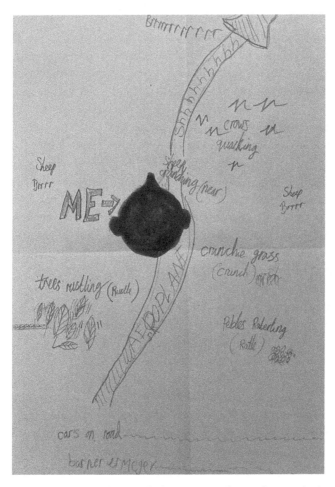

Figure 8.1 Children were asked to mark the sources of sound around a bird's eye view of their head (Photo: Barnes)

Case Study 8.3

Food and community building

Teachers and children in a nursery and infant school devoted extended lunchtimes every Wednesday to eating and singing together. Parents and carers brought and shared Somali, Ethiopian, Turkish, Pakistani and Jamaican food and each week were taught a children's song from the home culture of one of the attending adults. These simple and universal human activities were seen by parents and staff as building better communication between each other. During the 2020 pandemic many parents and carers who had established friendships through this sharing, supported each other in continuing inclusive and distanced activities in the streets surrounding the nursery (Barnes, 2021).

In Case Study 8.3, creativity arose from the unique mix of food, song, languages, cultural diversity and the human tendency to build community. After just a few weeks' involvement, parents/carers had made new connections with each other and were meeting outside school, sharing the school run and bringing new songs to the meetings. Children and teachers took their new songs back to class and added them to the class repertoire of 'clear up' or 'start the day' songs.

The food in our lives also confirms the fact of globalisation. The UK has around 10,000 Indian, Bangladeshi, Pakistani or Sri Lankan restaurants employing some 60,000 people and contributing more than 3 billion pounds to the economy. There are a further 5,000 Chinese, Thai, Singaporean, Japanese, Malaysian and Vietnamese restaurants and takeaways. Together with the many Italian, Spanish, Greek, Turkish, Lebanese, Mexican, Creole and Caribbean eating places, the UK has an incomparable range of different cuisines. While a 'Sunday Roast' remains Britain's most popular meal, pizza, spaghetti, lasagne, fajitas, chili con carne and chicken curry – all foreign imports – remain in the top 12 of favourite foods (Independent, 2021).

Educational engagement with food can be used to generate discussions on climate change, global resources, customs, cultural preferences, globalisation, interdependence and the ethics of world trade. A class cookery lesson such as constructing a vegetable curry, pizza, fried rice or fruit salad dish can be used to illustrate our global interconnections. So too can a visit to the local supermarket.

Your local supermarket sells products from a wide range of countries of the world. For a class session on the global aspects of UK food, purchase a range of foods from other countries. Many supermarket chains are generous with vouchers for food-based school projects. You may find the country of origin of most vegetables and fruits in the fresh food shelves. A brief survey is likely to indicate many are grown in distant countries like Kenya, Zimbabwe, Egypt, Israel, Morocco, The Canaries, Puerto Rico. Look also for spices and tinned fruits like pineapple, guava or lychees which often show the place of origin on their labels. In the flower section you may be surprised to find red roses from Kenya – one of Europe's main suppliers of cut flowers. Case Study 8.4 provides an example of how one teacher developed their supermarket visit.

Case Study 8.4

Globalisation in the supermarket

A Cardiff primary school used its supermarket purchases and food technology sessions to link science, geography and PSHE responses. After making labelled drawings of cross-sections of some of the imported fruits and vegetables, showing their structures and main features, children in Year 4 went on to make fruit salads, spicy rice and vegetable curry with the ingredients. They invited parents and carers to share in their dishes after school. These experiences motivated classwork on:

- Maps and graphs of the countries represented in their dishes
- Climates in the places of origin (e.g. children found fresh green beans and mangetout peas came from Kenya and discussed what this told them about the climate in parts of Kenya. They were asked to consider why they come all the way from Kenya if we can grow them?)
- Fair trade (e.g. children watched videos about tea and coffee production and considered the time and effort taken to harvest and process them. They discussed what had generated the idea of 'fair trade' and decided on ways the school could respond in its purchases)
- Supermarket pricing (e.g. Mangetout or snow peas cost around £1 for a small packet, yet the daily wage in Zimbabwe for collecting enough peas for hundreds of packs is little more than £1 – what does this tell us about global inequalities?)
- Discussions on the contrasting range of seasonal foodstuffs in shops available in their linked school in a small town in Uganda

---

The large variety of responses to class discussions and food-based activities in Case Study 8.4 generated many contrasting results. The class teacher was able to follow the interests of several groups of children. Their detailed drawings of cut fruit and vegetables sparked multiple and highly varied questions and ideas. Some children were keen to try out recipes with their foods, others were inspired to make fabric designs based on repeated prints using star fruit, pineapple slices, figs and coconut halves. Their drawings were used in science to provoke further analysis and words like Exocarp, mesocarp, endocarp, seed while others produced large-sized and simplified vegetable paintings in the style of artists Christopher Dina or Mary Feddern.

Our common values

In English and foreign languages

The concept of 'human universals' (Brown, 1992) suggests hundreds of commonalities apply across human communities past and present and beyond the shared need for food, shelter, nurture and security. Among these universals there are certain common values, for example: care and healing, conflict resolution, empathy, fairness, family, hope, hospitality, respect for law, sharing and taking turns. Since it is likely that every culture respects such values, it is highly probable that individuals in any class are familiar with and care about them.

Knowledge of shared values should inform a positive approach across the curriculum: turn-taking may be highlighted in music-making, games or dance, sharing might be stressed in food technology and art work, examples of respecting the law in PSHE or history, and community hospitality emphasised in geography or RE.

The language we use and the foreign language examples we introduce should also address common human values.

In English, sentences, stories and poems about care, conflict, empathy and fairness are common, but when it comes to other languages our examples often stick to the simple and banal. Teaching and learning foreign languages can be more emotionally involving however. Case Study 8.5 captures one teacher's attempt to illustrate human commonalities by provoking simple statements and conversations about values.

Case Study 8.5

Human values through French language

A Year 6 class in Glasgow had weekly French lessons. Their teacher started a term's work by preparing a number of large viewfinders (see Figure 8.2) labelled with French words for some positive personal values with their English translations, such as: (*gentile*) kind, (*optimiste*) hopeful, (*pacificateur*) peace-maker, (*réfléchi*) thoughtful, (*modeste*) humble, (*accueillant*) welcoming, (*optimiste*) optimistic, (*honnête*) honest, (*équitable*) fair, (*joyeux*) joyful. The class was divided into random pairs and each partner was asked to choose a viewfinder containing a word that described a positive aspect of the personality of the other. They were then asked to photograph their partner looking through the frame keeping both face and key French word in focus.

Later, the class was taught how to make simple French sentences about their classmate using the key descriptive word. The printed photos and written sentences were then displayed in the classroom to celebrate the positive characteristics recognised in each child. In a subsequent lesson each person extended their understanding of the word by making further sentences.

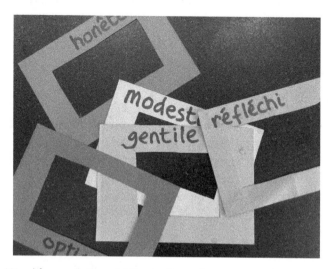

Figure 8.2 Word frames in French (Photo: Barnes)

Sharing our emotions

> **Case Study 8.6**

Emotional mapping in geography with creative writing about feelings

Schools are emotional places. Each school building has places where a child may feel insecure, happy, peaceful, sad, excited, safe, confident or interested. In a unit of work based on the plan of their school and its grounds, children in a Year 3/4 class were asked to make an 'emotional map' of the school. Throughout the day, their TA walked groups of four around the school and grounds with an A3 copy of an aerial view of their school taken by a drone. Supported by the TA, pupil groups first located their position on the photo and walked to pre-planned locations: entrance, stairs, the wild area, different parts of the playground, the outside toilets, the infants area, etc. In each place they shared feelings and memories about the place and labelled their photo with stickers that described their past or present emotions linked to the place. Discussions were rich and revealing.

The use of the school and grounds as a teaching resource continued when children were asked to visit parts of the site to 'collect' words. They took with them blank pages folded in half three times to make eight rectangular spaces. In twos and threes they were asked to visit a small chosen location in the school and take a short and reflective amble around the place. While on their walk they were each asked to write down random words (spelling and writing did not matter at this point) that came to mind. When they returned to their classroom, they were asked to tear out the rectangles filled with their words (see Figure 8.3) and try to construct a meaningful sentence using at least six of their collected words. They were allowed to add in any extra words or alter word endings if that helped their sentence make sense. When they had constructed their often quite poetic sentences each child pasted them onto 'their' place within an enlarged aerial photograph on their classroom wall.

The sentences constructed from random words generated from the short walk in Case Study 8.6 were undeniably creative. They had real meaning for the children because the work involved and validated their personal choices. The products were original, used their imaginations and were valued as such by their teacher and peers, fulfilling Robinson's definition of creativity (NACCCE, 1999). The emotional mapping exercise also had practical outcomes. The staff and students became newly sensitised to the physical areas of the school that felt uncomfortable to some and highlighted areas that might profitably be used as teaching resources more often.

Figure 8.3 Making sense of random words in place (Photo: Barnes)

Our shared experiences

School life should continually generate emotionally powerful shared experiences. Through authentic listening, doing, meeting, visiting, handling, making experiences children more easily become involved and motivated. The power of shared experience is often very evident in the last few weeks of primary school life. The end-of-Year 6 play, musical or activity holiday often serves as a 'rite of passage' for those transitioning from primary to secondary school, but was missing from the lives of children for two years. Teachers know that these trips and activities often become a nexus for meaningful learning, because the usual hierarchies and formalities are often relaxed, learning is outdoors or outside the normal confines of the classroom and timetable. They involve strongly defined meanings and end points. Achievements or deeply felt performances often culminate the experience.

Teachers at one school decided to use the Year 6 adventure trip to think about transition to Year 7 in a secondary school and other transitions. They articulated the idea of the adventure holiday being a kind of initiation into the new life they would follow in Year 7. Teachers were explicit about the many ways their activities would help their young people see the value of working with experts rather than generalists.

Consider the learning about self, confidence, growing up, peer support, change and friendship in the list shared by a school in Cornwall.

> **Case Study 8.7**
>
> On their adventure course in Cornwall children from a local Year 6 had choices between:
>
> - Using Zip wire suspended above magnificent views
> - Practising Bush craft, fire lighting, shelter building, cooking
> - Archery
> - Jumping from platforms into a flooded quarry
> - Designing and building rafts
> - Canoeing and kayaking
> - Rock climbing
>
> Back at school in the last week of Year 6, the children were given space to speak and write about the changes they had seen in themselves and the importance of the experience. Some spoke of new hopes, conquered fears, others of new achievements, some of new beauties and even of career choices. The teacher used this experiential focus on change and transition to introduce frank and open discussion and teaching on the physical, emotional and social changes they were about to see in themselves.

Assessing learning

Teachers continually assess. They could not get through a single lesson successfully without repeatedly making judgements on whether their words and actions were communicating their intentions. No dialogue between teacher and child would be effective unless each participant continually assessed the subtle, unsaid facial and body language between them alongside the words. Learners constantly assess too. Is this relevant, important, interesting to me? Am I going to get into trouble if I don't do it or don't do it well? Assessment does not just happen at the end of a session; it is probably always present somewhere in a classroom. Formal, planned assessment is, however, necessary to clarify if and what learning has taken place, what needs repeating, deleting, explaining, whether targets have been met and what should be the next step. Assessing the success of a lesson or unit of work should centrally concern itself with structural questions such as the ones shown in Table 8.1.

The questions in Table 8.1 are general and wide-ranging, but tell us little about the experience of or transformations within the individual child. For individual children the assessment questions have to be different. The meaning of education itself is different for them. Education for the individual may, for example, be thought of as:

Table 8.1 Structural teacher assessment

What was the overarching goal of this unit of work?
To what big question did this unit seek an answer?
What role was this lesson expected to play in reaching the overarching goal/answering the question?
Did the lesson/unit achieve the goal for all, some, a few or none?
What percentage of children were engaged in this lesson/unit?
What support was needed?
Did the session change children's minds or behaviours in any other way?
What were the positive knowledge outcomes?
What were the positive skills outcomes?
What were the positive attitude outcomes?
What unexpected outcomes arose?
What problems in understanding arose?
What skills would have helped achieve the objectives better?
What knowledge needed to be added to improve learning?
What needs changing?
What are the next steps in learning?

> ...individual acts of teaching conducted within institutions and in which one individual seeks to spur on development in another. In this case, the goals cannot be utilitarian, but rather seek to develop the individual for his or her own sake (even if the result also contributes to that societal goal or to an individual's own utilitarian goals). These acts focus on the development of the capacity for individual human flourishing along multiple dimensions ... (Allen et al., 2016, p. 10)

If individual flourishing (in the present and for the future) is a fundamental aim of education then questions related to changes in the individual's literacy, thinking, understanding, communicating, practical skills, attitudes, creative thinking, judgement and engagement should be the focus of assessment.

Children should be helped to flourish on multiple levels. Many lesson objectives, for example, involve the aim to introduce and learn new words that hold new concepts – some of these key words were listed under subject headings in earlier chapters; the first assessment questions might be variations on those in Table 8.2:

Table 8.2 Assessing literacy and languages

What new words have you learned today?
Can you put some of those new words in a sentence for us?
What new words are you going to use to test those at home?

But schools are charged with teaching much more than literacy. On social and economic levels they are expected to prepare children to become good citizens, good partners, good workers, educated voters wise with their money. On a personal level schools help children to be confident people, morally, mentally and physically healthy, reliable friends, cooperative team members, creative thinkers, keen, good and lifelong learners. Each personal quality is an attribute needed and worked upon in the present, not for some future role but for now. Indeed, the future-orientated economic functions of education fail when its present-tense and personal aspects are missing. To achieve this educational balance, as discussed in Chapter 1, the curriculum must be carefully thought about, discussed, planned and fully understood by teachers and support staff. This book has stressed the centrality of a curriculum coherently planned and taught around big or existential questions (Billingsley et al., 2018) and many new concepts and processes will necessarily be introduced. This developing literacy needs continual assessment. New words capture new concepts and groups of words put newly together often constitute the seeds of new knowledge, but knowledge is not internalised, part of the mind, until processed in some way. David Perkins' (1992) statement used earlier in this book, 'learning is a consequence of thinking', reminds us that children must be actively involved – pondering, questioning, doing, making, sharing – in order to learn. So, the next level of assessment questions might be as shown in Table 8.3.

If new knowledge is to become permanent it generally requires some emotional relevance. It will often involve being able to do something we have not been able to do before. The assessment questions might be as shown in Table 8.4.

Involving children in big questions aims to develop positive attitudes towards the world and life. Changed mindsets or personality traits may not be immediately easy to assess, but they are relatively easy to see and hear in real life. This aspect of assessment may happen sometime after specific teaching aimed at attitude change. An enhanced

Table 8.3 Assessing thinking

Question	Intention
What did you think of that activity/experience/thing?	Deepen thinking by asking for more detail, examples, other feelings
I wonder how you think best? What bits were tricky? What questions did you/would you like to ask? What do you look like when you are thinking?	Encourage thoughts about different ways of thinking, e.g. when using your hands, looking really carefully, watching others, listening carefully, talking to others
I wonder how you will remember what you have learned? Why? What do you think you will easily remember?	Focus on memory: Are you good at remembering? Do you like to talk to others about it? Can you use it in some way? How do you remember best?
What would you like to tell others about what you have learned?	The answers to this question will provide important feedback on what to do next time

Table 8.4 Assessing new skills

What new thing can you do today that you couldn't do yesterday?
How do you think you might use that skill in your everyday life? What kind of people use this skill in everyday life?
Do you think you could show someone else how to do this new thing? What would you need to help you?

attitude of care or sympathy or fairness shown in playground behaviour might arise from the fact that these words and concepts in translation had been understood and internalised during a foreign language lesson using words for human values. Sometime after a session on aspects of climate change a child might show a new concern for recycling or travelling less by motor car. Both examples might occur weeks after a lesson but if the planned objectives of a series of lessons was the development of inclusive values or awareness of what individuals can do to counter climate change, then such changes of attitude are valuable indicators of exemplary character development and should be recorded.

The level of understanding of a concept, skill or issue will be shown in its use. Assessing the depth of new abilities, understandings, appreciations or creative ideas is best done by seeing them applied. The idea of 'performing' a new mental, collaborative or physical ability was introduced in Chapters 3 and 4. The idea was trialled, developed and refined at Harvard Graduate School of Education (Project Zero, 2022) and detailed examination of their Teaching for Understanding (Blythe, 1997) programme is recommended. Put simply, children involved in meaningful learning projects should be given multiple opportunities to demonstrate what they have learned, first with strong teacher support, second with the support of resources and guides and finally in a culminating self or group-driven 'Performance of Understanding' (see Table 8.5) where they apply their new knowledge unaided in a new situation.

Table 8.5 Assessing understanding by performance in 'Big Question' projects

Type of Assessment	Level of support
Highly supported performance of understanding at the beginning of a unit	Teacher and peers heavily support children by brain storming, prompting, offering words, demonstrating, modelling
Interim and partly supported performance of understanding – half way through a unit of work	Teacher and support staff provide materials, resources and a plan for children to demonstrate what they have learned in an expected and familiar context
Culminating Performance of Understanding	Children singly or in groups put their understanding to work by applying their new knowledge in a novel, unexpected context

Social, moral, spiritual and cultural development

This book ends by considering the non-physical elements needed for our flourishing. The social, moral, spiritual and cultural (SMSC) aspects of the curriculum ultimately concern thinking about answers to the big questions concerning life, death, creation, values, purpose, war, peace, justice, love, beauty and so on. Such questions are as relevant to young children as to adults. They are the questions at the core of each of the subject disciplines. As outlined at the beginning of this book, a positive school with positive teachers and support staff seeking the flourishing of every child will plan aspects of these questions and issues into the heart of every curriculum subject. Equally, they will use the perspectives of several subjects together to widen and deepen the answers and express the integrated nature of knowledge.

The schools that have thought carefully about SMSC across their curriculum and teaching generally do well in community support and in inspections. In the Ofsted Framework (2019), these areas are included in judgements of the school's role in children's personal development. A school judged excellent in SMSC is one where the well-being of every child is paramount. In Ofsted terms such a school is described as follows:

> The school consistently promotes the extensive personal development of pupils. The school goes beyond the expected, so that pupils have access to a wide, rich set of experiences. Opportunities for pupils to develop their talents and interests are of exceptional quality. There is a strong take-up by pupils of the opportunities provided by the school. The most disadvantaged pupils consistently benefit from this excellent work. The school provides these rich experiences in a coherently planned way, in the curriculum and through extra-curricular activities and they considerably strengthen the school's offer. The way the school goes about developing pupils' character is exemplary and worthy of being shared with others. (Ofsted School Inspection Handbook, 2019, p. 62)

The positive pedagogue will strive to achieve an atmosphere and school culture that produces these things. Excellence is not enough, however. There must be soul and heart and soft skills too. The key words in Ofsted's guidance for the teacher here are: personal, rich, wide, coherence, curriculum, opportunities and experience, yet how these are exemplified must come from the teacher. There are also highly significant words missing from this document. Words that relate to the good social, moral, spiritual and cultural life in and beyond school: inclusion, diversity, meaning, interdependence, community and creativity. These words have been the key themes of this book because they are liberating. Inclusion liberates the excluded, respect for diversity frees the culturally, linguistically or mentally different, the search for meaning unites us all and surely only a full appreciation of our global interdependence will save humanity from the looming disasters we see ahead of us. Knowing how to build and sustain community will save us from isolation and selfishness and finally, thankfully, the human aptitude for creativity will and always has offered us liberation from the limits of our finite minds and bodies.

In practical and curriculum terms the development of SMSC connects all subjects. The gate keepers and heroes of every discipline have sought to address SMSC issues at least partly because social, moral, spiritual and cultural issues involve everyone. Through the 21st century, we have seen this interconnection expressed in exponential growth of multi-disciplinary teams who now lead decision-making in medicine, digital technology, manufacture, commerce, exploration, research and innovation across the globe. Education has been slow to catch up. Previous work on cross-curricular learning has argued the interrelationship of all knowledge for decades and yet our school curricula mostly continue to run in separated subject silos.

Here a compromise is presented, knowing that schools want to hold on to separate subject teaching, but firmly believing that humanity needs more integrated approaches to the problems that face us if it is to survive. I have outlined *double focus cross-curricular learning* in earlier work (Barnes, 2018) but not previously tied it to SMSC. The four case studies that follow illustrate ways in which primary schools have helped children use separately taught subject skills and knowledge to connect two or three subject/disciplines to real issues related to the big social, moral, spiritual and cultural questions relevant to us all.

Social

Case Study 8.8

Why do refugees come to this country and what should we do about it? (Year 5 geography, English, civics) (Big issues: nationalism, migration, war)

I was teaching in a school near the east coast of Malaysia in the 1980s. One weekend I was with my family at the nearby beach. Several of my class with their families were also there. Suddenly one class member spotted a shabby, broken and listing wooden fishing boat crowded with refugees appearing near the beach. They knew from the words they could hear from the boat that the occupants were Vietnamese. The boat had clearly been attacked by pirates who had beaten many of the occupants and abducted several. The boat grounded on the beach and the local hotel immediately brought food to the hungry occupants. The children from my class watched silently as the boat was cordoned off and eventually police arrived to take the boat people to safety.

The next day in school 'the boat people' was the main topic of excited conversation and the question, 'Why do these people come to this country?' arose many times. Two full days of English, geography and civics lessons followed. Children first had new teaching on the political background to the troubles in Vietnam at that time – a government that many were afraid of, lots of violence, increasing poverty and threats. These were agreed as reasons to want to escape. We then read the local newspapers that described the risks of sailing across the South China Sea at this time – which included frequent attacks by pirates who robbed refugees of everything they had. We had already studied maps of southeast

Asia in geography and used them to trace the journey the boat must have taken. Using their established map knowledge they offered reasons why Malaysia and Thailand were the two destinations for refugees. Using previous social studies work on Malaysia's multi-racial society we spoke about how these people could be helped to live in Malaysia, imagined their feelings and discussed the rapid humanitarian response of the beach hotel.

We then considered what we would do if we were in such a situation. How we would want to be treated and what would happen next to the survivors. In those two days of teaching, learning in English, geography and civics was demonstrably the most effective, sustained and transferable of any I have been part of.

Moral

Case Study 8.9

What shall we do about the lost watch found in the school grounds? (Reception class, Awra Amba, Ethiopia: Language, Citizenship) (Big issue: honesty, inclusion, inequality)

The small village of Awra Amba (Website) in an inhospitable area of Ethiopia receives thousands of relatively wealthy visitors every year interested in its utopian community aims to alleviate poverty, establish gender equality and provide an equally dignified life for all its 500 inhabitants. In 2018, I joined a lesson with its infant class of 5-year-olds. One of the children had found a watch dropped by a visitor to the village. The teacher called the class together and showed them the watch. Many had not seen one so they learned about what it did and how it worked. The teacher then asked the child where it had been found and the class all agreed it must have been dropped by one of the morning's visitors who had left and returned to Addis Ababa. They agreed that it must have been dropped today because the paths are thoroughly swept each morning – it would not have been missed. The teacher then asked the children, 'What is the right thing to do about this?' All agreed the watch had to go back to the owner. The children discussed the relative virtues of leaving it with the teacher, running to the main road to see if the bus was still there or putting it back where it was found. Some suggested taking it to the local police station, but the children agreed that the best thing to do was to take it to the village meeting room which had a computer and phone so that if someone called to enquire, it would be there on the spot. Three of the children were given the job of taking the watch to the meeting room.

This lesson began with an unplanned problem, the teacher grasped the opportunity to teach an aspect of civic duty and extend the children's use of language. The children were genuinely concerned and all offered answers and suggestions in the 20-minute discussion. They used complex sentence structures, past and future, conditional forms that were sometimes gently corrected in Amharic. Boys and girls equally, sustained a fluent, lively conversation and arrived collaboratively at a wise solution without interference from their teacher. Their teacher reminded them after the discussion of their duties to be good moral citizens and how their actions had so beautifully illustrated their duty. (The watch was returned to its owner, by the way.)

Spiritual

Case Study 8.10

Why are some places more special than others?
(Year 4, RE, history, mathematics) (Big issue: faith, meaning and inclusion)

Canterbury Cathedral has annual schools days where the building is thrown open to the many church schools in the county. Schools choose between a wide variety of site-specific activities like drawing, ceramics, dance, maths, storytelling, stained glass, poetry, history, reflection and prayer. One teacher wanted their three activities to be linked with the work on special places they had been doing earlier in the term. They came armed with the overarching question 'Why are some places more special than others?' and attended the history, reflection and Euclidian maths options. They went on a cathedral walk that took them past monuments to kings and princes, soldiers from the Hundred Years' War, poets, musicians, refugees and martyrs and learned different ways in which these people had been linked to the place. When they went to a quiet and dimly lit underground chapel they were given ideas to help each child reflect in silence and see what came to their minds, drawing a tiny detail of one of the columns there, looking at a candle, making marks in a sand tray, writing their own letter to God or composing a haiku. Finally, the class met a mathematics specialist who had written a thesis on the mathematics of the cathedral. They learned how the length and height and complex patterns in the ceiling and windows were all designed using just a ruler and compass and the expert showed them how. They constructed some simple versions of the patterns themselves and measured the spaces to find ratios between the height and width of columns. They identified 'sacred numbers' in the architecture, the numbers 3,4, 7, 12 and others each had a biblical significance and were used throughout the cathedral.

Their teacher used the three experiences in the cathedral to frame a debate on why some spaces are more special than others. History, mathematics and RE were used in synthesis to explain why the cathedral space attracted a million people each year before and since the Covid pandemic.

Cultural

Case Study 8.11

How can we turn anger to peacefulness? (Year 2, music, drama, PE) (Big issue: managing emotions)

Some children in a Year 2 class were showing difficulties with anger management. Their teacher decided to address the issue of anger through drama, music and movement. They used a special grant to ask a drama specialist to come to class for three mornings. The specialist brought recordings of instrumental music by Britten, Hindemith and Courtney Pine that used volume, discords, rapid speeds and high ranges of harsh sound to create an atmosphere of anger. Groups of children sat in circles each with a PE hoop at their centre, in the school hall. The groups were asked to place printed words in the ring to describe how the music made them feel. Between them the words: cross, scary, angry, horrible, loud, argument, dangerous, arose as the most common words. The drama practitioner generated from the children how and why the composer had made such angry sounds. They then were given instruments in groups to improvise their own sonic version of anger that lasted about a minute. The angry pieces were recorded and played back as they moved around the hall in regular slow but angry movements. The following day, peaceful, calm pieces – this time by Vaughan Williams, Ravel, David Binney and Coltrane – were played to them. Children listened on earphones and responded by describing the key characteristics of this music and again followed by making their own simple quiet and calm music and making bodily movements, shapes and gestures in response. On the third day, they were reminded of their two types of music and were asked to improvise a link between them that turned their angry sounds to peaceful sounds. They were guided in groups to make corresponding physical theatre movements in response to their music. Later, selected members of the class were asked to invent and speak their own 'anger to peace' story to go with the music.

Summary

This final chapter has attempted to bring together the main themes and principles discussed throughout the book. The global, the human, our dependence on community, the strengths of our diversity and human creativity as a maker of meaning have each been exemplified in pairs and trios of subjects brought together to address real and relevant 21st-century issues. The uncontroversial principle that education should be controlled by teachers and founded upon research has been illustrated and justified. The idea that classrooms and curricula should create models of a utopian society and that children should experience what being listened to and included feels like, has been exemplified. Throughout the chapter the issue of our overwhelming commonalities has been highlighted because the more teachers look for and celebrate our human likenesses and rejoice in our creative diversities, the closer they come to being positive pedagogues.

REFERENCES

Action for Children (2020) *Report on Children's Services Funding.* Available at: https://media.actionforchildren.org.uk/documents/Joint_report_-_childrens_services_funding_2018-19_May_2020_Final.pdf

Aiello, L. and Dunbar, R. (1993) Neocortex Size, Group Size and the Evolution of Language. *Current Anthropology*, 34(2), April 1993, pp. 184–193.

Ainscow, M. and Booth, T. (2020) *Index for Inclusion.* Bristol: Centre for Research in Inclusive Education.

Alexander, R. (2004) *Towards Dialogic Teaching: Rethinking Classroom Talk.* Cambridge: Dialogos.

Alexander, R. (2010) Children, Their World Their Education. *Cambridge Primary Review.*

Alexander, R. (2019) Whose Discourse? Dialogic pedagogy for a post-truth world. *Dialogic Pedagogy* online journal, 7.

Alexander, R. (2021) *Education in Spite of Policy.* Abingdon: Routledge.

Allen, D., Dean, C., Schein, S., Kang, M., Webb, A. and Walton, D. (2016) *Understanding the Contributions of the Humanities to Human Development.* Harvard, Project Zero.

Association of Citizenship Teaching (n.d.) About Citizenship Available at: https://www.teachingcitizenship.org.uk/about-citizenship

Awra Amba, Ethiopia (n.d.) Human Beings Are Mankinds Greatest Asset Available at: https://awraamba.net

Barnes, J. (2012) *What Sustains a Life in Education?* (Unpublished PhD thesis). Available at: https://repository.canterbury.ac.uk/item/86vy2/what-sustains-a-life-in-education

Barnes, J. (2015) *Speech Bubbles: An evaluation of the 2013-14 extended programme funded by the Shine Trust.* Canterbury: Sidney De Haan Centre.

Barnes, J. (2018) *Applying Cross-curricular Approaches Creatively.* Abingdon: Routledge.

Barnes, J. (2019) Teachers' Values: An international study of what sustains a fulfilling life in education. *Journal of Education and Training Studies*, 7(5), pp. 1–16.

Barnes, J. (2020) Improving Children's Social and Emotional Health by Dramatising Their Stories. *Perspectives in Public Health,* 140(5), pp. 255–256. doi: 10.1177/1757913920927068

Barnes, J., in Bower, V. (Ed.) (2020) *Debates in Primary Education.* Abingdon: Routledge.

Barnes, J. (2021) We Are Still Here: The impacts of street music and street art during the 2020 London lockdowns. *International Journal of Community Music*, Feb 2021, pp. 1–12. https://doi.org/10.1386/ijcm_000XX_XX

Barnes, J. (2023) *Speech Bubbles and the Teaching Assistant: Investigating the impact of a drama intervention on school support staff*. Drama Research 14.1, April 2023.

Barnes, J. and Scoffham, S. (2017) The Humanities in English Primary Schools: Struggling to survive. *Education 3–13*, Vol. 45(3), pp. 298–308.

BBC (2021) *Windrush Generation*. Available at: https://www.bbc.co.uk/news/uk-43782241

Bennett, T. (2017) *Creating a Culture: How school leaders can optimise behaviour*. Available at: https://assets.publishing.service.gov.uk/government/uploads/system/uploads/attachment_data/file/602487/Tom_Bennett_Independent_Review_of_Behaviour_in_Schools.pdf

Benson, J. (2020) *Advances in Child Development and Behaviour*. Cambridge, MA: Academic Press.

Biesta, G. (2011) *Good Education in an Age of Measurement*. London: Paradigm.

Biesta, G. (2016) *The Beautiful Risk of Education*. Abingdon: Routledge.

Billingsley, B., Nassaji, M., Fraser, S. et al. (2018) A Framework for Teaching Epistemic Insight in Schools. *Research in Science Education*, 48, pp. 1115–1131. https://doi.org/10.1007/s11165-018-9788-6

Birbalsingh, K. (2020) *The Power of Culture: The Michaela way*. Woodbridge: John Catt Educational.

Blacking, J. (1976) *How Musical Is Man?* London: Faber and Faber.

Blacking, J. (1995) *Music, Culture, and Experience: Selected papers of John Blacking (Chicago Studies in Ethnomusicology)*. Chicago, IL: University of Chicago Press.

Blatchford, R. (Ed.) (2020) *The Forgotten Third: Do one third have to fail for two thirds to succeed?* Woodbridge: John Catt Educational.

Blythe, T. (1997) *Teaching for Understanding Guide*. Hoboken, NJ: Jossey-Bass.

Bonnett, A. (2008) *What Is Geography?* London: Sage.

Booth, T. (2011) Curricula for the Common School: What shall we tell our children? *FORUM*, 53(1).

Booth, T. (2018) How Should We Live Together? Choosing the struggle for inclusive values. Available at: https://www.redalyc.org/journal/6198/619866756013/html/

Booth, J. and Ainscow, M. (2020) *The Index for Inclusion: Developing learning and participation in schools*. Bristol: Centre for Studies in Inclusive Education.

Bourdieu, P. (1985) The Forms of Capital. In J. Richardson (Ed.) *Handbook for Theory and Research for the Sociology of Education*. Westport, CT: Greenwood, pp. 241–258.

Bowlby, J. (1988) *A Secure Base: Parent-child attachment and healthy human development*. New York, NY: Basic Books.

Britten, B. (1962) Libera Mei. Available at: https://www.youtube.com/watch?v=hgVpjv7ebeA

Brooks, S., Webster, R., Smith, L., Wooland, L, Wessly, S., Greenberg, N. and Rubin, G. (2020) The Psychological Impact of Quarantine and How to Reduce it: Rapid review of the evidence. *Lancet*, 395, pp. 912–920. Available at: http://dx.doi.org/10.1016/S0140-6736(20)30460-8

Brown, D. (1992) Human universals. In Pinker, S. (2002) *The Blank Slate*. London: Penguin.

Bruner, J. (1996) *The Culture of Education*. Cambridge, MA: Harvard University Press.

Burnard, P. and Loughrey, M. (2021) *Sculpting New Creativities in Primary Education*. Abingdon: Routledge.

Charlton-Perez, A. (2021) *Climate Change Gaps in the UK School Curriculum at Key Stage 1 and 2*. Available at: https://www.carbonbrief.org/guest-post-the-climate-change-gaps-in-the-uk-school-curriculum

Centre for Research in Underachievement (2020) *Educational Underachievement in Northern Ireland*. Available at: https://www.stran.ac.uk/wp-content/uploads/2020/01/CREU-Educational-Underachievement-in-Northern-Ireland-Evidence-Summary-January-2020.pdf

Chartered College of Teachers (2021) *Teacher Researchers*. Available at: https://impact.chartered.college/article/dann-teacher-researcher-shaping-curriculum-pupil-learning/

Children and Young People Now (2021) Available at: https://www.cypnow.co.uk/best%20practice/article/london-primary-s-whole-school-approach-to-sustainability

Children's Commissioner (2022a) *Where Are England's Children? Interim findings from the Children's Commissioner's Attendance Audit*. Available at: http://files.localgov.co.uk/cc.pdf

Children's Commissioner (2022b) *Voices of England's Missing Children*. Available at: https://www.childrenscommissioner.gov.uk/report/voices-of-englands-missing-children/

Children's Society (2021) Good Childhood Report (2021). Available at: https://www.childrenssociety.org.uk/sites/default/files/2021-08/GCR_2021_Full_Report.pdf

Clarke, S. and Muncaster, A. (2018) *Thinking Classrooms: Metacognition lessons for primary schools*. London: Rising Stars.

Cohen, H. (2019) *Emotions and School Inspection*. Available at: https://repository.canterbury.ac.uk/item/8v4xv/emotions-and-school-inspection-an-exploration-of-the-way-primary-and-prepartory-school-teachers-in-the-state-and-independent-sector-experience-ofsted-and-isi

Communication Trust (2017) *Talking about a Generation*. Available at: https://ican.org.uk/media/3215/tct_talkingaboutageneration_report_online_update.pdf

County Councils Network (2021) https://www.countycouncilsnetwork.org.uk/number-of-children-in-care-could-reach-almost-100000-by-2025-as-county-leaders-call-for-an-unrelenting-focus-on-keeping-families-together/

Craft, A. (2005) *Creativity in Schools: Tensions & Dilemmas*. London: Routledge.

Craft, A., Gardner, H. and Claxton, G. (2008) *Creativity, Wisdom and Trusteeship: Exploring the roles of education*. London: Sage.

Cremin, T. (2022) *Teaching English Creatively* (3rd Edition). Abingdon: Routledge.

Crick, B. (1998) *The Crick Report*. Available at: https://dera.ioe.ac.uk/4385/1/crickreport1998.pdf

Csikszentmihalyi, M. (1990) *Flow: The psychology of optimal experience*. New York, NY: Harper and Row.

Csikszentmihalyi, M. (1997) *Creativity: The psychology of discovery and invention.* New York, NY: Harper and Row.

Csikszentmihalyi, M. (2002) *Flow: The classic work on how to achieve happiness.* New York: Ebury Press.

Cushing, I. (2022) *Word Rich or Word Poor?* Available at: https://www.tandfonline.com/doi/full/10.1080/15427587.2022.2102014?src=

Damasio, A. (1995) *Descartes Error: Emotion reason and the human mind.* London: HarperCollins.

Damasio, A. (2003) *Looking for Spinoza: Joy sorrow and the feeling brain.* Orlando, FL: Harcourt.

Damasio, A. (2010) *Self Comes to Mind.* New York, NY: Pantheon.

Damasio, A. and Carvalho, G. B. (2013) The Nature of Feelings: Evolutionary and neurobiological origins. *Nature Reviews Neuroscience*, 14, pp. 143–152. doi: 10.1038/nrn3403

Damasio, A. (2021) *The Strange Order of Things: Life, feeling and the making of culture.* London: Penguin.

Dann, R., Czerniawski, G. and Chris Hanley, C. (2018) Teacher-as-Researcher: Shaping the curriculum for pupil learning. *Impact Magazine.* Available at: https://impact.chartered.college/article/dann-teacher-researcher-shaping-curriculum-pupil-learning/

Darwin, C. (1872/2012) *Origin of Species, by Means of Natural Selection.* New York, NY: Dover.

Decety, J. (Ed.) (2020) *The Social Brain: A developmental perspective.* Cambridge MA: MIT Press.

Dempster, H., Leach, A. and Hargrave, K. (2020) *Public Attitudes Towards Immigration and Immigrants.* Available at: https://cisp.cachefly.net/assets/articles/attachments/83372_202009_odi_public_attitudes_towards_immigration_wp_final_0.pdf

DfE (2013a) *The National Curriculum in England, Key Stages 1 and 2 Framework.* Available at: https://assets.publishing.service.gov.uk/government/uploads/system/uploads/attachment_data/file/425601/PRIMARY_national_curriculum.pdf

DfE (2013b) *Design and Technology Programmes of Study.* Available at: https://assets.publishing.service.gov.uk/government/uploads/system/uploads/attachment_data/file/239041/PRIMARY_national_curriculum_-_Design_and_technology.pdf

DfE (2013c) *English Programmes of Study.* Available at: https://assets.publishing.service.gov.uk/government/uploads/system/uploads/attachment_data/file/335186/PRIMARY_national_curriculum_-_English_220714.pdf

DfE (2013d) *Mathematics Programmes of Study.* Available at: https://assets.publishing.service.gov.uk/government/uploads/system/uploads/attachment_data/file/335158/PRIMARY_national_curriculum_-_Mathematics_220714.pdf

DfE (2013e) *Science Programmes of Study for Key Stage 1 and 2 in England.* Available at: https://assets.publishing.service.gov.uk/government/uploads/system/uploads/attachment_data file/425618/PRIMARY_national_curriculum_-_Science.pdf

DfE (2014) *Promoting Fundamental British Values as Part of SMSC in Schools.* Available at: https://assets.publishing.service.gov.uk/government/uploads/system/uploads/attachment_data/file/380595/SMSC_Guidance_Maintained_Schools.pdf

DfE (2015) *Non Statutory Programme of Study for Citizenship at Key Stages 1 and 2*. Available at: https://assets.publishing.service.gov.uk/government/uploads/system/uploads/attachment_data/file/402173/Programme_of_Study_KS1_and_2.pdf

DfE (2019a) *Core Content Framework*. Available at: https://assets.publishing.service.gov.uk/government/uploads/system/uploads/attachment_data/file/974307/ITT_core_content_framework_.pdf

DfE (2019b) *Early Career Teacher Framework*. Available at: https://www.gov.uk/government/publications/early-career-framework-reforms-overview/early-career-framework-reforms-overview

DfEE (1999a) *Archived National Curriculum in Art (England)*. Available at: https://dera.ioe.ac.uk/4410/7/cAD_Redacted.pdf

DfEE (1999b) *Archived Geography Curriculum (England)*. Available at: http://archive.teachfind.com/qcda/curriculum.qcda.gov.uk/uploads/Geography%201999%20programme%20of%20study_tcm8-12055.pdf

DfEE (1999c) *Archived History Curriculum (England)*. Available at: https://dera.ioe.ac.uk/4404/1/cHi.pdf

Dewey, J. (1897) *My Pedagogic Creed*. Harvard: E Kellogg.

Dewey, J. (1938) *Experience and Education*. New York: Collier.

Diversity in the UK website. Available at: https://diversityuk.org/diversity-in-the-uk/

Dunbar, R., Kaskatis, K., MacDonald, I. and Barra, V. (2012) Performance of Music Elevates Pain Threshold and Positive Affect: Implications for the evolutionary function of music. *Evolutionary Psychology*, 4(10), pp. 688–702.

Dweck, C. (2017a) *Mindset: Changing the way you think to fulfil your potential*. London: Robinson.

Dweck, C. (2017b) From Needs to Goals and Representations: Foundations for a unified theory of motivation, personality, and development. *Psychological Review*, 124(6), pp. 689–719.

East Lothian. (2023) Curriculum for Excellence. Available at: https://www.eastlothian.gov.uk/info/210557/schools_and_learning/12018/educating_children_and_young_people_about_citizenship

Economist (2021) Britain a Diverse Country for Decades Is Now Superdiverse. Available at: https://www.economist.com/britain/2021/06/24/britain-a-diverse-country-for-decades-is-now-superdiverse

Education Development Trust (2014) *Inspiring Teachers: How teachers inspire learners*. Available at: https://www.educationdevelopmenttrust.com/EducationDevelopmentTrust/files/b9/b9a42c3c-93b0-4baf-896b-d85af91afa66.pdf

Education Scotland (2022a) *Curriculum for Excellence*. Available at: https://education.gov.scot/education-scotland/scottish-education-system/policy-for-scottish-education/policy-drivers/cfe-building-from-the-statement-appendix-incl-btc1-5/what-is-curriculum-for-excellence

Education Scotland (2022) https://education.gov.scot/education-scotland/scottish-education-system/policy-for-scottish-education/policy-drivers/cfe-building-from-the-statement-appendix-incl-btc1-5/experiences-and-outcomes/#arts

Education Wales (2022a) *Expressive Arts Guidance.* Available at: https://hwb.gov.wales/curriculum-for-wales/expressive-arts

Education Wales (2022b) *Curriculum for Wales Proposals.* Available at: https://cdn.cyfoethnaturiol.cymru/media/689700/draft-curriculum-for-wales-2022-have-your-say.pdf?mode=pad&rnd=132085197690000000

Egermann, H., Fernando, N., Chuen, L. and McAdams, S. (2015) Music Induces Universal Emotion-Related Psychophysiological Responses. *Frontiers in Psychology.* Available at: https://www.frontiersin.org/articles/10.3389/fpsyg.2014.01341/full

Ekman, P. (1989) The argument and evidence about universals in facial expressions of emotion. In H. Wagner and A. Manstead (Eds) *Handbook of Social Psychophysiology.* Chichester: Wiley, pp. 143–164.

Ekman, P. (2004) Emotions Revealed: Understanding Faces and Feelings, London: Phoenix.

End Child Poverty Coalition (2022) *1 in 4 Children Living in Poverty.* Available at: https://www.lboro.ac.uk/media-centre/press-releases/2022/july/1-in-4-children-living-in-poverty-cost-of-living/

End Child Poverty website. Available at: https://endchildpoverty.org.uk/key-facts/

Epistemic Insight project website. Available at: https://www.epistemicinsight.com/

Equality and Human Rights Commission (2020) https://www.equalityhumanrights.com/sites/default/files/childrens_rights_in_great_britain_0.pdf

Fancourt, D., Williamon, A., Carvelho, l., Steptoe, A., Dow, R. and Lewis, I. (2016) Singing modulates mood, stress, cortisol, cytokine and neuropeptide activity in cancer patients and carers. *Ecancermdeicalscience,* 2016, Vol 10: 631 doi: 10.3332/ecancer.2016.631

Feldman, D. (1994) Creativity: Proof that development occurs. In D. Feldman, M. Csikszentmihalyi and Gardner, H. (Eds) *Changing the World: A framework for the study of creativity.* Westport, CT: Praeger, pp. 85–101.

Feuerstein, R. (1970) A dynamic approach to causation, prevention and alleviation of retarded performance. In H. C. Haywood (Ed.) *Social-cultural Aspects of Mental Retardation.* New York, NY: Appleton-Century-Crofts, pp. 341–377.

Feuerstein, R. (2013) *What Learning Looks Like: Mediated Learning in Theory and Practice, K-6.* New York, NY: Teachers College Press.

Feuerstein, R., Klein, P. and Tannenbaum, A. (Eds) (1999) *Mediated Learning Experience (MLE): Theoretical, Psychosocial and Learning Implications.* Freund Publishing House Ltd.

Forest Schools website. Available at: https://forestschoolassociation.org/the-forest-school-association/

Forster, E. M. (1910) *Howards End.* London: Edward Arnold.

Frankl, V. (1992) *Man's Search for Meaning.* London: Rider.

Fredrickson, B. (2010) *Positivity.* New York, NY: Crown.

Fredrickson, B. (2013) Positive emotions broaden and build. Available at: https://asset-pdf.scinapse.io/prod/186242951/186242951.pdf

Fredrickson, B. and Joiner, T. (2018) 'Reflections on Positive Emotion and Upward Spirals,' Perspectives on Psychological Science. Available at: https://journals.sagepub.com/doi/full/10.1177/1745691617692106

Fredrickson, B., Tugade, M., Waugh, C. and Larkin, G. (2003) What good are positive emotions in crisis? A prospective study of resilience and emotions following the terrorist attacks on the United States on September 11th, 2001. *Journal of Personality and Social Psychology*, 84(2), pp. 365–376. https://doi.org/10.1037/0022-3514.84.2.365

Freire, P. (1970) *The Pedagogy of the Oppressed*. New York, NY: Continuum.

Froebel, F. (1887) *The Education of Man*. (W.A. Hailman, Trans.). New York, NY: D. Appleton.

Gandhi, M. (1922) Young India. https://www.jetir.org/papers/JETIR2105274.pdf)

Gandhi, M. (1937) Pedagogical https://www.mkgandhi.org/articles/Gandhis-educational-thoughts.html

Gardner, H. (1993) *Creating Minds*. New York, NY: Basic Books.

Gardner, H. (2000a) *The Disciplined Mind*. London: Penguin.

Gardner, H. (2000b) *Intelligence Reframed*. New York, NY: Basic Books.

Gardner, H. (2009) *Five Minds for the Future*. Boston: Harvard Business School Press.

Gardner, H. Csikszentmihalyi, M. and Damon, W. (2001) *Good Work: When Excellence and Ethics Meet*. New York: Basic Books.

Giroux, H. (1988) *Teachers as Intellectuals: Toward a Critical Pedagogy of Learning*. Westport, CT: Bergin & Garvey.

Gladwell, M. (2006) *Blink: The Power of Thinking without Thinking*, London: Penguin.

Global Dimension website. Available at: https://globaldimension.org.uk/

Goldsmiths (2015) Why does singing make us feel good? Available at: https://www.gold.ac.uk/news/why-does-singing-make-us-feel-good/

Goleman, D. (2007) *Social Intelligence: The new science of human relationships*. New York, NY: Bantam.

Goren, E. (2013) Economic effects of domestic and neighbouring countries' cultural diversity. Available at: https://www.etsg.org/ETSG2013/Papers/042.pdf

Goswami, U. (2015) *Cognitive Development and Learning*. Available at: https://cprtrust.org.uk/wp-content/uploads/2015/02/BRIEFING-Goswami-Cognitive-Development-and-Learning.pdf

Goswami, U. (2019) *Cognitive Development and Cognitive Neuroscience: The Learning Brain*. Abingdon: Routledge.

Gove, M. (2010) *Times*, 6 March 2010.

Gove, M. (2013) *Mail Online*, 23 March 2013. Available at: https://www.dailymail.co.uk/debate/article-2298146/I-refuse-surrender-Marxist-teachers-hell-bent-destroying-schools-Education-Secretary-berates-new-enemies-promise-opposing-plans.html

Gov.Scotland (2017) Benchmarks Expressive Arts. Available at: https://education.gov.scot/nih/Documents/Expres(2017) BenchmakrsiveArtsBenchmarksPDF.pdf

Gov.Scotland (2019) *Citizenship advice, Curriculum for Excellence*. Available at: http://www.moray.gov.uk/downloads/file70312.pdf

Gov.Scotland (2019) Guidance on Citizenship Available at: https://education.gov.scot/media/qz0cl2pa/weatherclimatechange_climate.pdf

Gov.UK, DfE (2010) *The Case for Change*. Available at: https://assets.publishing.service.gov.uk/government/uploads/system/uploads/attachment_data/file/526946/The_case_for_change_The_importance_of_teaching.pdf

Gov.UK (2013a) *National Curriculum for History Key Stage 1 and 2*. Available at: https://assets.publishing.service.gov.uk/government/uploads/system/uploads/attachment_data/file/239035/PRIMARY_national_curriculum_-_History.pdf

Gov.UK (2013b) *National Curriculum in England: Geography*. Available at: https://assets.publishing.service.gov.uk/government/uploads/system/uploads/attachment_data/file/239044/PRIMARY_national_curriculum_-_Geography.pdf

Gov.UK (2013c) *Climate Change*. Available at: https://www.gov.uk/government/news/climate-change-in-the-draft-national-curriculum

Gov.UK (2013d) *Art and Design Programmes of Study for Key Stages 1 and 2*. Available at: https://assets.publishing.service.gov.uk/government/uploads/system/uploads/attachment_data/file/239018/PRIMARY_national_curriculum_-_Art_and_design.pdf

Gov.UK (2013e) *National Curriculum in England, PE*. Available at: https://www.gov.uk/government/publications/national-curriculum-in-england-physical-education-programmes-of-study/national-curriculum-in-england-physical-education-programmes-of-study

Gov.UK (2014) *Guidance on Promoting British Values in School*. Available at: https://www.gov.uk/government/news/guidance-on-promoting-british-values-in-schools-published

Gov.UK (2019a) *Timpson Review of School Exclusion*. Available at: https://assets.publishing.service.gov.uk/government/uploads/system/uploads/attachment_data/file/800028/Timpson_review_of_school_exclusion_literature_review.pdf

Gov.UK (2019b) *Core Curriculum Framework*. Available at: https://assets.publishing.service.gov.uk/government/uploads/system/uploads/attachment_data/file/974307/ITT_core_content_framework_.pdf

Gov.UK (2019c) *Early Career Framework*. Available at: https://www.gov.uk/government/publications/early-career-framework-reforms-overview/early-career-framework-reforms-overview

Gov.UK (2020) *Ofsted State Funded Schools Inspections and Outcomes Report*. Available at: https://www.gov.uk/government/statistics/state-funded-schools-inspections-and-outcomes-as-at-31-march-2020/main-findings-state-funded-schools-inspections-and-outcomes-as-at-31-march-2020

Gov.UK (2021a) *Initial Teacher Training Market Review*. Available at: https://www.gov.uk/government/publications/initial-teacher-training-itt-market-review/initial-teacher-training-itt-market-review-overview

Gov.UK (2021b) *ITT Market Review Report*. Available at: https://assets.publishing.service.gov.uk/government/uploads/system/uploads/attachment_data/file/999621/ITT_market_review_report.pdf

Gov.UK (2021c) *Annual Report of Chief Inspector of Education: Children's services and skills*. Available at: https://www.gov.uk/government/publications/ofsted-annual-report-202021-education-childrens-services-and-skills/the-annual-report-of-her-majestys-chief-inspector-of-education-childrens-services-and-skills-202021

Gov.UK (2021d) *Early Years Foundation Stage Framework*. Available at: https://assets.publishing.service.gov.uk/government/uploads/system/uploads/attachment_data/file/974907/EYFS_framework_-_March_2021.pdf

Gov.UK (2021e) *PSHE Guidance*. Available at: https://www.gov.uk/government/publications/personal-social-health-and-economic-education-pshe/personal-social-health-and-economic-pshe-education

Gov.UK (2021f) *National Curriculum in England: Music programmes of study*. Available at: https://www.gov.uk/government/publications/national-curriculum-in-england-music-programmes-of-study/national-curriculum-in-england-music-programmes-of-study#:~:text=understand%20and%20explore%20how%20music,structure%20and%20appropriate%20musical%20notations

Gov.UK (2022a) *Special Needs in England: National statistics*. Available at: https://explore-education-statistics.service.gov.uk/find-statistics/special-educational-needs-in-england

Gov.UK (2022b) *Promoting Children's and Young People's Mental Health and Well Being*. Available at: https://assets.publishing.service.gov.uk/government/uploads/system/uploads/attachment_data/file/1020249/Promoting_children_and_young_people_s_mental_health_and_wellbeing.pdf

Gravesend Grammar (2019) Page 10. Available at: https://gravesendgrammar.com/wp-content/uploads/2019/10/19-October-Newsletter.pdf

Groundswell Arts website. Available at: https://groundswellarts.com/

Gruber, H. (1981) *Darwin on Man*. Chicago: University of Chicago Press.

Gu, S. *et al*. (2019) A model for basic emotions using observations of behavior in drosophila. *Frontiers in Psychology*, April, 2019. Available at: https://www.frontiersin.org/articles/10.3389/fpsyg.2019.00781

Guardian (2021) Available at: https://www.theguardian.com/uk-news/2021/apr/08/one-in-three-uk-teachers-plan-to-quit-says-national-education-union

Guardian (2021a) Available at: https://www.theguardian.com/education/2021/oct/22/deprived-schools-in-england-getting-less-money-after-funding-overhaul-report

Halpin, D. (2002) *Hope and Education: The Role of the Utopian Imagination*. Abingdon: Routledge.

Hancox, G. and Barnes, J. (2004) Young gifted and human. *Improving Schools*, 7(1), pp. 11–21.

Hicks, D. (2002) *Lessons for the Future: The Missing Dimension in Education*. London: Routledge.

Hicks, D. (2018) *Educating for Hope in Troubled Times: Climate change and the transition to a post-carbon future*. London: Trentham. https://www.eastlothian.gov.uk/info/210557/schools_and_learning/12018/educating_children_and_young_people_about_citizenship

Hirsch, E. D. (1988) *Cultural Literacy: What every American needs to know*. New York, NY: Random House.

Ikeda, D. (2020) Available at: https://www.daisakuikeda.org/main/educator/edu/edu-03.html

Immordino-Yang, M. (2015) *Emotions, Learning, and the Brain: Exploring the Educational Implications of Affective Neuroscience*. New York, NY: W.W. Norton & Co.

Immordino-Yang, M. (2019) Nurturing nature: How brain development is inherently social and emotional, and what this means for education. *Educational Psychologist*, 54(3), pp. 185–204, DOI: 10.1080/00461520.2019.1633924

Immordino-Yang, M. and Gottlieg, R. (2020) Understanding emotional thought can transform educators understanding of how students learn. In M. Maraschal Thomas, M. and I. Dumonthell (Eds) (2020) *Educational Neuroscience: Development across the lifespan.* New York, NY: Routledge.

Immordino-Yang, M., Christodoulou, J. and Singh, V. (2012) Rest Is not idleness: Implications of the brain's default mode for Human Development and Education, *Perspectives on Psychological Science*, 7(4) 352–364.

Independent (2021) *Britain's Favourite Family Meals*. Available at: https://www.independent.co.uk/life-style/uk-favourite-family-meals-b1814446.html?amp

Institute for Fiscal Studies (2021) Available at: https://ifs.org.uk/publications/15858

Isen, A. (1987) Positive affect, cognitive processes, and social behavior. *Advances in Experimental Social Psychology*, Vol. 20, pp. 203–253.

Johnson, K. and Fredrickson, B. (2005) 'We all look the same to me': Positive emotions eliminate the own-race bias in face recognition. *Psychological Science*, 16(11), pp. 875–881. doi:10.1111/j.1467-9280.2005.01631.x

Jung, C. (1953) *Two Essays on Analytical Psychology: Collected works, vol. 7*. R. F. C. Hull, trans. Bollingen Series XX. Princeton, NJ: Princeton University Press.

Jung, C. (1971) *Psychological types: Collected works, vol. 6*. R. F. C. Hull, trans. Bollingen Series XX. Princeton, NJ: Princeton University Press. Originally published in 1921.

Juslin, P. and Sloboda, J. (2011) *Handbook of Music and Emotion: Theory, Research, Applications,* Oxford: Oxford University Press.

Keller, M. M., Hoy, A. W. and Goetz, T. (2016) Teacher enthusiasm: Reviewing and redefining a complex construct. *Educational Psychology Review*, 28, pp. 743–769.

Keltner, D. (2023) *Awe: The transformative power of everyday wonder.* London: Allan Lane.

Kidd, D. (2020) *A Curriculum of Hope: As rich in humanity as in knowledge.* Carmarthen: Independent Thinking Press.

Kings College London (2021) *Racial Disparity*. Available at: https://www.kcl.ac.uk/events/racial-disparity-within-the-legal-profession-tackling-the-failure

Kwauk, C. (2020) Available at: https://www.brookings.edu/wp-content/uploads/2020/02/Roadblocks-to-quality-education-in-a-time-of-climate-change-FINAL.pdf

Laevers, F. (2004) *Involvement of Teacher and Children Style: Insights from an International Study on Experiential Education.* Leuven: Leuven University Press.

LeDoux, J. (2002) *The Synaptic Self.* New York, NY: Viking.

LeDoux, J. (2012) Rethinking the emotional brain. *Neuron*, 73, pp. 653–676. doi: 10.1016/j.neuron.2012.02.004

Lieberman, M. (2015) *Social: Why our Brains are Wired to Connect.* Oxford: Oxford University Press.

Lucas, B. and Spencer, E. (2018) *Developing Tenacity: Teaching learners how to persevere in the face of difficulty.* Carmarthen: Crown House.

Makiguchi, T. (2002) *A Geography of Human Life*. D. Bethel (Ed.). San Francisco, CA: Caddo Gap Press.

Malloch, S. and Trevarthen, C. (2019) The human nature of music. *Frontiers in Psychology*, 9. 16380 https://www.ncbi.nlm.nih.gov/pmc/articles/PMC6180173/

Manchester Church Schools guidance (2017) Available at: https://www.horwichparish.net/serve_file/683757

Manera, L. (2022) Art and aesthetic education in the Reggio Emilia approach, *Education 3-13*, 50(4), pp. 483–493.

Mann, K. (2015) *The Musical Tradition in Latin America*. Oxford: Oxford University Press.

Marmot, Sir M. (2020) *Health Equity in England: The Marmot Review Ten Years On*. Available at: https://discovery.ucl.ac.uk/id/eprint/10106434/3/Bockenhauer_BMJ%20Ten%20years%20essay2pg3.pdf

McGilchrist, I. (2021) *The Matter With Things: Our Brains, Our Delusions, and the Unmaking of the World*. London: Perspectiva.

Migration Observatory (2022) *Public Opinion Towards Immigration*. Available at: https://migrationobservatory.ox.ac.uk/resources/briefings/uk-public-opinion-toward-immigration-overall-attitudes-and-level-of-concern/

Mirror On Line (2021) Available at: https://www.mirror.co.uk/news/uk-news/parent-shaming-new-tsar-flunks-25261762

Mithen, S. (2005) *The Singing Neanderthals: The Origins of Music, Language, Mind and Body*. London: Weidenfeld and Nicolson.

Mokuria, V. G. and Wandix-White, S. F. (2020) *Care and Value-Creating Education Put into Action in Brazil: A Narrative Inquiry*. Available at: https://files.eric.ed.gov/fulltext/EJ1265800.pdf

NACCCE (1999) *All Our Futures, the Report of the National Advisory Committee on Creative and Culture and Education*. Available at: https://sirkenrobinson.com/pdf/allourfutures.pdf

NASUWT (2021) Available at: https://www.politics.co.uk/opinion-former/press-release/2021/10/22/urgent-investment-needed-in-teachers-pay/

National Research Institute (US) website. Available at: https://www.genome.gov/genetics-glossary/Race#:~:text=Definition&text=Race%20is%20a%20social%20construct,nations%2C%20regions%20and%20the%20world.

Noddings, N. (2005) *Happiness and Education*. Cambridge: Cambridge University Press.

Northern Ireland Council for Curriculum Education and Assessments (2020) *Key Stage 1 and 2 Drama*. Available at: https://ccea.org.uk/learning-resources/key-stage-1-2-drama-lessons

Northern Ireland Curriculum Primary (2019) Available at: https://ccea.org.uk/downloads/docs/ccea-asset/Curriculum/The%20Northern%20Ireland%20Curriculum%20-%20Primary.pdf

Nuffield (2022a) *Little Change in Inequalities*. Available at: https://www.nuffieldfoundation.org/news/little-change-early-childhood-inequalities

Nuffield (2022b) *Mental Health Indicator Update*. Available at: https://www.nuffieldtrust.org.uk/news-item/mental-health-indicator-update

Nunez, I. and Goulah, J. (2021) *Hope and Joy in Education.* New York, NY: Teachers College Press.

NUT (2001) *Teachers Leaving Report.* Available at: http://www.alansmithers.com/reports/TeachersLeaving2Nov2001.pdf

O'Donoghue, B. website. Available at: http://www.bernodonoghue.com/bernodmecom

Oates, T. (2015) 'So who says that a 12-year-old should learn that?' Confused issues of knowledge and authority in curriculum thinking. *Knowledge and the Curriculum.* London: Policy Exchange. Available at: https://policyexchange.org.uk/wp-content/uploads/2016/09/knowledge-and-the-curriculum.pdf

Observer, 5 December (2021) *UK is failing Fostered Children Report.* Available at: https://www.theguardian.com/society/2022/jun/26/uk-is-failing-fostered-children-with-mental-health-problems-warns-charity

Ofsted (2013) *Unseen Children Access and Achievement 20 Years On.* Available at: https://www.gov.uk/government/publications/unseen-children-access-and-achievement-20-years-on

Ofsted (2019) Available at: https://www.gov.uk/government/publications/education-inspection-framework, London: Gov. UK.

Ofsted (2021a) *Music Research Review.* Available at: https://www.gov.uk/government/publications/research-review-series-music/research-review-series-music

Ofsted (2021b) *Teacher Well-being Report.* Available at: https://assets.publishing.service.gov.uk/government/uploads/system/uploads/attachment_data/file/936253/Teacher_well-being_report_110719F.pdf

Ofsted (2021c) *Ofsted Annual Report.* Available at: https://www.gov.uk/government/news/ofsted-annual-report-we-must-do-all-we-can-to-make-sure-this-generation-is-not-denied-its-opportunities

Ofsted (2022) *School Inspection Handbook.* Available at: https://www.gov.uk/government/publications/school-inspection-handbook-eif/school-inspection-handbook

Ovenden-Hope, T., Blandford, S., Cain, T. and Maxwell, B. (2018) *'RETAIN' Early Career Teacher Retention Programme: Evaluating the role of research informed continuing professional development for a high quality, sustainable 21st century teaching profession.* Available at: https://marjon.repository.guildhe.ac.uk/id/eprint/17249/1/RETAIN%20Early%20Career%20Teacher_Ovenden-Hope.pdf

Pan, Y., Novembre, G., Song, B., Zhu, Y. and Hu, Y. (2021) Dual brain stimulation enhances interpersonal learning through spontaneous movement synchrony. *Social Cognitive and Affective Neuroscience.* 16(1–2), pp. 210–221.

Panksepp, J. (2004) *Affective Neuroscience: The Foundations of Human and Animal Emotions.* New York, NY: Oxford University Press.

Parsons, C. (2018) The continuing school exclusion scandal in England. *FORUM.* Volume 60, Number 2.

Parsons, C. (2020) A curriculum to think with: British colonialism, corporate kleptocracy, enduring white privilege and locating mechanisms for change. Available at: http://www.jceps.com/wp-content/uploads/2020/09/18-2-6.pdf

Perkins, D. (1992) *Smart Schools*. New York, NY: Free Press.

Pew Research Center (2013) *The Most (and least) Culturally Diverse Countries in the World* Available at: https://www.pewresearch.org/fact-tank/2013/07/18/the-most-and-least-culturally-diverse-countries-in-the-world/

Pew Research (2014) *US doesn't rank high in religious diversity*. Available at: https://www.pewresearch.org/fact-tank/2014/04/04/u-s-doesnt-rank-high-in-religious-diversity/#:~:text=By%20this%20measure%2C%20Singapore%20is,%2C%20China%20and%20Hong%20Kong

Piaget, J. (1954) *The Construction of Reality in the Child*, trans. M. Cook. New York, NY: Basic Books.

Pinker, S. (2002) *The Blank Slate: The modern denial of human nature*. London: Penguin

Primary Science Teaching Trust website. Available at: https://pstt.org.uk

Policy Exchange (2018) Available at: https://policyexchange.org.uk/publication/it-just-grinds-you-down/org.uk/resources/curriculum-materials/citizen-science-air-pollution

Project Zero (2018) *Towards a Pedagogy of Play*. Available at: http://www.pz.harvard.edu/sites/default/files/Towards%20a%20Pedagogy%20of%20Play.pdf

Project Zero (2022) *Teaching for Understanding*. Available at: http://www.pz.harvard.edu/projects/teaching-for-understanding

PSHE Association website. Available at: https://pshe-association.org.uk/resources-landing

Ravel, M. Adagio from Piano Concerto in G. Available at: https://www.youtube.com/watch?v=ud6nbX5XKVk

Rees, P. et al. (2016) *The Future is Diversity*. Available at: https://epc2016.princeton.edu/papers/161123

Researching Arts in Primary Schools (2022) *West Rise Junior School Report*. Available at: https://artsprimary.com/2022/04/28/west-rise-juniors/

Ritchhart, R. and Perkins, D. (2008) Making learning visible. *Educational Leadership*, 65(5), pp. 57–61.

Rights Respecting Schools website. Available at: https://www.unicef.org.uk/rights-respecting-schools/

Roach, P. (2022) *Education International*. https://www.ei-ie.org/en/item/22156:in-the-uk-racial-inequality-in-schools-is-deep-rooted-endemic-and-institutionalised

Robinson, K. (Ed.) (1989) *Arts in Schools: Principles, Practice and Provision*. London: Calouste Gulbenkian Foundation.

Robinson, K. (Ed.) (1990) *The Arts 5-16: Practice and Innovation*. Harlow: Oliver and Boyd.

Robinson, K. (2006) *Do Schools Kill Creativity? TED talk*. Available at: https://www.ted.com/talks/sir_ken_robinson_do_schools_kill_creativity?language=en

Robinson, K. and Aronica, L. (2014) *The Element: How Finding Your Passion Changes Everything*. London: Penguin.

Robinson, K. and Aronica, L. (2015) *Creative Schools: Revolutionising education from the ground up*. London: Alan Lane.

Robinson, Sir K. (2022) *Imagine If: Creating A future for us all*, London; Penguin.

Royal Society of Arts (RSA) (2020) Partridge, L. *Pinball Kids: Preventing School Exclusions*, RSA Blog, 16th March 2020.

RSA (2014) *Schools with Soul*. Available at: https://www.thersa.org/globalassets/pdfs/reports/schools-with-soul-report.pdf

Ryff, C. (1989) Happiness is everything, or is it? Explorations on the meaning of psychological well-being. *Journal of Personality and Social Psychology*, 157, pp. 1069–1081.

Salovey, P. and Mayer, J. D. (1990) Emotional intelligence. *Imagination, Cognition and Personality*, 9(3), pp. 185–211.

Sammons, P., Kington, A., Lindorff-Vijayendran, A. and Ortega, L. (2014) *Inspiring Teachers: Perspectives and practices*. Reading: CfBT Education Trust.

SAPERE website. Available at: https://www.sapere.org.uk/about-us.aspx

Sarafoleanu, C., Mella, C., Georgescu, M. and Perederco, C. (2009) The importance of the olfactory sense. Available at: https://www.ncbi.nlm.nih.gov/pmc/articles/PMC3018978

Segerstrom, S. and Miller, G. (2004) Available at: https://www.ncbi.nlm.nih.gov/pmc/articles/PMC1361287/

Scioli, A. and Biller, H. (2009) *Hope in an Age of Anxiety*. New York, NY: Oxford University Press.

School Curriculum & Assessment Authority (SCAA) (1997) *The Arts & the Curriculum*. London: SCAA.

Schoolsweek (2022) Available at: https://schoolsweek.co.uk/five-year-teacher-retention-rate-worsens-and-5otherschoolworkforcefindings/#:~:text=Of%20the%20nearly%2040%2C000%20teachers,lower%20than%209.6%20in%202018

Scott, C. (2021) *Arts for Health: Drawing*. Bingley: Emerald.

Seligman, M. (2004) *Authentic Happiness*. New York, NY: Basic Books.

Sherrington, T. (2015) *Knowledge and the Curriculum*. Policy Exchange.

Simonton, D. K. (1984) *Genius, Creativity, and Leadership*: Historiometric inquiries. Cambridge, MA: Harvard University Press.

Smith, E. (2005) *Analysing Underachievement in Schools*. London: Continuum.

Snyder, B. (1971) *The Hidden Curriculum*. New York, NY: Knopf.

Social Market Foundation (2013) *Michael Gove speaks at the SMF*. Available at: https://www.smf.co.uk/michael-gove-speaks-at-the-smf/

Speech Bubbles website. Available at: https://www.speechbubbles.org.uk/

Sternberg, R. (1997a) *Thinking Styles*. Cambridge: Cambridge University Press.

Sternberg, R. (1997b) *Successful Intelligence*. New York, NY: Plume.

Sternberg, R. (2003) *Wisdom, Intelligence, and Creativity Synthesized*. Cambridge: Cambridge University Press.

Sternberg, R. and Gluck, J. (2019) *The Cambridge Handbook of Wisdom*. Cambridge: Cambridge University Press.

Takazawa, M. (2016) *Exploration of Soka Education Principles on Global Citizenship: A Qualitative Study*. Available at: https://repository.usfca.edu/cgi/viewcontent.cgi?article=1327&context=diss

Timpson, E. (2019) *The Timpson Review of School Exclusion*. Available at: https://assets.publishing.service.gov.uk/government/uploads/system/uploads/attachment_data/file/807862/Timpson_review.pdf

Tomkins, S. and Tunnicliffe, S. D. (2015) *Darwin Inspired Learning*. Boston, MA: Brill.

Trainor, L., Austin, C. and Desjardins, R. (2000) Is infant directed speech prosody a result of the vocal expression of emotion? *Psychological Science*, 11(3). Available at: https://www.researchgate.net/profile/Laurel-Trainor-2/publication/12060527_Is_Infant-Directed_Speech_Prosody_a_Result_of_the_Vocal_Expression_of_Emotion/links/59f8d5dc458515547c26a6c5/Is-Infant-Directed-Speech-Prosody-a-Result-of-the-Vocal-Expression-of-Emotion.pdf

Trevarthen, C. (2008) The musical art of infant conversation: Narrating in the time of sympathetic experience, without rational interpretation, before words. In *Musicae Scientiae*, Special Issue 2008, pp. 15–46. Available at: https://www.researchgate.net/profile/Colwyn-Trevarthen/publication/258173164_The_musical_art_of_infant_conversation_Narrating_in_the_time_of_sympathetic_experience_without_rational_interpretation_before_words/links/5d80a6e892851c22d5dd7643/The-musical-art-of-infant-conversation-Narrating-in-the-time-of-sympathetic-experience-without-rational-interpretation-before-words.pdf

Trevarthen, C. (2020) Discovering our Music with Infants. *Enfance*, 1(1), pp. 17–39.

Tummeltshammer, K. and Kirkham, N. (2013) Learning to look: probabilistic variation and noise guide infants' eye movements. *Developmental Science*, 16(5), pp. 760–771.

Tutu, D. and Allan, J. (2011) *God Is Not A Christian*. London: Random House.

UK Parliament (2021) *Home Affairs Committee Report*. Available at: https://committees.parliament.uk/committee/83/home-affairs-committee/news/157006/urgent-action-needed-to-tackle-deep-rooted-and-persistent-racial-disparities-in-policing/

UK Parliament (2022) *Home Education in England*; Research Briefing. Available at: https://researchbriefings.files.parliament.uk/documents/SN05108/SN0518.pdf

UK Parliament (2021) *Mental Health Statistics: Prevalence, services and funding in England*. Available at: https://researchbriefings.files.parliament.uk/documents/SN06988/SN06988.pdf

Vertovec, S. (2007) Superdiversity and its implications. *Ethnic and Racial Studies*, 30(7). Available at: https://www.tandfonline.com/doi/abs/10.1080/01419870701599465

Vygotsky, L. (1930/2004) (Translation) Imagination and creativity in childhood. *Journal of Russian and East European Psychology*, 42(1), January–February 2004, pp. 7–97.

Vygotsky, L. (1978) *Mind in Society: Development of higher psychological processes*. Cambridge, MA: Harvard University Press.

Wales Education (2022a) *Foundation Stage*. Available at: https://media.bloomsbury.com/rep/files/curriculum_framework-for-1.pdf

Wales Education (2022b) Available at: https://hwb.gov.wales/api/storage/bfb53832-463a-409d-a284-9edfc2389116/history-in-the-national-curriculum-for-wales.pdf

Wheway, D., Miles, H. and Barnes, J. (2018) *How to Teach Primary Music: 100 inspiring ideas*. London: Collins.

World Economic Forum (2021) *Ranked: The countries with the most linguistic diversity*. Available at: https://www.weforum.org/agenda/2021/03/these-are-the-top-ten-countries-for-linguistic-diversity/

WHO (2020) Health Behaviour in School-aged Children: World Health Organization Collaborative Cross National Study, Findings from the 2018 HBSC study for England. Hatfield: CRIPACC. Available at: https://www.researchgate.net/publication/340165667_HBSC_England_National_Report_Findings_from_the_2018_HBSC_study_for_England

Witherspoon, D. J., Wooding, S., Rogers, A. R., Marchani, E. E., Watkins, W. S., Batzer, M. A. and Jorde, L. B. (2007) Genetic similarities within and between human populations. *Genetics*, 176(1), pp. 351–359.

World Population Review (2022) *Country Rankings.* Available at: https://worldpopulationreview.com/country-rankings/most-diverse-countries

Woodhead, C. (2005) *Times,* 3rd April, Worthwhile knowledge.

Woodhead, C. (2017) *What Matters Most: A Collection of Pieces,* Buckingham: University of Buckingham Press.

Zoological Society of London (2019) Conserving orangutans one classroom at a time. Available at: https://zslpublications.onlinelibrary.wiley.com/doi/10.1111/acv.12513

INDEX

Note - *Page number with 'f' indicates figure, 't' indicates table.*

action and values, 14
Ainscow, M.
   The Index for Inclusion, 16
Alexander, R., 118
All Our Futures, 7
Applying Cross-Curricular Approaches Creatively (Barnes), 129
art(s)
   biodiversity in, 101, 101f–102f
   case studies across, 98–104
art and design, 81, 143t
   beginnings, 81–83
   concepts, 81–86
   creativity, 83–85
   digital media, 85–86
   personal development, 83–85
   sketchbooks, 85–86
   skills, 81–86
Arts in Schools Project (Robinson), 86
assessing learning, 167–170
assessing literacy, 168t
assessing new skills, 170t
assessing thinking, 169t
assessing understanding by performance, 170t
australopithicus, 80

Bandura, A., 48
Barnes, J.
   Applying Cross-Curricular Approaches Creatively, 129
behaviour, 54–56
   classroom, 11
   human and animal, 27
   moral, 24, 31
Bennett, T., 43
Biesta, G., 118
biodiversity, 154
   conservation of, 61
   in drama, dance and art, 101, 101f–102f
Birbalsingh, K., 10
Black, Asian, and minority ethnic (BAME), 9–10, 26
Booth, J.
   The Index for Inclusion, 16
Booth, T., 47, 126
Bourdieu, P., 9–10
brain to brain coupling, 5
British Nationality Act of 1948, 26
Britten, B.
   War Requiem, 103
Broaden and Build Theory, 28
broader curriculum, 146
Bronze Age dwelling on Eastbourne, 76–77, 77f
Bruner, J., 48, 126

CAMHS (child and adolescent mental health service), 13
cardinal virtues, 24
Caribbean, 75
case studies, 158–164, 167
   adventure course in Cornwall children, 167
   atmospheric pollution, 108–109
   drawing for understanding, 109
   D&T and history in concentric castle, 112–113
   emotional mapping in geography with creative writing about feelings, 165
   faith, meaning and inclusion, 174
   food and community building, 161–162
   food technology and geography of food, 113–114
   globalisation in the supermarket, 162–163
   honesty, inclusion, inequality, 173
   human values through French language, 164
   managing emotions, 175
   nationalism, migration, war, 172–173
   refugees, 172–173
   sensory trails in Canary Wharf, 159–160
   talking about and to refugees (English), 117–119
   telling my story (English), 115–117
   thinking about home, 158–159
   three bowls for three bears (mathematics), 119–120, 121f
   turning anger to peacefulness, 175
   year 4/5 maths in forest school (mathematics), 122–124, 123f
celebrating diversity, 16
child/children, 126
   in London Nursery School, 75
   in year 3 class in Leicester, 72, 75
Children's Society, 11
citizenship
   concepts, 68–69
   dominant attitudes, 70
   skills, 69–70
   vocabulary, 69
classrooms
   models of inclusion and positivity, 6–7
   physical features of, 46–47
   values-conscious, 47–48
climate change, 3
collaborative curriculum, 147
commonality, 155–156
common humanity, 4
community, importance of, 5–6
compassionate curriculum, 147
computing, 145t
confidence-building curriculum, 147
connecting, 16–17
   with culture, 141–142
   curriculum, 129–132

the disciplines, 145–151
  with the locality, 140–141
  with others, 138, 139t
  with self, 135–138
  through expert teachers, 132–135
  through friendships, 139t
The Connecting Curriculum, 17
connections in the community, 139t
connections on the web, 139t
controlled/controlling sound, 93
  starter activities to develop skills of, 94t
Core Content Framework (CCF), 10
core knowledge, 9–10
Covid-19, 8, 12, 19, 142
Craft, A., 48
creative curriculum, 147
creativity
  art and design, 83–85
  defined, 7–8
  kinds of, 8
  value of, 7–8
critical pedagogy, 31
cross-curricular work, on school campus, 73t–74t
Csikszentmihalyi, M., 7, 27, 30, 51
cultural capital, 9–10, 42
cultural development, 175
cultural diversity, 154–155
Cultural Understanding, 65
curriculum, 125–151
  changes, 45–46, 46t
  child, 126
  connecting curriculum, 129–132
  connecting the disciplines, 145–151
  connecting through expert teachers, 132–135
  connecting with culture, 141–142
  connecting with others, 138, 139t
  connecting with self, 135–138
  connecting with the locality, 140–141
  disciplined knowledge, 127
  drama across, 88
  global connections, 142–143, 143t–145t
  hidden, 12
  humanising the, 15
  impact, 46t
  implementation, 46t
  intent, 46t
  learning environment, 127
  making relevant, 128–129
  sequencing knowledge, 128
  stories across, 15

Damasio, A., 4
dance, 95
  biodiversity in, 101, 101f–102f
  skills and concepts in, 95–97
  starter ideas for, 96t–97t
  talking about war and peace, 102–104
Darwin, C., 27
design and technology (D&T), 110, 120, 160–161
  across the curriculum, 111–112
  case studies, 112–114
  languages used in, 111t
  skills and concepts of, 110–111
Dewey. J., 32, 48
  My Pedagogic Creed, 31
Dickens, C.
  Hard Times, 40

digital media, art and design, 85–86
dimensions of music, 91
disaffection, 11–12
disciplined knowledge, 127
diversity, 73t
  celebrating, 16
  cultural, 154–155
  humanities, 72, 75
  music, 93
  representation, 7–8
  teachers role in inclusion and positivity, 6–7
  values and, 26–27
double focus cross-curricular learning, 9, 146, 172
drama, 86–87
  across the curriculum, 88
  biodiversity in, 101, 101f–102f
  mental health and, 89–90, 89f
  skills, techniques and concepts, 87–90
  talking about war and peace, 102–104
  techniques, 88t–89t
drama practitioner (DP), 116
drawing for understanding, 109
Dunbar, R., 90
Dweck, C., 48, 51

Early Career Teacher Framework, 10
Early Career Teachers (ECT), 133
education, 41–42
  change, 43
  funding, 12–13
  linking values with, 25t
  policy, 3–4
  practice, 5–6
  traditional, 9
Education, Health and Care (EHC), 129
embodied connections, 139t
emotionally positive classrooms, 48, 49t
emotions, 4, 49t, 165
  managing, 175
English, 114–115, 145t
  case study, 115–119
  drama, 116–117
  and foreign languages, 163–164
  oracy, 117–118
English National Curriculum in History, 64
Environmental, Social and Governance (ESG), 25, 25t
exciting experience curriculum, 147
experiencing world around child, 17–18

Feldman, D., 7
Feuerstein, R., 48, 49
flow theory, 55
Floyd, G., 3
Forster, E.M., 16
Fredrickson, B., 28, 85
freeze-frame dance, 99, 100f
Freire, P., 31
'Fridays for the Future' climate action campaign, 47
Froebel, F., 24
funding, education, 12–13. See also education

Gandhi, M., 32
Gardner, H., 7, 48, 53, 127
geography, 73t, 76f, 77, 144t, 145t
  concepts, 59
  defined, 59

dominant attitudes, 61–62
emotional mapping in, 165
knowledge progression in, 130t
skills, 61
vocabulary of, 59–60, 60t–61t
Giroux, H., 31
global connections, 142–143, 143t–145t
Goldsworthy, A., 123
Gove, M., 40
government, expectations from, 10–11
Gruber, H., 7

haiku, 99, 100f
Hard Times (Dickens), 40
Hicks, D., 60
hidden curriculum, 12. See also curriculum
hierarchical cross-curricular learning, 150f
history, 73t, 77
  concepts, 62
  dominant attitudes, 64–65
  sample of progression in, 131t
  skills, 64
  vocabulary, 63, 63t–64t
hokey-cokey education, 11
homo erectus, 80
homo neanderthalis, 80
homo sapiens, 90
Human Genome Project, 155
humanitarian competition, 32
humanities, 58–59. See also common humanity
  case study, 72, 75
  and human search for meaning, 5–6
  to work, 71–72
human universals, 163
human values, 32

inclusion and positivity, classrooms models of, 6–7
inclusive values, 143f
The Index for Inclusion (Booth and Ainscow), 16
information and communications technology (ICT), 111
Initial Teacher Education (ITE), 14, 22
Initial Teacher Training (ITT) Market Review, 10
inspectorate, expectations from, 10–11
intellectually positive classrooms, 50–52
intelligences, 54f
inter-disciplinary cross-curricular learning, 123, 148f
Isen, A., 27

Key Stage 2, 131t

language of music, 91–92
leadership, 43–44, 44t
learning environment, 127

Makiguchi, T., 32
making relevant, 128–129
Malloch, S., 91
mathematics, 119
  case studies, 119–124
memorable curriculum, 147
mental commonalities, 5–6
mental health, 89–90, 89f
mental representation, 4
Montessori, M., 24
Moore, H., 103
moral development, 173–174
multi-disciplinary cross-curricular learning, 148f

music, 90–91
  concepts in, 92–95
  culture of, 93, 95
  and dance, 144t
  dimensions of, 91
  freeze-frame dance and, 99, 100f
  history of, 93, 95
  language of, 91–92
  playing with sound, 93
  skills in, 92–95
  talking about war and peace, 102–104
My Pedagogic Creed (Dewey), 31

Nash, P., 103
National Advisory Committee on Creative and Cultural Education (NACCCE), 7
National Health Service (NHS), 26
need for positivity, 13
negative emotions, 4, 29
negativity, 29
Northern Irish Curriculum, 65

Oates, T., 9
Ofsted, 11
Ofsted Framework, 171
opportunistic cross-curricular learning, 147f
oracy, 144t
oracy skills, 115, 117–118

pedagogy, 31–32
  positive, 52–56, 90, 95, 97
  praxis and, 52–54
personal, social, health and economic education (PSHE), 58, 59, 70–71, 138, 146f
Personal, Social and Emotional Development curriculum, 75
personal development, art and design, 83–85
Pestalozzi, J. H., 24
Philosophy for Children, 70
physical commonalities, 5–6
physical education (PE), 15, 95, 97–98
  games and, 157–159
physical features of the classroom, 46–47
physical needs, 160–163
Piaget, J., 48
Piano Concerto in G (Ravel), 103
playing with sound, 93
positive approaches to teaching, 33
positive curriculum, 146
positive emotional climate, 35
positive emotions, 4
positive environments for learning, 39–56
  behaviour, 54–56
  curriculum changes, 45–46, 46t
  education, 41–42
  emotionally positive classrooms, 48, 49t
  intellectually positive classrooms, 50–52
  intelligences, 54f
  leadership, 43–44, 44t
  pedagogy and positivity, 52–56
  physical features of the classroom, 46–47
  praxis and pedagogy, 52–54
  in schools, 42–46
  socially positive classrooms, 49–50
  teacher responses to challenge, 51t–52t
  thought-provoking words and phrases, 51t
  traditional *versus* progressive, 40–42
  values-conscious classrooms, 47–48

positive intellectual atmosphere, 35
positive moral environment, 33
positive pedagogy, 13, 31, 32, 90, 95, 97, 153–176. See also pedagogy
    assessing learning, 167–170
    case study, 158–164, 167, 172–175
    commonality, 155–156
    cultural development, 175
    cultural diversity, 154–155
    emotions, 165
    moral development, 173–174
    physical education (PE) and games, 157–159
    physical needs, 160–163
    senses, 159–160
    shared experiences, 166–167
    social development, 172–173
    spiritual development, 174
    values, 163–164
positive physical surroundings and resources, 35
positive relationships between adults and children, 34–35
positive spiritual environment, 37
positivity
    need for, 13
    power of, 27–31
    towards others, 68
praxis and pedagogy, 52–54
primary education, 59
    current context in UK, 8–13
progressive education, 9. See also education
progressive versus traditional education, 40–42

Ravel, M.
    Piano Concerto in G, 103
relevant curriculum, 146
religious education (RE), 59, 76f, 77, 145t
    concepts, 66
    dominant attitude, 68
    skills, 68
    vocabulary, 66, 67t
research-informed reports, 133
RETAIN project, 133
Robinson, K., 7, 8, 45, 86
Rousseau, J.-J., 24, 122
Royal Society of Arts, 47, 70

Save the Children, 47–48
school drama, 87–88, 87t
schools, positive environment in, 42–46
science, 107, 144t
    case studies, 108–109
    concepts of, 107t
    in cross-curricular contexts, 108
Scottish Curriculum for Excellence, 65
self portrait, 135f
Seligman, M., 27, 126
senses, 159–160
sequencing knowledge, 128
shared experiences, 166–167
similarities that connect us, 139t
Simonton, D. K., 7
single transferable subject cross-curricular learning, 149f
six degrees of separation, 16
sketchbooks, art and design, 85–86
social, moral, spiritual and cultural education (SMSC), 58, 59, 70–71, 138, 171

social commonalities, 5–6
social development, 172–173
social intelligence, 138
socially positive classrooms, 49–50
special educational needs (SEN), 10, 11
Special Educational Needs and Disabilities (SEND), 129
spiritual development, 174
staff development for teachers, 134t
Steiner, R. J. L., 24
Sternberg, R., 27, 48, 52–53
Strong, R., 9
structural teacher assessment, 168t
students of year 5 and 6, 76–77, 77f
superdiversity, 154
sustainability school, 140
sustained curriculum, 3–4

teacher-led curriculum, 3–4
teachers
    promoting acts, products and connections in every child, 8–13
    responses to challenge, 51t–52t
    role in inclusion and positivity, 6–7
teaching assistant (TA), 90, 116
teaching school hubs, 10
'Team Around the Child' (TAC), 13
theme-based cross-curricular learning, 149f
theme of identity, 76
thought-provoking words and phrases, 51t
traditional education, 9
traditional versus progressive education, 40–42
Trevarthen, C., 91
Triarchic and Multiple Intelligence theories, 53
Tutu, D., 27

Ubuntu philosophy, 24
Understanding the World curriculum, 75
UNESCO, 47

values-conscious classrooms, 47–48
values/valuing, 14–15, 21–37, 163–164
    and action, 14
    defined, 14
    diversity, 26–27
    general thinking about, 24–26
    linking education with, 25t
    pedagogy, 31–32
    positivity, power of, 27–31
    think about, 22–24, 22f
    wordle, 23f
virtuous values, 24–25
Vygotsky, L., 5, 8, 49, 126

War Requiem (Britten), 103
'wholly different year,' 11
Woodhead, C., 9
word experience around child, 17–18
wordle, valuing, 23f
World Health Organisation (WHO), 11, 12, 129
worthwhile knowledge, 9

zone of proximal development, 5, 49